OUTDOOR
ADVERTISING

HUGH E. AGNEW

GARLAND PUBLISHING, INC.
NEW YORK & LONDON
1985

For a complete list of the titles in this series
see the final pages of this volume.

This facsimile has been made from a copy in
the Yale University Library.

Library of Congress Cataloging in Publication Data

Agnew, Hugh E.
 Outdoor advertising.
 (The History of advertising)
 Reprint. Originally published: New York : McGraw-Hill,
1938.
 Includes index.
 1. Advertising, Outdoor. I. Title. II. Series.
HF5843.A64 1985 659.13'42 84-46055
ISBN 0-8240-6749-5 (alk. paper)

Design by Donna Montalbano

The volumes in this series are printed on
acid-free, 250-year-life paper.

Printed in the United States of America

OUTDOOR ADVERTISING

(Frontispiece.)

The lithographing plant of the Latham Litho Company, Inc., Long Island City, N. Y. C. H. Sprague, Professor of Decorative Arts at New York University, thinks that theaters and other buildings needing display space in the future will arrange for it as did the architects of this building.

OUTDOOR ADVERTISING

BY

HUGH E. AGNEW, A.B., M.Pd., Litt.D.

Professor of Marketing, Chairman of Marketing Department, New York University; Author of "Co-operative Advertising by Competitors" (Harper & Brothers); "Advertising Media—How to Weigh and Measure" (D. Van Nostrand Company, Inc.); Coauthor of "Advertising Principles" (Alexander Hamilton Institute); "Outlines of Marketing" (McGraw-Hill Book Company, Inc.)

First Edition

McGRAW-HILL BOOK COMPANY, Inc.

NEW YORK AND LONDON

1938

Preface

Why Write a Textbook on Marketing about the Outdoor Advertising Industry?

The purpose of advertising is to help move goods from the point at which they originate to the point at which they are consumed. It is a fundamental, basic force. With those who are so close to business that they become engrossed with the day-to-day details, it is sometimes wise to halt long enough to get a perspective of the whole scheme; in other words, to analyze one's own part and see how it fits into the general pattern. The following pages are calculated briefly to aid such a survey for the outdoor advertising industry.

The marketing system of the United States and Canada changes so rapidly that it is necessary to follow it closely and make frequent checks on progress in order to keep abreast of the times. In evidence of this, consider the marvelous improvement in posters in the last 20 years. It is not merely in the improvement in making the poster, in the art work or lettering that the fundamental change has come. Outdoor advertising now is much more closely tied up with the actual movement of goods than it has been in the past. Each advertisement is now designed with a very definite aim. It has a clearly defined objective, and this objective is part of the general campaign—the marketing plan.

Even for the leaders of an industry, it is often wise to stop and reconsider the fundamentals. Practice cannot be kept sound unless the theory underlying that practice is sound. It is the purpose of this book to review the more fundamental problems of marketing and to show how outdoor advertising plays an intimate and effective part in the great movement of goods.

It is believed that reviewing these fundamentals in the light of the most recent developments contributed by art, psychology and economics will provide new material for the salesman; give him fundamentals out of which he can construct his sales talk and apply it to any problem which he meets.

Schools and colleges have come to regard marketing, advertising and salesmanship as worthy subjects for their curricula. On some of these subjects there are numerous and able books, but the outdoor advertising industry has been left with much too limited consideration for the important part that it plays in the field of marketing. An occasional chapter in a textbook on advertising or, more often, one or two paragraphs supply all the information that is available to the large number of students who are interested in the study of marketing as a specialized business and to many more students who expect to enter the field of business and want to know marketing as an essential part of that business. The present text is designed to give the fundamentals of the outdoor advertising industry and adequately to show how it is related to the general marketing system. The author is advised that this material will be welcomed by both professors and students.

The two aims of the book are not antagonistic but rather complementary. Most progressive businessmen continue to be students; they study, make researches and analyze their problems along the same methods that are taught in the best schools and colleges. Indeed, it is the very methods used by businessmen in surveying and analyzing marketing problems that are taught young men and women preparing for business. The author of the book has attempted to treat the subject matter in line with this modern practice.

The book could not have been written without the help
and assistance of many men active in the outdoor advertis-
ing industry. Among these are representatives from the
Outdoor Advertising Association of America, Inc.: W. Rex
Bell, President; J. B. Stewart, Vice-president; H. E. Fisk,
General Manager. From Outdoor Advertising Incorporated:
Kerwin H. Fulton, President; C. O. Bridwell, Vice-Presi-
dent; Leonard London, Art Director; C. D. McCormick
and Robert A. Sprague. From the Traffic Audit Bureau:
Harrison Atwood, President; Dr. Miller McClintock,
Auditor; and John Paver. And from the National Outdoor
Advertising Bureau, Inc.: Frank T. Hopkins, President.
And in addition, Senator George Wharton Pepper and
Judge E. Allen Frost.

HUGH E. AGNEW.

NEW YORK CITY,
July, 1938.

Table of Contents

xi

Introduction

It always gives me a great deal of satisfaction to review the phenomenal progress which organized outdoor advertising has made during the past twenty-five years.

Many significant changes have been made and are continually being made to increase the effectiveness of this major medium as a means of bridging the gap between mass production and mass consumption.

First among these changes was the standardization of structures and service which enabled advertisers to secure uniform coverage with accumulative advertising effect throughout the length and breadth of the land.

Another important development was the formation of O. A. I.—Outdoor Advertising Incorporated—the national selling representative of the outdoor advertising industry.

Still another step of far-reaching importance was the formation of T. A. B.—Traffic Audit Bureau—the authority on outdoor circulation and coverage.

Great strides also have been made within very recent years in plant improvement, such as the reduction of the average number of poster panels per location and their placement at an angle to show head-on to traffic.

Because of these and many other changes in the industry and the decided trend of the daily habits of people to outdoor life, there is a need for an up-to-date and authoritative textbook on outdoor advertising.

Dr. Hugh E. Agnew, the author of this book, enjoys an enviable national reputation as a teacher and writer in the field of marketing. It gives me pleasure to compliment him and those who assisted him upon the preparation of this very comprehensive and practical treatise.

Those who read it will have a more intelligent understanding of outdoor advertising in all its phases and a clearer picture of its function in modern business.

KERWIN H. FULTON
President, Outdoor
Advertising Incorporated

OUTDOOR ADVERTISING

CHAPTER 1

Outdoor Advertising
as an Industry

What Constitutes Organized Outdoor Advertising[1]

Outdoor advertising has come to be a highly organized, well-regulated business. In the United States, there are approximately 1,050 operators of standard outdoor advertising facilities, of which more than 95 per cent are members of the national trade association, the Outdoor Advertising Association of America, Inc. That association is made up of plant owners, and its bylaws make standard construction obligatory upon members, and it is through this regulation that the pleasing uniformity of present displays has been attained. The owner of each display—not the advertiser—places his name upon each unit, so it is immediately apparent who is responsible for the construction and maintenance of the display.

The organized outdoor advertising industry represents an invested capital of $125,000,000 in poster panels, painted display bulletins, electric spectaculars, automotive equipment, machinery, buildings and real estate. The annual purchases of products, equipment and services amount to approximately $12,000,000.

[1] A formal definition of the Outdoor Medium-Industry as prepared by H.E. Fisk, general manager of the Outdoor Advertising Association of America, Inc., is as follows: "The Outdoor Medium-Industry is an advertising service for others including selling, erecting, placing and maintaining outdoor advertising displays *on premises owned, leased or controlled by the producer of the service.*"

3

Approximately 250,000 property owners receive income for rent of space. About 33,000 persons are employed in the operation of organized outdoor advertising plants, including carpenters, steel workers, tinsmiths, electricians, roofers, painters, poster hangers, laborers, and the necessary foremen, superintendents, clerks and managers. This does not include those commercial artists and lithographic industry employees which are largely dependent upon the outdoor medium.

The lithographic industry represents an investment of $80,000,000 and employs thousands of men and women in the production of posters used in the medium. In addition to this industrial employment, the medium directly and indirectly employs thousands of advertising agency executives, creative artists, and sales and promotional personnel.

Of course, there is nothing to prevent the advertisers of a product or service from erecting and maintaining their own display structures and copy. Years ago, this was a common practice, and there are still a few advertisers who follow this method of advertising outdoors. Most advertisers, however, have welcomed the development of a national standardized poster and painted display service, because they found that their private ventures in the establishment and maintenance of outdoor advertising were too costly, ineffective, and many times were considered unattractive by those whom it was intended to impress favorably.

Posters

There are three classes of outdoor advertising: posters, painted bulletins, and electrical spectaculars. In poster advertising, there are two standard size posters, the twenty-four-sheet and the three-sheet. The twenty-four-sheet is the most widely used.

The term twenty-four-sheet is derived from the fact that it represents 24 multiples of the basic one-sheet unit which measures 28 inches high by 41 inches long. When collated, a twenty-four-sheet poster is four sheets high and six sheets wide. The over-all dimensions of a twenty-four-sheet poster when posted are 8 feet 10 inches high and 19 feet 8 inches long.

The basic one-sheet unit is not often the paper size used in poster production, as the size and arrangement of the sheets are controlled to a considerable extent by the design to be reproduced. Therefore, from a poster manufacturing standpoint, a sheet is one of the finished pieces that makes up the complete poster regardless of its size. Usually the completed poster consists of from twelve to eighteen such sheets. Designs are reproduced on posters by four processes, namely, lithography, printing, screen process, and hand painting. Posters are pasted on a steel-surfaced, standard structure erected for this purpose, known as a poster panel. The poster panel measures 12 feet high by 25 feet long. The poster is centered in the panel, and the space between the poster and the green molding frame is covered with white blanking paper.

The three-sheet poster when collated is three sheets high and one sheet wide. The over-all dimensions of a three-sheet poster when posted are 6 feet 10 inches high and 3 feet 5 inches wide inside the blanking.

The three-sheet poster panel measures 8 feet 7 inches high and 4 feet 10 inches wide. As in the case of the twenty-four-sheet, the three-sheet is centered on the panel and is surrounded with white blanking paper. Illustrations of the twenty-four-sheet poster and panel and the three-sheet poster and panel are shown on pages 38 and 115. Twenty-four-sheet poster advertising plants are established, maintained and operated to deliver general market coverage distributed over the important streets. Three-sheet poster advertising is essentially a point-of-purchase medium.

Painted Display and Electric Spectaculars

The term "painted display" is applied both to painted bulletins and painted walls. Painted bulletins may be located on roofs or walls of buildings or on the ground.

In cities and their principal suburbs, bulletins are of a standard structural design and ornamentation and are

The above is an evening view of electrical spectaculars located on Seventh Avenue and Broadway in New York City, looking north. The descriptive matter for Chevrolet and Planters Peanuts is merely the order which was sent to the plant operator. For descriptive matter see opposite page.

painted white. Ground bulletins measure 12½ feet high by 47 feet long. Roof and wall bulletins vary somewhat in size based primarily on perspective and space availability.

The standard highway and railroad bulletins, used outside of cities and their suburbs, are somewhat simpler in design and ornamentation and are painted cream color. They measure 12½ feet high by 42 feet long.

On highway and railway approaches to metropolitan areas, a metropolitan unit is available of the same structural design, ornamentation, and color as the standard highway-railroad bulletin, 18 feet high and 72 feet long, for locations where the space permits and perspective requires a larger unit.

Painted walls, as the term indicates, are spaces on the walls of buildings on which copy is to be directly painted. They are available in cities, their suburbs and towns generally. They vary in size based on space availability and

---

ELECTRIC SPECTACULAR

Name:	Planter's
Description	Broadway, 7th Avenue; faces south into Times Square from 47th Street. Can be seen from as far south as 41st Street on Broadway and 39th Street on 7th Avenue
Circulation:	1,091,000 daily
Dimensions:	55 feet high by 49 feet wide; 2,600 square feet
Number of electric bulbs:	approximately 6,700 lamps
Number of feet neon tubing:	3,340
Colors:	note attached data sheet describing Planter's sign in complete detail.
Action:	note attached sheet.

ELECTRIC SPECTACULAR

Name:	Chevrolet
Description:	Broadway, 7th Avenue and 47th Street
Circulation:	1,091,000
Dimensions:	45 feet 6 inches by 60 feet
Number of electric bulbs:	7,069
Number of feet neon tubing:	. . .
Colors:	Letters in the large title word CHEVROLET are white. Letters within the trade-mark are red, trade-mark is outlined with yellow. Colors in the corona and rays of the sunburst are green, red, yellow and white.
Action:	First part of the display to light up is the 60 foot word CHEVROLET, extending right across the board in brilliant white lamps. Then six semicircular rows of colored lamps come on showing the beginning of the sunburst build-up. Then the rays begin to light up, and continue all the way out the edge of the display.

The 60-foot word CHEVROLET burns steadily, scintillating. The motograph across the bottom runs constantly with the Chevrolet sales message, and the correct time flashes at 1-minute intervals.

The build-up of the sunburst starts at the center, one row at a time starting from the innermost semicircle. When the six semicircles are filled, the rays start to build up and fill right out to the edge of the frame. After they have reached the edge of the frame, the rays start to work in a chaser action, and they continue this chaser or ripple action for a few seconds. Then the large CHEVROLET trade-mark comes on. And now the entire display is on, and it burns steadily for about 5 seconds.

Then it goes off, and the action starts again from the beginning in the same sequence.

visibility. Illustrations of the various types of painted bulletins and painted walls are shown on pages 117 to 121. Painted display plants are established, maintained and operated to deliver selective coverage of a dominant character at strategic points of high circulation.

Electric spectaculars are located on the roofs or walls of buildings and on specially constructed steel towers. They

Painted bulletin, located at Astor Place, New York City.

are available in the larger cities. They are located at points of unusually heavy night and day circulation. The size is dictated by perspective, visibility and space availability. Illustrations of electric spectaculars are shown on page 6.

Each of the three classes of display will be discussed in detail as to its use, but it may be said here that each unit of each class is constructed according to definite standards, plans and specifications adopted by the Outdoor Advertising Association of America, Inc.

Commercial Signs

The essential difference between the sign industry and the outdoor advertising medium, as defined above, is that

Commercial sign for retail store identification.

signs are manufactured and sold outright for installation and maintenance by a sign contractor on premises *not* owned, leased or controlled by the contractor or his agent.

Commercial sign for factory identification.

Signs are primarily used for the purpose of identifying a business, its products or its services at the point of manufacture, distribution or sale.

The sign industry consists of three recognized divisions:

1. Electric and luminescent tube signs in retail or wholesale quantities.
2. Commercial signs of any material in retail or wholesale quantities.
3. Commercial point of purchase signs of various materials, such as metal, porcelain, wood, etc., in wholesale quantities.

In the United States, there are approximately 15,000 sign shop owners, manufacturers, contractors, and distributors. The majority of the operators in the sign industry are members of one or more of the following national trade associations: National Sign Association, Advertising Metal Sign and Display Manufacturers Association, and Porcelain Enamel Institute.

The outdoor advertising structures of the organized medium and the signs installed by the sign industry are erected and maintained under lease or consent of the owner of the property on which they are placed and in accordance with the building code of the related municipality.

Advertising copy or signs of any character posted, painted, placed or affixed in any way upon rocks, trees, fences or barricades are not the work of members of the organized outdoor advertising medium or the organized sign industry.

Organization in Outdoor Advertising

In order to provide a national poster and painted-display service, maintain the necessary physical facilities and equipment, determine the advertising values, promote and sell the medium, buy the space and carry out the details of the advertising plan, an extensive organization setup on a functional basis is necessary.

At first sight, this organization seems complex, but further examination discloses very little duplication or waste effort between the several functional units, which are:

1. Outdoor Advertising Association of America, Inc., and its subordinate state associations.

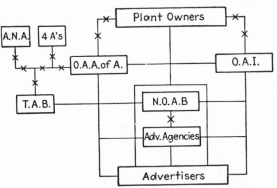

This shows the relationship of the various organizations which make up the operating part of the outdoor advertising industry.

A.N.A.—Association of National Advertisers
4 A's—American Association of Advertising Agencies
O.A.A. of A.—Outdoor Advertising Association of America
O.A.I.—Outdoor Advertising Incorporated
T.A.B.—Traffic Audit Bureau
N.O.A.B.—National Outdoor Advertising Bureau

The crossed line indicates ownership; for example, the plant owners own O.A.I. and O.A.A. of A., while the advertising agencies own N.O.A.B.

2. Outdoor Advertising Incorporated.
3. Traffic Audit Bureau, Inc.
4. National Outdoor Advertising Bureau, Inc.
5. Poster Lithographers.

A brief description of each of these organization factors follows:

Outdoor Advertising Association of America, Inc.

This organization was mentioned briefly in the first paragraph of this chapter. It has resulted from the stable organization which first came into existence in outdoor advertising in 1891. Those engaged in the business realized that individually they could not develop the inherent values of the medium as a national trade facility. The objectives of organization originally adopted and those of the present are practically identical in principle, intended to accomplish the establishment and maintenance of a nation-wide standardized outdoor advertising service.

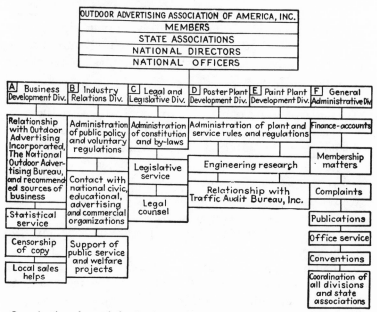

Organization chart of the Outdoor Advertising Association of America, Inc.

The following statement of objectives is quoted from the Constitution and Bylaws of the Association:

1. To provide for the American business community an efficient and economical instrument of distributing, merchandising and advertising.
2. To insure, through standardization of practice, facilities and structures, a readily available and flexible, scientific advertising medium.
3. To conduct the business with due consideration of the public interest and welfare.
4. To advance the common interests of those engaged in the business of advertising.

The code of ethics of the organization under which these objectives are to be achieved is as follows:

1. To provide an efficient advertising service outdoors.
2. To give to the advertiser's message coverage of the population as it moves within and through the retail trading and wholesale distribution areas.
3. To conduct the business of outdoor advertising so that there will exist at all times an equal opportunity for all advertisers and their accredited advertising representatives.
4. To recognize the economic and social value of other media of advertising and to coöperate with them in the general interest of the advertiser and the public.
5. To serve the public through giving publicity to meritorious products and services conducive to the general welfare of the consumer.
6. To give the encouragement of our organization and the support of our medium to projects either community, state or national in scope, which are of benefit to the public.
7. To place and maintain the advertising facilities of this medium in such a way that they will be acceptable to reasonable-minded persons and to the end that the natural beauties of the rural landscape and the amenities of historical and public shrines will be protected and preserved.

Important Developments

A few of the important standards, policies, and activities which have been established, developed and carried on by the Association which would have been impossible for the individual outdoor advertising operator are as follows:

1. The standard poster and painted display structures.
2. The standard twenty-four-sheet poster, in coöperation with the lithographic industry.

3. The establishment of an industry-owned and stabilized sales and promotion representative company (Outdoor Advertising Incorporated) and the policy governing the recognition of sources of business (advertising agencies).
4. The poster showing allotment and market-coverage principle and procedure and the supplying of statistical information regarding coverage allotments and costs to recommended sources of business.
5. The determination of the circulation, space position, and coverage values of the medium. (The researches at the Universities of Wisconsin and Harvard and the formation of the Traffic Audit Bureau, Inc.)
6. The procedure for the handling of advertisers' contracts (through sources of business to plant operators).
7. The public relations policy and voluntary regulations and censorship of copy.
8. Methods of defense against discriminatory legislation.
9. The relationship with other advertising media and civic and commercial groups through contact with their national organizations.
10. The development of factual data with respect to all phases of the business through academic, laboratory and field research.

There are 995 plant-operator members of the Association, each having an equal voice in the establishment of policies and activities of the organization.

In each State, there is a subordinate association charged with the responsibility of carrying out the requirements of membership, service to advertisers, and the protection of the invested interests of the members. The governing body is the national board of directors and is made up of the national association officers and a representative from each State.

Outdoor Advertising Incorporated

Outdoor Advertising Incorporated is the national selling representative of the outdoor medium. It does not place or sublet business. It performs the primary functions of national selling.

The multiple activities of national selling may be grouped under three main divisions: *selling, research and plans, creative.*

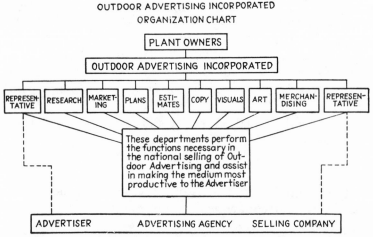

OUTDOOR ADVERTISING INCORPORATED
ORGANiZATION CHART

PLANT OWNERS

OUTDOOR ADVERTISING INCORPORATED

REPRESEN-TATIVE · RESEARCH · MARKET-ING · PLANS · ESTI-MATES · COPY · VISUALS · ART · MERCHAN-DISING · REPRESEN-TATIVE

These departments perform the functions necessary in the national selling of Outdoor Advertising and assist in making the medium most productive to the Advertiser

ADVERTISER · ADVERTISING AGENCY · SELLING COMPANY

Organization chart of Outdoor Advertising Incorporated. This is the selling agency of the associated plant owners.

Selling involves the presentation and sale of the medium to advertisers and agencies on the basis of planned advertising and coöperation with the advertiser and agency after the sale to secure the maximum results in accordance with the plan.

Research and plans include the preparation of presentations of the medium from original research to complete plan. The steps involved are:

1. Conduct of market and product investigations and research work covering all sections of the country for firsthand information as a basis for developing business.

2. Maintenance of research files and library of information on advertising and marketing.
3. Preparing marketing studies which show the application of outdoor advertising to specific markets. Examples are ''96 Metropolitan Markets,'' ''College-town Plan,'' ''Main Street Plan.''
4. Preparation of specific plans for the use of outdoor advertising to serve the particular needs of individual advertisers, including research data, definition of markets, marketing information, estimate of outdoor advertising costs, attributes of the medium and other data required in making a complete presentation.
5. Preparation of descriptive literature in explanation of outdoor advertising, its various forms and uses.
6. Maintenance of general presentations of outdoor advertising in New York, Chicago and other cities where they are used extensively for group meetings of advertisers' sales, distributor and dealer organizations.
7. Collection of factual data regarding outdoor campaigns for use in preparing case histories on the success of outdoor advertising.
8. Coöperation in the merchandising or promotion of outdoor campaigns to the trade, such as the preparation of dealer helps, letters to the trade, posterettes, broadsides, etc.
9. Educational work in helping associations interested in advertising, teachers of marketing and students. Also publicity and promotional work in the interests of the medium.

Creative includes writing copy for outdoor advertising, both pictorial and word copy, rough visuals and complete finished sketches; consultation with and assistance to the art departments of sources of business regarding art and copy.

Outdoor Advertising Incorporated is owned by the outdoor advertising plant owners and conducted on a nonprofit basis, whereas the special representatives of other media are privately owned and organized for profit.

Plant owners pay 5 per cent to Outdoor Advertising Incorporated on national business billed.

The Traffic Audit Bureau, Inc.

Circulation is the factor that indicates the number of times the advertisement may be seen, or the number of messages delivered. It is the measuring rod by which the buyer can ascertain the values in a medium or between media. It is one of the fundamentals in advertising. In the publication field years ago, the Audit Bureau of Circulations developed a means of securing authentic circulation statements which were uniform, exact and reliable.

In recognition of the same need for outdoor displays, the Association of National Advertisers, Inc., in October, 1931, requested the coöperation of the Outdoor Advertising Association of America, Inc., and the American Association of Advertising Agencies in sponsoring a research in Harvard University looking toward the establishment of a scientific foundation for a method which all concerned could accept with confidence and use with practical value. After a period of 18 months, in which comprehensive field studies were made in more than 150 cities, the sponsoring groups adopted a set of basic principles to govern the circulation evaluation of outdoor advertising. The method and procedure for applying these principles are set forth in Chapter 8.

In June, 1933, the sponsoring associations established by agreement the Traffic Audit Bureau, which was subsequently incorporated in May, 1934.

The Traffic Audit Bureau Organization

The Traffic Audit Bureau is a nonprofit membership corporation operating under the laws of the State of New York. Its corporate members and board of directors comprise sixteen unpaid representatives; eight selected by the Association of National Advertisers, four by the American

Association of Advertising Agencies, and four by the Outdoor Advertising Association of America. In addition, the president of the Association of National Advertisers, the president of the American Association of Advertising Agencies and the general manager of the Outdoor Advertising Association of America are ex officio members of the board. Control is thus vested exclusively in a body representative of the principal interests concerned in the accurate

ORGANIZATION

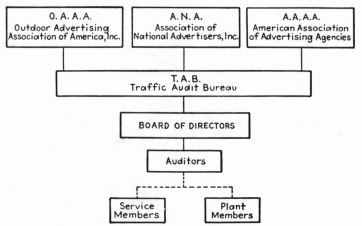

Organization chart showing the relationship of the Traffic Audit Bureau, Inc., to its sponsors.

and scientific evaluation of outdoor advertising circulation values.

The supervision of the board of directors is exercised through an auditor and his organization. Dr. Miller McClintock, who directed the basic Harvard researches, is in charge of the national audit activities.

Participation by advertisers, agencies and outdoor advertising plant operators is through several classes of membership. Service memberships are provided for those who desire to receive the annual publications of "Standard Circulation Values of Outdoor Advertising," the first volume of which was published June, 1934.

Plant memberships are provided both for poster and paint plant operators. The dues for plant membership are $2 per year. Plant members are eligible to enter into audit service agreements and have their plants audited annually

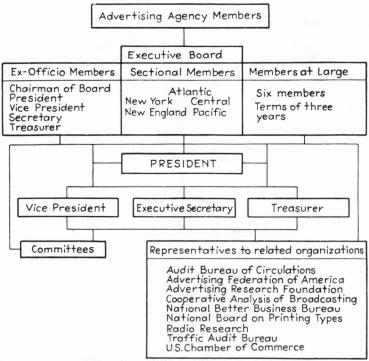

Advertising Agency Members		
	Executive Board	
Ex-Officio Members	Sectional Members	Members at Large
Chairman of Board President Vice President Secretary Treasurer	Atlantic New York Central New England Pacific	Six members Terms of three years

PRESIDENT

Vice President	Executive Secretary	Treasurer

Committees	Representatives to related organizations
	Audit Bureau of Circulations Advertising Federation of America Advertising Research Foundation Cooperative Analysis of Broadcasting National Better Business Bureau National Board on Printing Types Radio Research Traffic Audit Bureau U.S. Chamber of Commerce

Organization chart of the American Association of Advertising Agencies. As will be noted, the Traffic Audit Bureau, Inc., is a related organization, owned in part by the A.A.A.A.

for a service fee of 50 cents per poster panel and $1.00 per painted bulletin.

National Outdoor Advertising Bureau, Inc.

The National Outdoor Advertising Bureau, Inc., is a nonprofit coöperative organization owned by 226 leading advertising agencies.

Its functions are as follows:

1. To furnish statistical information and estimates of coverage, rates, allotments, specifications, and costs

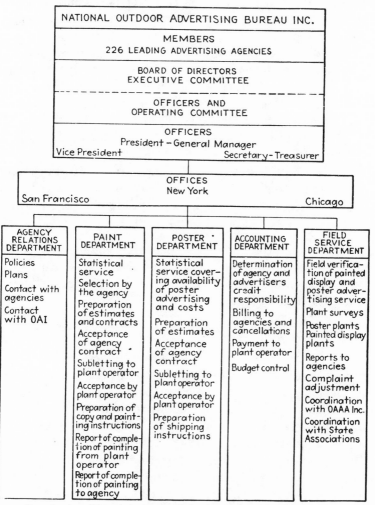

Organization chart of the National Outdoor Advertising Bureau, Inc.

of poster and painted display and electrical spectaculars to agency members of the Bureau.

2. To place sublet contracts for space with outdoor advertising plant operators in accordance with the governing contract.
3. To prepare and furnish to lithographers shipping instructions and labels to cover shipment of posters to plant operators, and to prepare and furnish to plant operators working copy for painted display.
4. To secure, receive and record reports of service rendered under sublet contracts by plant operators and advise the related agency member accordingly.
5. To bill the agency member for service rendered under the governing contract, collect monies due and pay the related plant operators for service rendered under the sublet contracts.
6. To travel field representatives throughout the country for personal contact with plant operators in the interest of good will and understanding and for first-hand verification of service delivered.

Plant operators pay 16⅔ per cent commission to the Bureau on business billed. The Bureau compensates the agency members out of this commission after deducting the cost of handling.

Poster Lithographers

There are about twenty-five lithographers in the United States equipped to manufacture twenty-four-sheet posters.

Dependent upon the character of the poster design the individual colors are hand drawn or photographed direct to the press plates. Many twenty-four-sheet posters are today a combination of process and straight lithography. The introduction of the projection machine method in combination with straight lithography has tended to economy and enabled the lithographer to give quicker service at no increase in cost.

However, some few twenty-four-sheet posters are produced even today by the use of wood blocks which are cut away leaving the raised parts for printing. This method is available for flat color or line work.

Posters are produced on rotary lithographic presses, either direct or offset, depending upon the nature of the design.

The inks and paper used in the manufacture of posters are of prime importance, as they must withstand the posting process and exposure to the weather. Poster lithographers have contributed directly to the development of better inks and better types of paper, which have resulted in the improvement of posters in general.

The progressive improvement in lithographic processes is in large measure due to the work of the Lithographic Technical Foundation, a research institution founded and financially sponsored by the Lithographers National Association, its members, and others directly and indirectly interested.

The poster lithographers coöperated with the Outdoor Advertising Association of America, Inc., in establishing the present standard twenty-four-sheet poster as to specifications and layout arrangement.

The functions of a twenty-four-sheet poster lithographer are:

1. To determine from the artist's sketch to be reproduced the layout arrangement and the number of printings, as well as the cost thereof, based on the number of posters required.
2. To sell the advertiser or his agent.
3. To manufacture and collate the posters.
4. To ship the posters to plant operators in accordance with shipping instructions furnished by the source of business which placed the contract.
5. To bill the advertiser or his agent for the posters and shipping charges and to collect therefor.

CHAPTER 2

Steps in the Development of Outdoor Advertising [1]

Earliest Advertising

The earliest advertising known to history occurred in Egypt and was in the nature of signs. These appeared both upon walls and on the specially erected signposts of which the obelisks are the most generally known. There were many of these in Egypt 2,500 years ago, and it was doubtless from them that Rome developed its idea of important historical monuments. It seems to be clearly established that the famous Rosetta stone, which supplied the key to Egyptian literature, was one of a series erected by the Memphis Synod of Priests, giving notice to all, and particularly to the tax gatherers, that by royal decree the taxes in arrears and the penalties therefor had been cancelled for the sacerdotal body. This would constitute an outdoor advertising campaign, to use the modern phraseology.

The fundamental differences between a commercial sign and outdoor advertising are: a commercial sign is nearly always used to identify a place of business, such as a warehouse, store, factory, bank, theater, and hotel. Or it may refer to a product that is sold at that particular location, such as Dependable Batteries, All Steel Automobiles, etc.

---

[1] Judge E. Allen Frost prepared a manuscript which supplied the facts for the early history of advertising, as given in this chapter. Frank T. Hopkins told the interesting story of how outdoor advertising was sold. References to other authors have been acknowledged in footnotes.

Outdoor advertising, on the other hand, may be restricted to one announcement, but this need not be at the place

The famous Rosetta Stone was one of a series of road signs which appeared in ancient Egypt. This is the first outdoor advertising of which there is an authentic record. The permanent form in which it appeared might indicate that it was common practice to use a series of signs in communicating with the public.

where the product or service is offered for sale. If a hotel has just one painted bulletin along a railroad track or public highway giving its location and means of identification, it would be regarded as an outdoor advertisement. If the same hotel placed its name on the roof, or other sign helping the traveler to identify it, that would be regarded as a commercial sign. Another difference is that the outdoor advertisement nearly always carries a sales message, while the commercial sign may, and usually does, mark or identify a location.

The fact that there was a series of Rosetta stones would plainly place those monuments in the category of outdoor advertising. Also, the notice in two languages was intended both for the tax gatherers and for those from whom the tax might be collected. Such an impressive message, presented with all the dignity that surrounds the erection of a monument, would carry authority to all who could read.

The Emperor Trajan of Rome greatly expanded the idea of erecting monuments and of using them for decrees and other state proclamations. The earliest letters which composed our alphabet were found upon these monuments, and so beautifully were they proportioned and carved that in most of the alphabet there has been little change. The curve at the bottom of the capital U is one of the most significant changes. In the old Roman, it was made as we make our capital V, and on some of our formal monuments of today this form of the letter U is still found. J, W, Y and Z are other letters which were added after the Roman period, at least in the form now used. J was not differentiated from I until the sixteenth century, and in strictly classical inscriptions the I is still used for J.

The invention of movable type by Johannes Gutenberg, about 1450, facilitated the printing of handbills, most of which were distributed, as the name implies, from hand to hand. It is extremely probable that many of these were pasted up in public places, thus being the forerunner of our posters.

Perhaps the next great invention that contributed to outdoor advertising was the process of printing from a smooth, flat-topped stone. This process, which was invented by Aloys Senefelder, in 1796 or 1798, is called "lithography." This was also a German invention. It was by the lithographic process that the first pictures were reproduced in large size and at a cost within the reach of advertisers.

The study of heraldry and coats of arms is interesting and has a definite relationship to the early commercial signs. Rivers[1] states that, when the favored families who maintained castles and had coats of arms were away on vacation, their castles were frequently used as hostelries and the coats of arms helped to identify the place, and it is his belief that from these coats of arms came many of the signs of inns that were so common to Europe. The red lion is one to which he gives particular emphasis. We still find hotels in the United States bearing this historic name. Space forbids further discussion of these ancient but interesting signs, which at best are not very closely related to outdoor advertising.

The Beginnings of Outdoor Advertising in America

The early poster advertising in the United States was started quite spontaneously. Notices of sale of farm stock and equipment, county and state fairs, theatricals, circuses, horse races, Fourth of July celebrations, carnivals, and medicine shows constituted the early patrons of the industry. Perhaps the circuses were the most active and the most extensive users of posters in the early days of the medium. Barnum, in this field as in many others, is credited with being one of the pioneers.

Because of a tax on British newspapers, poster advertising received a degree of attention in England that America was slow in copying. As early as 1860, the hoardings through many cities of England were utilized for posting in an orderly and attractive manner. It was necessary to have some legal claim to the space occupied before posting could

[1] Hugh W. Rivers, "Ancient Advertising and Publicity." A. Kroch Co., Chicago.

develop in a businesslike way. That came in America about ten years later, or 1870.

Even though outdoor advertising in the United States had developed without plan or purpose, it was so effective that by the close of the war between the states, there were 275 billposting firms employing from two to twenty men each.[1]

Until the beginning of the present century, the manager of the local theater frequently had charge of the outdoor advertising for his city. That came about in a perfectly natural way, as a large part of the posting was from the theater. The manager was well supplied in advance with posters for road shows which were to appear later. If there was no one else available to do the posting, the local manager of the theater would arrange to have it done. The active season for the theater was 32 weeks, roughly from the middle of September to the following May, and during this season there was much posting for the theater. During the other 20 weeks, business was built up for other advertisers who had posting to do. This should not be interpreted to mean that these city plants were wholly taken over during the fall and winter months by the theaters, but during that time theaters were the principal customers of the poster stands. Consequently, during the summer, local advertisers who had posting to do were encouraged to place advertising, and constituted the principal business of the poster plant.

Tacking in the early days of outdoor advertising was almost as important as billposting itself. This was particularly true of advertising that was done in the country districts, such as farm sales, Fourth of July notices, fence signs for stores and the miscellaneous advertising that was offered. A new implement that came in before tacking went into disuse was the magnetized hammer with a long handle. This permitted the posting of large sheets in places that were otherwise inaccessible.

---

[1] Frank Presbrey, "History and Development of Advertising," p. 500, Doubleday, Doran & Co.

Of the strictly commercial posting, which was largely employed by food products, patent medicines, soap, cleansing compounds and the like, it was a common practice to secure protection for the position by giving the landlord or tenant in the case trinkets or tickets of admission to a circus. These were freely, if not lavishly, conferred. Subscriptions to magazines, kitchen and pocketknives, watches and even jewelry were used in payment for posting.

Painted signs were somewhat more elaborate and required a much higher degree of personal skill than the posting. The sign painters were employed to a much larger extent than the bill posters. This was true even of firms which produced the same kinds of goods that were advertised on posters.

1870—Modern Advertising Began

There are many reasons why the year 1870 may be considered the dividing line between ancient and modern advertising. The perfection of a web-fed printing press, of stereotyping, of paper-folding machines and of a new lithograph half-tone had provided improved mechanical equipment that gave printing and lithography a new field.

Jules Chéret, the first real poster artist, was just getting into his stride in France, and his influence was quickly felt throughout Europe and ultimately reached America. Barnum organized his circus and soon became the most extensive user of outdoor advertising in America, if not in the world. It was in 1867 or 1870 that the earliest recorded leasings of boards occurred in the United States,[1] one being the board fence around the new post office under construction in New York City. The firm of Bradbury and Houghteling was formed to give a country-wide paint service, the first of its kind. Previously there had been some 250 firms which offered a limited paint service. Their "services" overlapped, as did those of the early billposters, even to the

---

[1] Frank Presbrey, "History and Development of Advertising," p. 501, Doubleday, Doran & Co.

This is an early advertisement for the Ford Motor Cars. Notice that the prices range from $750 to $2,800.

extent of painting over signs recently placed by a competitor.

A little later, 1872, the firm of Kissam and Allen was formed with the idea of owning and erecting their own poster panels. It was also in this year that the International Bill Posters' Association of North America was formed at St. Louis. This organization continued to function for twelve years when it was allowed to lapse. But a new and larger association, under the awkward name of Associated Bill Posters' Association of United States and Canada, was organized in 1891, seven years later.[1] The second organization will be considered later. In course of time, other advertising organizations were formed, and all came into existence for furthering the purpose announced by the members at the first meeting, improving and standardizing the service provided advertisers.

Also the decade 1870–1880 brought the first real space selling by magazines—in which the early *Century* pioneered. The names of three men appeared who were to have a great influence on outdoor advertising in the next half century.

[1] See list of Outdoor Advertising conventions in Appendix.

Two of these came from Chicago. R. J. Gunning entered the field in 1873, and two years later came Thomas Cusack, who began as a sign painter. O. J. Gude came into the business in Brooklyn in 1878.[1] It was also during this decade that the first of the state billposters' associations was formed. Michigan led off in 1875, and was followed by Indiana, New York, Minnesota, Ohio and Wisconsin, all of which had active associations by 1891.

The entrance of the theaters into poster advertising occurred during the seventies, and has continued. The improvement in lithographic process for reproducing pictures was largely responsible for this extension in the use of posters. These posters were limited in size to sheets about 28 by 42 inches. The legitimate use of posters for reputable theaters soon spread to the burlesque shows where such lurid portrayals began to appear, that they gave public offense, and the billposters, through association action, refused to handle offensive "paper." Although that came some years later, it was the earliest recorded censorship exercised by an advertising medium over copy.

After the permanent organization was launched, developments in the field of outdoor advertising came rapidly. It was in 1891, only twenty-one years after the first announcement of a nation-wide paint service by Bradbury and Houghteling, that a meeting of the most enterprising men engaged in the industry was arranged and a national association of poster men formed. It was called the Associated Bill Posters' Association. This association has functioned continuously for forty-seven years, and has never ceased to be a live and driving influence. So far as records reveal, this was also the first national association of advertising men. The purpose of the new organization was to improve the service, particularly by standardizing it. It is an interesting sidelight on the organization of this association that the leading plant owners from New York City, which took an

[1] Frank Presbrey, "History and Development of Advertising," p. 501, Doubleday, Doran & Co.

active interest, were the same group that had previously established a billposting service in a considerable number of cities, and who were represented by the same Houghteling.

1891 Began the Long Process of Standardization

One of the purposes in calling the convention at which the first national association was formed was to establish standards and adopt uniform practice as far as possible.

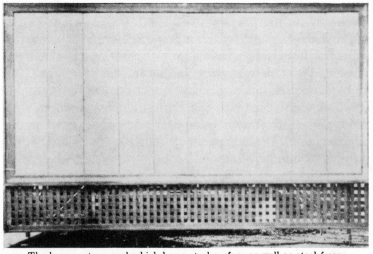

The bare poster panel which has a steel surface as well as steel frame.

At that time, the unit sheet for lithographing posters was 28 by 42 inches. Units in which displays were printed were one sheet, two sheet, three sheet, four sheet, six sheet, eight sheet, twelve sheet, sixteen sheet and twenty-four sheet. Also, thirty-two-sheet and forty-eight-sheet posters were found occasionally. Hawkins,[1] writing as late as 1910, stated that "the most popular poster in vogue is the 8 sheet." But the difficulties of standardizing did not end with securing a uniform number of sheets for each display. A study by Hawkins of thirty 8-sheet posters showed a variation in size of from 109 by 75 inches to 114 by 76 inches. This difference resulted from the unequal margins

[1] G.H.E. Hawkins, "Poster Advertising," published by the author, Chicago.

Rear elevation of an all-steel poster panel. The only wood used in construction is the molding and latticework. Such a structure withstands winds and storms without being wracked out of shape.

which lithographers permitted. Truly, even the mechanics
of posting have gone a long way since the early organization
of the Outdoor Advertising Association!

A definite size of poster was not adopted until the annual
meeting of the Association in 1912, twenty-one years after
the first convention where the movement was started. Not
only was the twenty-four-sheet poster made the standard,
but its size was determined as 8 feet 10 inches high by
19 feet 8 inches long, approximately the size which now
universally prevails. Also, the poster "stand," as it was then
called, was standardized with blanking paper and a frame.
This was called the "AA" (usually pronounced "double
A") structure. Many refinements have been added, and are
still being added, but no fundamental change in the poster
structure has been made since its adoption twenty-five
years ago.

Meanwhile, in 1909, the interests owning the painted
bulletins had met and organized, with purposes similar to
those of the poster plant owners. Both organizations early
adopted resolutions binding their members to the observ-
ance of rules of display which would avoid creating animos-
ity of reasonable-minded people. The day of indiscriminate
—"as-chance-may-offer"—posting was over, in so far as
the members of the Association were concerned. Before
the policy of leasing had been inaugurated, no assurance
was asked or given as to the time the display was to be
exhibited. The contracts merely called for "posting." With
the leasing of space, the term "listed and protected showings" was adopted. This meant that each poster was listed
as to location and recorded. No other poster would be
assigned to that position during the term of the contract. At
that time the contracts scheduled posters at 1 week, 2
weeks, etc. The monthly service was unknown. Both associations soon adopted the compulsory plan of using only
display space which they controlled, that is, bulletins by
the paint interests and poster panels by the poster plants
on owned or leased ground.

The adoption of "showings" as the basis for displays was slower of adoption, involving as it did a more complete survey of traffic than was available for many members. A further, and perhaps more important, difficulty was the opposition of advertisers who had followed the policy of advertising in each city or county directly in proportion to sales. When the appropriation was secured from an allowance of so much for each case or pound, or from a given percentage of sales in the territory, the amount available did not necessarily correspond with the cost of a showing. Making an appropriation in this way was illogical, as it provided too much where sales were good and too little where they were poor. In course of time, this was recognized, and possibility of sales was chosen as a better base for advertising budgets. The prime purpose of the showing —to give every advertiser a service equal in extent and cost to every other advertiser—was early adopted and is pretty nearly universally applied.

Early Selling of Outdoor Advertising

In the earlier stages of the development of outdoor advertising as a national medium, it was sold to the advertiser principally through special solicitors who devoted themselves exclusively to this one medium. Some of these solicitors were also plant operators, while some were simply selling agents and others were advertising agents. Hawkins, in his "Poster Advertising" (published in 1910), listed 3,100 in the United States and 200 in Canada who were on the "official list" of the Associated Bill Posters.

During the long period when general advertising agencies were not recognized by the outdoor medium (that is, when they could not secure a commission upon business placed) they were literally in direct competition with the special solicitors for the advertisers' appropriations. In the very early stages of agency development, agencies were hardly more than brokers of space—publication space. But the effectiveness and efficiency of the agencies in serving the advertiser in respect to publications led to the natural and normal growth in the importance of the agency to the advertiser.

The agency, handling the major part of most advertising appropriations, became the confidential and respected adviser of the advertiser. The scope of agency service was gradually broadened until it took in the whole field not only of advertising but of merchandising and sales. Even at the same time that this growth of agency activities was taking place, the outdoor medium was forging ahead under its policy of direct representation.

With the growth of the medium and its ability to deliver a truly national advertising coverage, it gradually assumed more importance to agencies and came to be looked upon as an important factor in national advertising. If agencies were to reach and maintain their position as unbiased advisers in respect to all advertising, then they must of necessity include outdoor advertising in their consideration of national media available for the use of the advertiser whether they were paid an agency commission or not. Obviously, if agencies could not profit from their recommendations of outdoor advertising, they could not be expected to be entirely unbiased. Although the medium was very successfully developed under the direct selling method, actually its position became more and more vulnerable as it increased in importance and as the volume grew. Competition was more intelligent and more aggressive.

In the very early stages of the medium, some agencies were recognized as official solicitors. Hawkins listed forty-one in the United States and thirteen in Canada. But his list included a number that would not now be recognized as advertising agents. For example, the Cusack Company was listed. But in 1910 the status of the advertising agent was not fixed. Anyone could have the designation, if he proclaimed himself an agent.

There was a confusion of policy within the medium and conflict between the two schools of thought—one sponsoring the recognition of general agencies and one sponsoring the direct selling method. For a time, the direct selling policy gained the ascendency so completely that even those agencies who had previously been recognized as official sources of business had their privileges withdrawn.

Out of the handling of solicitorships and other matters, there eventually developed a suit in the Federal Courts, and the result of this was a decision that at least in theory left the outdoor advertising door open to advertising agencies but in fact gave them nothing more than legal ground to wage a competitive battle against the overwhelming odds in favor of the direct solicitor.

Directly out of this situation grew the idea of a coöperative organization supported by many agencies and serving all of them. Some years before this, the agencies had already formed an association known as the American Association of Advertising Agencies. It was from the deliberations and consideration of the outdoor advertising committee of this Association that the idea of a special organization to represent the agencies collectively in outdoor advertising was born.

A number of important agencies agreed to subscribe funds to make a start, and a charter was secured for the National Outdoor Advertising Bureau, Inc. This charter was granted in the year 1915 and the organization began to function in a small way.

Developments, 1915–1925

By 1915, some very definite accomplishments had been achieved in outdoor advertising. The national association was firmly established with hundreds of members representing several thousand cities and towns. The standard twenty-four-sheet poster had been adopted as the most desirable unit, and the principal features of the panel structure had been worked out. The frame, design and structural dimensions for the display, the space for white paper blanking and other similar regulations had been adopted which consti-

These two illustrations show the great improvement that has been made in grouping posters. This is the same corner with the displays reduced from nine to four. The shrubbery at the base of the more modern display also adds to its attractiveness.

tuted the AA panel. The National Outdoor Advertising Bureau had been established, and the painted bulletin owners had formed a national association in 1909, so that the outdoor field had become well organized.

In 1923, Wilmot Lippincott wrote a text "Outdoor Advertising." This purported to be the last word in outdoor advertising practice at the time, but is of interest now only from an historical standpoint. This of itself is an indication of how rapidly the business has developed and the vast scope of improvement which has been made in the last fifteen years. It was during this period that the idea of "showings" was being developed. Before the adoption of that plan, the Outdoor Advertising Association sent out inspectors who visited the different plants and checked up on the positions of the different panels. The purpose of this inspection was to check up on the physical service, such as the construction and distribution of the panels and the appearance and distribution of the posters, and to see that it was in accord with the service rules and regulations of the association. These inspectors commented in a general way upon the circulation value of the posters, such as being opposite railroad stations or inter-urban stations, near the post office, etc.

Lippincott reports that posters could be found in most denominations of sizes, from one sheet up to twenty-four sheets. Apparently the thirty-two-sheet poster had been discontinued at the time of his writing. The electric spectacular had come into its own. This was due in part to the great improvement in electric light bulbs, which were far more effective and less expensive to operate than the earlier carbon filaments had been.

Lippincott relates the following incident concerning the Federal government's interest in outdoor advertising and possibly an explanation of how the government was sold on the medium:

. . . The great growth of this industry since the war may be attributed to the war itself. Some of the incidents which brought

This is an illustration of what was called "poster fence" or, more often, a "fence." The practice of connecting displays in this way has been discontinued in up-to-date poster plants.

outdoor advertising into such vogue in those days are significant. In 1917, someone suggested that a tax levied on outdoor advertising would prove a valuable source of revenue to the government. Government officials, not being aware of the fact that a

The above is an illustration of the present display where the fence on the opposite page formerly stood. The crack in the pavement, with the sewer inlet, is evidence of the location. Instead of five boards, all parallel, there is one for each direction of traffic in the present display. This also is typical of the new grouping of posters.

small number of boards in well-chosen locations gives the effect of being much more numerous than they really are, assumed that since approximately $700,000,000 was being spent annually in this country for advertising, surely one-half of this sum was being appropriated for outdoor purposes. Their investigation showed, however, that, instead of the amount being $350,000,000 available for taxation, the annual expenditure was amounting to only about $13,000,000.

This total was so small that the officials deemed it inexpedient to levy a tax; but they learned a lesson which they were soon to put to a great use—namely, that a $13,000,000 medium was producing a $350,000,000 impression. . . .

Organization of Outdoor Advertising, 1915–1925

Lippincott divided the outdoor advertising business among three classes of operators:
1. Those who handle painted and electric display.
2. Solicitors.
3. Posting companies.

While it was true that a great many concerns at that time solicited their own business, most of it came through the personal selling companies, the largest and most successful of which was the Poster Advertising Co., Inc., formed in 1917, and through the Outdoor Advertising Bureau. The large posting companies—plant owners—were able to supply a full service. They maintained an art service and a copy service, as well as posting service.

To quite an extent it was due to the solicitors that duplicate coverage was discouraged. The solicitors favored the posting company which gave the best service and refused to place business with competitors, and so in many instances they forced competitors to withdraw from the field. Also, the difference in rates for posting was gradually brought into force, according to which plants maintaining an AA service were given a higher rating. The effect of this was to speed up the rebuilding of plants and the standardization of the twenty-four-sheet AA panel, which, at the time Lippincott wrote, provided that the posting surface must be of steel, as it is at present.

The Association issued two publications at the time in which Lippincott wrote. One of these, *The Poster*, was a house organ circulated outside of the Association for the promotion of the business. Its name was subsequently changed to *Advertising Outdoors* and was continued until the end of 1931, then abandoned. The other, *The Association News,* was an internal organ sent only to members. It is still active, with a slight change in the name, *Outdoor Advertising Association News.* The *News* first appeared in January, 1910.

The standards for the Association were high fifteen years ago, just as they are at present. In general, the plant owner who was a member of the Association was required to keep panels up to the Association standards. The locations were restricted as to residential districts, and then, as now, panels could not be placed where they would create resentment in the minds of reasonable men and women. The rules required that the premises be kept neat and free from weeds. The molding of the panel was to be repainted green at least once a year. Also, a new regulation forbade the accepting of any business by a member of the Association which could not be accommodated by a standard showing and AA panel. It will be remembered that this was before the union of the painted bulletin interests and poster interests. A novel and somewhat naïve regulation required that a typewriter and proper stationery must be used in connection with the transaction of the firm's business. A recognition of the social importance of outdoor advertising was expressed in the following requirement: "The plant owner must always keep in mind that poster advertising is business conducted outdoors, and that other people are concerned in its proper conduct, and have rights as well as the plant owner."

The Syndicated Posters

The syndicated poster was widely used, either singly or in series. These were prepared primarily for banks, bakers, dairies, coal and lumber dealers, laundries and the like. The Donaldson Lithograph Company was the major promoter in this field, and for many years secured business through their own traveling representatives. The nature of these posters was such that they could apply to a local business in almost any city, and by adding his name and address, the local advertiser presented a finished poster. The Thomson-Symon Company perfected a silk-screen poster for the same purpose, which they sold through the Outdoor Advertising Association to operators or direct to advertisers. The Thomas Cusack Company also syndicated posters of the same character, which were lithographed for them by the Morgan Lithograph Company.

This type of business flourished in the period 1915–1925. The Donaldson Company continued until about the height of the depression, but the Outdoor Advertising Association discontinued the practice in 1931. The Thomson-Symon Company has continued in the field with a greatly increased volume of business. There are also several other companies who operate on the same basis.

Reorganizations

Among the dominant owners were the Thomas Cusack Company, which had lately absorbed the R. J. Gunning interests of Chicago. Then the Barney Link interests of Brooklyn, Chicago, St. Louis, Pittsburgh, and other cities, which had passed into the management and part ownership of Kerwin H. Fulton, together with Mr. Fulton's other extensive properties, were combined with the O. J. Gude properties and with the Cusack Company. The combination of these companies into one constituted the establishment of the General Outdoor Advertising Company, Inc., of which Kerwin H. Fulton was made president. He continued in this office until the organization of Outdoor Advertising Incorporated in 1931, and was made president of the new corporation.

The new General Company was the largest plant owner and operator of poster plants, painted bulletins and electrical spectaculars. Foster and Kleiser was the second largest operating company. Other outstanding operators were: John Donnelly and Sons, Boston; Walker and

Company, Detroit; United Advertising Corporation, Newark; and the O'Mealia Outdoor Advertising Company, Jersey City. With the largest operators equally interested in painted bulletin and poster plants, it was inevitable that the two associations, namely, the Poster Advertising Association and the Painted Outdoor Advertising Association, of which these companies were the dominant influence, should be combined. This combination occurred in the annual meeting of the two associations, which was held jointly at Kansas City in October, 1925. Since then the Outdoor Advertising Association of America, Inc., has been the one dominant association which has represented the outdoor advertising industry.

The principal purpose of the promoters who effected the amalgamation of the two associations was well presented by Mr. Fulton. In his formal address to the Association, he said in part:

We have now come to another definitely important period of refinement in outdoor advertising. . . . In every step we have taken, the public interest has been carefully considered, and it is worth noting here that this public interest coincides absolutely with the desires and best interests of the advertiser. We realize that our medium is peculiarly a public medium, and it is our responsibility to see that it pleases the people.

The enforcement of these new standards will no doubt be burdensome to the industry, but the final result will be worth all it may cost.

Since 1925, new organizations have been formed which are given consideration in other chapters in this book. They are the Outdoor Advertising Incorporated, which came into existence in 1931; and the Traffic Audit Bureau, which was organized in 1934.

Extent of the Outdoor Advertising Industry

From a promiscuous part-time employment of unorganized men carried on over the country, to the present well organized, well conducted and highly responsible association of businessmen, is a long distance. The industry at the present time includes 1,050 plant owners, distributed throughout the United States in 17,000 cities and towns. In Canada there are fifty-three plant owners covering 280 cities and towns. Approximately 33,000 are directly employed in the industry. These are divided as follows:

Real estate and leasing division	2,500
Plant and structures division	15,000
Service division	7,500
Management and clerical division:	
Men	2,500
Women	3,000
Solicitors	1,500
Artists	500

To these should be added 1,000 men and 200 women who are plant owners.

Indirectly, there are thousands of others given employment because of the supplies consumed by the industry. Paper manufacturers, lumber and steel mills, lithographing plants, automobile companies, and manufacturers of paint and lacquer, wire, adhesive products, electric current, electric accessories and supplies, brushes, tools and machinery, office equipment of all kinds, printing, color and art supplies, concrete, hardware, stencil silk, and many others find valuable customers in the outdoor advertising industry. The annual purchase of steel and other equipment and supplies for its structures has mounted to as much as 15 million dollars. The lithographing plants of the country supply upwards of 4 million posters a year, which constitutes a substantial part of the business of that 80 million dollars industry. Transportation and insurance companies are among the others who sell service on a large scale to the outdoor advertising industry.

The investment of the members of the Outdoor Advertising Association of America, Inc., in plant and equipment is more than $125,000,000. In this sum the public has a substantial interest. Stockholders in outdoor advertising companies are found in every State in the Union.

CHAPTER 3

Elements of Marketing

Marketing

In the most comprehensive sense, marketing means the transfer of goods from the hands of those who produce them to the hands of consumers. It includes all the changes of ownership; all the transportation and warehousing involved; all the financing and risk taking necessary to the movement and preservation of those goods; all the educational and investigational effort first to determine what to provide and then to convince the consumer that the product is what he wants. In the course of a year, literally hundreds of different items are bought by each family. In the space of a few years these hundreds increase to thousands. This statement may be verified by consulting a few retailers from whom the family supplies are bought. The grocer has about two thousand to offer, the druggist and hardware dealer each about five thousand. Clothing, furniture, jewelry, dry goods, notions and miscellaneous supplies make a formidable list. And all these refer only to consumption goods, which are replaced or replenished frequently.

All the construction work involved in erecting buildings, bridges and transportation machinery; the equipment and supplies of factories; building highways and sewer systems; supplying business with incidentals necessary to conduct its routine; and supplying institutions with their numerous and varied requirements are all parts of marketing—the most conspicuous parts.

Consumer and Industrial Goods

The marketing and consumption of consumer goods rather than durable goods are the chief interest of this text. These goods are supplied to consumers primarily by retail stores. Some are sold direct to consumers by the producers; some are sold by peddlers, either foot or wagon. But these are really itinerant merchants with limited stocks. The house-to-house canvasser usually represents some manufacturer as agent. This constitutes a form of selling direct.

Consumption goods, as the name implies, are those items of merchandise which are bought frequently by consumers and in comparatively small amounts. They are not necessarily consumer goods, although the greatest volume does go for household supplies. Fuel is an item classed under consumption, as it is used currently and by both consumers and industries. Food is another consumption product, or, perhaps better, group of products.

Durable goods also are sold to general consumers and to industry. Any item is classed as durable when its period of consumption cannot be definitely determined, but which is expected to continue in use for a term of years. Everything ultimately wears out and so is consumed. But building materials, most kinds of machinery, heavy furniture and floor coverings are expected to last for an indefinite period and so are called durable goods. The volume of sale of these goods fluctuates to a much greater extent between times of prosperity and depression than is true of consumption goods.

The consumption of durable goods is vastly more in industry than in the home. One of the principal uses of durable goods is to produce consumption goods. The equipment of factories and of transportation companies and even farm equipment are all largely employed for this purpose.

In 1929 the United States Bureau of the Census reported a gross wholesale business of $68,950,108,000 as compared with retail sales of $49,114,653,000. But this figure for wholesaling included the sales of industrial distributors—those who sold supplies and equipment only to the industrial field—as well as the sales to retailers.

While the 1933 business census showed a decrease in retail sales of from $49,114,653,000 to $25,037,225,000 representing a drop of 49 per cent, the wholesale business decreased from $68,950,108,000 to $32,151,373,000 or 52.6 per cent. These figures include all the consumption goods sold by wholesalers to retailers as well as the durable goods sold both to retail stores and to the industrialists.

By eliminating the whole industrial market from consideration, and disregarding the sale of all durable goods except those sold by retailers, the field of marketing is so simplified that it can be adequately treated in the space available in this text. Our purpose is to give consideration only to mass markets which are influenced by mass advertising.

How Goods Are Selected

A very human and practical question presents itself. How are all these goods and materials selected? Is each item carefully scrutinized? Is it weighed, or measured, or tested? The reader has but to review some of his recent purchases to get a partial answer. The intrinsic merits of very few articles are ascertained before purchase. Rather, one relies on one or more of the following aids to selection:

1. Recommendations of friends or of sellers. These recommendations may have many forms. The storekeeper, by act, if not by word, recommends merchandise that he displays prominently. The same thing is true in a slightly different way when a consumer makes a conspicuous exhibit of the brand of an article he owns or uses.

2. Knowledge of the product through experience.
3. Belief in the product because of advertising. This in reality is the written recommendation of the maker.

The trade-mark supplies a convenient means of identifying a product made familiar by any of the three processes. Far more than that, the trade-mark makes familiar many products that may never have been purchased. Then when the need arises it is human nature to select the known rather than the unknown. The common saying, "It must be good, it is so extensively advertised," aptly describes the buyer's attitude toward the product which he has seen mentioned so many times. Each individual buyer may not stop to analyze his mental processes—probably very few do—but some such reasoning as this has probably been at the basis of the common belief in advertised goods. The advertiser has so much invested in good will that he could not afford to skimp his product or otherwise to let it fall below its accepted standard. A rumor that "Beecher's soup is not nearly as good as it used to be" travels so fast that it takes months or even years for the correction to overtake it. Furthermore, the saving that comes from cheapening the product is almost sure to be much more than offset by the added expense in selling it, unless the price is dropped. That usually is a confession of change of quality, which may require the development of a wholly new market.

If tradition may be believed, it was once the common practice of cigar manufacturers to build up a brand of cigars with first quality tobacco and advertising. Then to "milk" the brand by cheapening the product. The General Cigar Company was organized with a plan and purpose which was the antithesis of this. This company realized that it was so difficult and so expensive to create a market for a product that the loss through destroying such a market was far more than any profits that might result from a saving on the materials which went into the product. They reduced the number of brands from over fifty to five and proceeded vigorously to extend the market for those five. Subsequently, the number of brands was reduced to four.

Dealer Influence

With a large number of goods, dealer influence is highly influential. With a few, it practically amounts to dictation. For example, your car has not been giving satisfactory performance. You talk to the mechanic at the garage. He advises new piston rings. You ask somewhat timidly whether the Elkins is a good ring. You have seen it extensively advertised. "Naw," the mechanic replies, "I wouldn't put that piece of junk on an ice wagon."

As a result of this colloquy you will probably accept the mechanic's recommendation, or go elsewhere for your repairs. This lies at one side of the zone of dealer influence, at the other is the old man at the newsstand. It is impossible to conceive of him switching his customers from one newspaper to another by a good sales talk.

Dealers, being human, like to have their recommendations accepted. So, other things being equal, they will recommend purchases which will meet with favor. The grocer may never have eaten Budlong cheese, but if he has seen it advertised extensively, he will recommend it with confidence, believing that his recommendation will be accepted, and accepted for the reason that the advertising has created the same good impression in his customer's mind as it has in his mind.

With technical goods, such as watches, clocks, radios, power washing machines and ironers, and electrical refrigerators and ranges, it is evident that the dealer is expected to know much more about his product than his customer knows. If he really does know the comparative values of the different makes, and is fair with his customers, his advice and recommendations will be valued. The same thing is true of style goods. The retailer knows all that his manufacturers tell him; all that his customers tell him; and all that he can learn by investigation. He should know goods better than the consumers know them. But seldom is a storekeeper wholly free from the suspicion that he has a monetary interest in pushing one item rather than another. If he is to retain the confidence of his customers, he must be able to advise them as to what will best satisfy *their* needs. It is by that kind of service that a store builds a reputation and gains an extended patronage.

Primary Interests of Retailers

It is seldom that a retailer thinks through his economic relationship with the community from which he gets his support. He is in business to make a profit. But profit should be the reward of a real service. The store has no legitimate claim to support from those in the trading area which it serves. People of the district are under no obligations to patronize or support a store. They did not ask the store to come to them. The only sane or business reason for opening a new store is that it can offer some service which the people who are supposed to constitute its customers will welcome. That is, they will appreciate this service to such an extent that they will give the store their patronage. The store must demonstrate its ability and willingness to provide such service.

The idea that a store is the purchasing agent for a community is largely a fiction. An agent is deliberately chosen by his principal, and subject to the supervision, direction and control of that principal. To say that when a child of five runs to the nearest store with his newly acquired nickel to invest in a package of chewing gum, that the store is his purchasing agent is ridiculous. Is it any more logical to say that, when a woman stops her automobile in front of a store to buy some of her favored laundry soap, she has constituted the store as her purchasing agent?

No doubt the great stores in many respects do act as purchasing agents for their clientele. They often interpret the needs of their patrons to manufacturers who then design a product that is more acceptable than any the manufacturer had designed before. One great store periodically surveys the shoppers who visit it, to learn their preferences; what they like and about what they are willing to pay. Such a store does constitute a purchasing agent.

In 1935, there were 1,649,081 retail stores in the United States. All but a very few of them were manufacturers' outlets, rather than purchasing agents for customers. They did not and do not go to the people who constitute their clientele to see what they want, but rather to manufacturers, or to the wholesalers, who are the manufacturers' representatives, to see what they have to sell. It is the one who produces the goods that assumes the trouble and expense of determining what will sell and in what amounts, and then *he* tells the retailers.

Stores have three definite objectives in mind in selecting their stocks of merchandise:

1. They want goods with an ample margin.
2. They want those articles which sell in quantities.
3. They want well-known goods which will repeat and so create prestige for their stores.

Retailers as Businessmen

Probably no businesses are conducted with greater skill than some of the leading department stores of the country. Some of the independents, some of the chains, and a large number of specialty stores are real business institutions, operated with admirable efficiency. But a vast majority of the country's retail establishments are in the same class with peanut venders. Of the 1,543,158 stores in the United States in the prosperous year of 1929, there were 673,846 which did less than $10,000 business in a year. That is just about $30 a day, excluding Sundays and holidays, for the best of them. Another 31.51 per cent registered sales of between $10,000 and $30,000 a year. That means that the best of the group sold only about $100 a day on an average.

Slightly more than three-quarters—75.17 per cent, to be exact—had annual sales of $30,000 or less. More than two-fifths had sales of $10,000 or less. These are the stores which make the cost of selling goods high. These are the stores that have a high percentage of failures. These are the ones that make collection costs high. Together they provide only 23.28 per cent of retail sales, which is less than one-quarter. To summarize, 75 per cent of the stores sell less than 25 per cent of the goods which constitute the retail

The Coca-Cola Company has created a great volume of business for its distributors. Because of the confidence druggists have in Coca-Cola advertising, they are willing to display and advertise this popular product. They do this knowing that an extensive demand has been created, and they advertise it, too, to share in supplying the demand.

sales of the country, while the remaining 25 per cent of the retailers—the businessmen who run stores—secure 75 per cent of sales.

It is this vast number of stores that exist on business that is created for them by wholesalers or manufacturers. Some of these have gone to great trouble and expense to educate the dealers who supply their products for the public, but their efforts have nearly always ended in failure. This, of course, does not mean that none of the retailers have benefited by the help offered them. Some have taken advantage of it and have developed into real merchants. These are the exception and their number is so small that it does not justify the trouble or expense that the efforts have cost.

The great automobile manufacturers leave little for their distributors to decide for themselves. They are told minutely what to do and what not to do. One of the leading manufacturers, for example, does not permit his dealers to have any opening between the sales room and the machine shop. Even with such close supervision, from 20 to 25 per cent of the automobile dealers go out of business every year.

Although 75 per cent of the stores sell only 23 per cent of the goods, that represents an immense business in itself; over $12,000,000,000 in 1929 and $6,000,000,000 in the very lean year of 1933. As we have already seen, 673,846 stores do a gross business of $10,000 a year, or less. Most of them do less. Add to these 486,094 stores with maximum sales of $30,000 and the surprising total is 1,159,939 stores which together sell only 23 per cent of the goods bought at retail. And that was for the prosperous year of 1929. But the larger the number of stores and the weaker they average, the more effort is necessary on the part of the manufacturer to create a demand for his goods. To attempt to make efficient merchants out of the vast horde of retail distributors in any line of goods is a much greater undertaking than to create an acceptance on the part of the public for the goods which those stores sell.

Goods Sold in Small Stores

With the exception of exclusive shops in the large cities, goods sold in small stores are primarily in the class of staples. Branded products will be included, but for the most part they will be the kind of merchandise that is regarded as staples by consumers, even though technically they might be classed as specialties. An example is laundry and toilet soap. Very little of either is now sold without the manufacturer's brand. Women who buy a trade-marked laundry soap think of it as being a staple quite as much as bulk granulated sugar. Marketing men who insist on treating

such branded merchandise as a specialty are slaves to
definitions in defiance of common sense.

Convenience goods constitute a major part of the stocks
of small retailers in the food group, in general and country
stores, in cigar stores, in drugstores, and in some of the
others as hardware, coal and lumber yards, and in farmers'
supply stores. These storekeepers—the ones in the class of
$30,000 sales and less—are seldom able to trust their own
judgment of goods. They like branded merchandise, the
quality of which is not open to question. And if complaint is
made, they want the protection of a well-known label to
shield them from a wrathy customer. Yet many of these
little merchants prefer to handle goods bearing a distributor's brand for which they can get an exclusive agency. This
usually gives them a wider margin, and dealers feel that
they are "just as good," or, if slightly inferior, that their
customers will not detect the difference. Also, an item for
which they have exclusive sale tends to protect them in
meeting competition.

The convenience goods sold through the stores mentioned
in the preceding paragraph constitute a large part of the
home supplies. Food is approximately 22 per cent; tobacco,
1 per cent; drugstore products, 3 per cent; coal and wood, 2
per cent; general merchandise group, 13 per cent; farmers'
supply, 2 per cent; hardware and farm implement stores,
$2\frac{1}{2}$ per cent; filling stations, 6 per cent. That means that
for a large part of the population over 50 per cent of retail
purchases come through the smaller stores. Not only does
this apply to the rural population, but to all the urban
population which gets its supplies from the neighborhood
stores and from the secondary trading centers.

This also means that manufacturers who supply this
class of staple goods under their own brands cannot hope to
get adequate representation from the vast number of stores
they must depend on for distribution. To put it bluntly,
these small retailers know little about the goods they sell,
and still less about competing goods which they do not

sell. Even in the great department stores, most of the sales people who pass out goods of the staple class know little about them.

One of the leading merchants[1] of the country frankly admitted, "The department store is weakest where it should be the strongest—at the point where store and customer meet."

Two Philosophies of Marketing

There are two philosophies as to how goods should be sold. One is that the manufacturer who makes the product has the chief interest in it. He wants his product to be popular, to be satisfactory. If so, he can sell more of it. Increased sales lead to mass production, and mass production to decreased manufacturing costs. The consumer will then buy for less, the manufacturer will sell more and make more profit. He is so vitally interested in the popularity of his product that he will make good on every item that proves unsatisfactory. This is a protection to the buying public. In order for a manufacturer to build up such a market, he may need to advertise—not only advertise to his distributors, so that they will know his product, but advertise to consumers, so that they will accept the product. In that case the consumers will be *his* customers as distinguished from his distributors' customers.

The other philosophy is that manufacturing and selling are two different kinds of business. They require wholly different kinds of abilities, and should be so separated that there would be no conflict between them. It is maintained that when a manufacturer undertakes to run a sales campaign that he divides his energies and so does not do either as efficiently as if he devoted his whole time to one. Under this doctrine, the wholesalers and retailers are held up to be the merchants upon whom the public depends. They buy what the public wants and go to those manufacturers who are the most efficient for their supplies. Mr. Patman,

[1] F.MacL. Radford, President of Bon Marché, Seattle, Wash.

coauthor of the Robinson-Patman Act, believed this theory so fanatically that he wanted a law passed by Congress that would forbid the manufacturers of goods sold in interstate trade from selling to retailers. There was a time, he points out, when that condition prevailed. It still prevails with the great majority of imported goods. It is also true of much of the merchandise which the chains and department stores buy from manufacturers to sell under their brands.

When Wholesalers Failed

That system broke down when the new inventions began to make their appearance. The manufacturer of power farm equipment had to go to the farmer and demonstrate his product before the farmer could be induced to buy. In a different way the same thing was true of a large part of electrical equipment for homes—which included refrigerators, washing machines, vacuum cleaners, ranges, sewing machines, radios—automobiles, and of nearly all industrial equipment. Of the proprietary medicines, it has been true for more than a century. They were among the first products to be extensively presented under a distinguishing label—trade name or trade-mark. With industrial equipment, especially automatic machines, there never has been a wholesale system of selling. But industrial distributors supply even the largest manufacturers with a considerable amount of their supplies, such as small tools, belting, waste, etc. The United States Census of Distribution classes them as wholesalers.

Neither the chains nor department stores can be trusted to go out and create a market for such an item as a vacuum cleaner. The same is true of wholesalers. Once the vacuum cleaner has been introduced into a market and there is a demand for it, any of these distributors may make strenuous efforts to get a substitute made for them which they can sell in place of the original. What has just been said of specialty selling also applies to merchandise of strikingly superior quality. When a manufacturer brings out an article that is strikingly superior to others, it is natural to want the credit for it, and also to want the future business which will come from the word-of-mouth advertising that results from its superior service. So, first, he puts his trade-mark on it, then he goes to the public and tells them about it. He can seldom trust a distributor to demonstrate a product of small value. An example of this occurred with a manufacturer of a vacuum bottle made of light steel instead of glass. It was practically unbreakable. Of necessity, it sold at a higher price than the breakable glass competitor. With considerable selling effort, some of the large New York stores were induced to put in a limited stock. Sales were very slow. One day the sales manager dropped into one of these stores and asked to be shown vacuum bottles. The young lady at the counter brought out two; his own and a cheaper one. "Why is this one priced so high?" he asked innocently. The young lady was puzzled. "It does seem kinda high, but I guess it's an awful good bottle," was her weak explanation. A label on the container explained that it was made of steel and would not break. The young lady had not read the label. Other stores did little or no better in explaining the merits of the bottle.

Perhaps it is not too much to say that if wholesalers and other distributors had been sufficiently alert to take on new articles and go out and *create* new markets for them, manufacturers would have been content to turn the whole selling job over to competent distributors. But where the idea has to be sold first, the manufacturer soon learned that he must sell the public himself, even though he permitted the established distributors to pass it along. As he created the market, he felt that he controlled the whole situation, both manufacturing and selling. Then he began to look at wholesalers and retailers as his agents. Furthermore, he felt that when he paid outdoor advertising, newspapers and other media for selling his product, that those who did the physical handling were not entitled to get paid also for selling it.

The Wholesalers' Predicament

The original idea of a wholesaler was a kind of super-merchant who sold to stores rather than to individuals. The economy of this arrangement is easily presented. Suppose that one wholesaler supplied a thousand stores with the goods made by fifty different manufacturers. Each manufacturer then sold to but one account in the district, instead of the thousand that was necessary in selling direct. The wholesaler employed twenty salesmen who adequately covered the territory. The fifty manufacturers each had but one salesman who spent part of one day a month with each wholesaler. Had these manufacturers all sold direct to the stores, each would have had to employ twenty salesmen to cover the same ground. That would have required a thousand salesmen full time to dispose of the same amount of goods that fifty salesmen (one for each manufacturer) could sell the wholesaler in a small fraction of their time.

The questions naturally arise, Why did not this system continue? What happened that led to all the present-day confusion? The questions are not easily answered, because there were so many things that exerted an influence. One thing was the rise of the great stores. When a merchant in a metropolitan district rose to such prominence that he could buy by the carload, he saw no reason to have a wholesaler intervene between him and his source of supply. The services of storage, extending credit, giving aid and advice in the selection of goods might be valuable to the little store, but to the metropolitan merchant such services meant nothing. He had his own warehouses, his credit might have been equal to or better than the wholesalers, and in selecting goods he was not benefited by any help that the wholesaler could give.

When manufacturers yielded to these arguments and sold the large stores direct, wholesalers complained that they carried many accounts for the manufacturers at no profit, or even at a loss, that they should not be deprived of the profitable business of the larger stores. Then when manufacturers began to sell hotels, steamship, and other large buyers direct, many wholesalers rebelled and began to sell goods put up specially for them by small manufacturers. Soon they became active competitors of the very manufacturers whose goods they distributed. The wholesale grocer who carried Arbuckle's coffee might also have a brand of his own, which he sold to his customers instead of Arbuckle's wherever possible. This kind of treatment often resulted in a break between wholesaler and manufacturer, and the latter increasingly sold direct to dealers in many classifications of goods.

The chain stores from the start proposed to "do their own wholesaling." That is, they bought in large quantities, ran their own warehouses and made their own deliveries. At least in theory they did all this. But, as a matter of fact, they often added much to the manufacturers' difficulties. First, the general buyer had to be sold. Then it was found that getting goods approved and put on the permitted list did not bring immediate orders, even though the prices were as low and sometimes lower than were quoted to wholesalers of the district. Each store manager had to be followed up and sold. Then instead of one large shipment to a central warehouse, too often the manufacturer was asked to make deliveries to separate stores. That was true especially in cities where the manufacturer carried stocks of goods in warehouses.

But it was cold comfort to the wholesalers to know that manufacturers were not finding the chains such profitable customers as had been anticipated. The wholesaler was losing business and in many classifications of goods he was losing out.

Many Kinds of Wholesalers

The 1929 Census of Distribution listed twenty-nine different classes of business, all of which came under the general head of wholesaling. But that included industrial distributors who sold only to manufacturers, importers, exporters, commission men and manufacturers' sales agencies, many of whom had little or nothing in common with the old line wholesaler who was the chief source of supply for the retailer and the chief outlet for the manufacturers.

But even with all those eliminated, there are still left a confusing number of different kinds of business, all of which are contributing something to the distribution of goods. The chief of those who are active in marketing manufactured goods will be given below, and their chief contributions to marketing enumerated.

Wholesale merchants and *jobbers* are terms used to mean the same thing. They are the wholesalers who supply retailers. They buy in large quantities and sell in small quantities. They keep a stock of merchandise on hand. They extend credit and help in the selection of goods.

Drop shippers, or *desk jobbers*, as they are sometimes called, do not actually handle the goods they sell. They have merchandise shipped to their customers on their order, but charged to them. They supply credit to their customers as occasion justifies.

Mail-order or *catalogue wholesalers* perform most of the functions of regular wholesalers, but instead of employing salesmen they sell by means of catalogues sent to dealers.

Cash-and-carry wholesalers carry stocks of merchandise at a location convenient to customers, but they do not repack or ship merchandise. Their customers come to them with trucks, load their purchases themselves and pay cash for it. This kind of business can exist only in the larger cities where retailers are within a short distance of the wholesale stock.

Wagon jobbers perform most of the functions of the regular wholesalers. The difference is that the salesman carries his stock of goods with him and delivers at the time the order is taken. This type of wholesaler is active in several fields, prominent in which is the candy business.

Brokers are in a sense superwholesalers, as they sell largely to wholesalers. Usually they do not come into physical possession of the goods, and they do not become responsible for the goods or the payment for the goods. They buy or sell on commission, but are not permitted to accept remuneration from both buyer and seller. Often their chief function is to bring buyer and seller together.

Manufacturers' Agents sell only a part of the output of a factory. They are, as the name implies, agents of the manufacturer. As such, they are limited to territory and to terms of sale.

Selling Agent is a broader term than Manufacturers' Agent. As defined by the Committee on Definitions of the National Association of Marketing Teachers, "A selling agent is a type of broker who generally operates on an extended contractual basis; sells the entire output of his principal and has full authority with regards to prices, terms, etc." For example, the General Motors Export Company is the selling agent for the General Motors Corporation, in so far as their sales in foreign countries are concerned.

These are the most important of the distributors from whom retailers get supplies, although there are numerous others, like resident buyers and coöperative buying agencies, which are active with some of the large stores, especially in the larger cities.

The Manufacturers' Sales Problems

A Pacific Coast manufacturer of food products has, among other things, nine different spices, about the same number of extracts, four different kinds of tea and several other products. The whole family is one of distinctive merit. The quality of many of these items is so high that there is a demonstrable difference between them and competing items. To the real student, each one of the spices and all of the extracts offer interesting topics for study. But to understand why they are superior also requires study. This manufacturer has perhaps 15,000 stores to which he sells direct. These stores vary all the way from tiny "bedroom" groceries to the largest and best food stores in the country. They are scattered over some 2,225,000 square miles of territory. The average life of these storekeepers is at best 8 years. That means 2,000 or more go out of business every year. Yet that manufacturer goes on year after year trying to teach that vast horde of shopkeepers the difference between good goods and poor. Think of the immensity of the task!

Salesmen come and go, requiring a constant effort to educate these representatives so that they in turn can educate storekeepers and they in turn educate their patrons to know good spices, good extracts, good teas and the same of other products. In all but a few cases, they have failed. Fortunately for this manufacturer, there are enough discriminating people in the vast district which he covers to recognize the merit of his products, to use them and to recommend them.

The territory referred to is nearly half the area of the United States but only about 20 per cent of the population. Suppose this manufacturer decided to extend his territory to become really national. There are nearly a half-million food stores in the country. To canvass each of these, or even a representative number of them, would be an appalling task, if the same method were adopted as is now used in the territory which has been intensively cultivated for the past fifty or sixty years.

Every worthwhile manufacturer has something to offer which is of distinctive value to his customers—the ultimate consumers. He will have a better product, or he will offer more in style or convenience or value than his competitors, or there is no reason for his existence. He will succeed or fail largely in proportion to the extent in which he convinces people of the superior value he offers. The modern way is to go to those who consume his products; tell of the products, proclaim their values, make people feel familiar with them.

Very few men know the real difference between a good hat and a poor one. Most recognize that there is a difference in quality. They associate that quality with two or three of the leading brands. They do not care to "bother their heads" with the technical information necessary to understand how better hats are made. The same is true of women. Within the space of a year, the housekeeper will buy several hundred different items. Even if told why some pepper, or mustard, or cinnamon is better than other peppers and mustards and cinnamons, she probably will not remember. She is content to know which is the best and where she can get it. This attitude, as we have seen, is characteristic for half or more of her purchases. In buying a high-priced rug, a sewing machine, a mechanical refrigerator or a power washing machine, she may want to know something about the construction, why some cost so much more than others. But even here it is only the more intelligent women who will really investigate.

What has just been said of buyers for the household, is true of all but a few retailers. They do not know much about their products and are not greatly interested, further than to know if they generally give satisfaction, that they will bring repeat sales and that there will be a profit in selling them. Retailers are influenced by advertising just as are their customers, the consumers. Many of them have learned all they know about the quality of merchandise they handle by reading consumer advertising. They believe, as do their customers, that products extensively advertised "must be good." What they regard as even more important is that advertised goods have the confidence of the public and consequently can be sold, as they have a ready acceptance.

One of the chief weaknesses of some advertising media is that dealers seldom, if ever, see them. This is true of farm papers. It is a rare grocer or druggist who even knows which agricultural papers come into his trading area. It behooves the advertiser who is using this medium to see to it that his consumer advertising is brought to the attention of his dealers. On the other hand, outdoor advertising is sure to catch the eye of the dealer, and sooner or later he will realize that that advertising is helping him to sell goods.

In summarizing, it may be said that a large part of the goods which come into the home are bought on reputation. With other goods, the recommendation of friends is highly influential. The dealer's recommendation is effective with technical goods, but with most consumer goods, it is taken with reservation unless something is already known about the goods recommended. A well-advertised laundry soap may be accepted rather than some other well-known soap, if recommended by the storekeeper. But between a familiar name and one never heard before, a dealer will have difficulty in having his advice accepted, unless it is for the known merchandise. The exceptions to this are technical products, like the piston rings discussed on page 51.

It is necessary, or at least advantageous, to have the confidence of the merchant, even when the product is a staple. This can be gained through advertising more easily and at less expense than through personal salesmanship. The exceptions again are technical goods and those of high unit cost.

CHAPTER 4

Circulation and Media

Circulation Defined

There has been much written on the subject of circulation, and vast quantities of statistics have been collected. Charts, graphs, illustrated books, broadsides and almost every other conceivable form of printed matter have been used to discuss the subject. In spite of all this, the term "circulation" has come to have something of a mystery surrounding it. Many men who spend huge sums of money for advertising frankly admit it is all a puzzle to them.

As a matter of fact, the whole idea is extremely simple. "An advertising medium is a means of transmitting a sales message."[1] The message may be of designated form and size, and the advertising medium faithfully delivers it as specified. With publications, that involves preparing duplicates. In sending advertising telegrams, the telegraph company prepares the duplicates. In a different way, it also is true of outdoor advertising. In form, size and color the message is reproduced and carried to the designated audience. But if it is a poster, the advertiser provides the duplicate copies.

The circulation in all cases is the number of messages delivered. That is perfectly plain to anyone who will give it an analytical thought. When an advertiser talks about "buying so much circulation," he means that he is paying

[1] Hugh E. Agnew, "Advertising Media," D. Van Nostrand Company. Inc.

to have this message delivered to a certain number of people. They may not heed this message. They may not even notice it. But it is circulation nonetheless. When a solicitor for a newspaper, magazine or broadcasting station says that he is selling advertising, he means that he is making contracts to deliver a designated number of sales messages for the advertiser. Some advertising writers have confused message and medium. They have defined circulation in terms of "impressions." It is not the carrier of the message that makes the impression, but it is the message itself. One may not know what the boy looked like who brought the telegram, however well he remembers the message. It is not the postman who makes an impression, but the message he brings. ·

The Medium Cannot Deliver Readers

After delivering the message in its specified form and size, the medium is in no way responsible for securing reading or other attention to the message. That is the responsibility of the one who writes the message—the advertiser. If a man is too indifferent, too excited, or too much engrossed otherwise to read a telegram which he receives, it is not the fault of the telegraph company. They performed their duty when they delivered the message to him. So with the paid space in a newspaper or magazine, the message may not interest the one who buys the newspaper or magazine, but the function of each of these media has been fulfilled when it is delivered to the buyer. With the broadcasting company, the message cannot be delivered unless there is a receiving set tuned in in the home to which the message is sent. Therefore, its circulation would be the number of messages sent to the homes, provided the receiving sets were tuned in when the message was sent. Of course circulation is limited to the zone reached by the broadcasting station. If the owners of these sets are not interested at the time, they may not get the message, but, nevertheless, they constitute part of the circulation of the broadcasting company, for it sent the message and the message was available. The fact that a circular or other advertisement or letter is thrown into the wastebasket without being read is not the fault of the postman. He delivered the message. One of the fundamental differences between the mail message and that of the radio is that if the listener is not attentive at the time the radio message comes, he will lose it irretrievably. Messages that are printed can be referred to on future occasions. Again, we repeat that the reader must be won. He cannot be bought. Circulation is the number of delivered messages.

Probably most of the confusion has resulted from the term "circulation," which is borrowed from common parlance. Its original meaning was to move from place to place in an irregular circuit, finally returning to the starting place. The government *circulated* money. The government sent it out to be passed from one to another, that is, circulated, until it finally returned to the starting place for redemption. Circulation, in advertising, has been given a restricted specialized meaning, which has not heretofore been satisfactorily defined. In so far as direct mail and publications are considered, the original meaning has a fairly logical application, although it does not return to the starting place.

With posters, painted displays, car cards, electrical spectaculars and even more with radio, to apply the term circulation to the number of messages delivered is a wholly new use of the word—unwarranted in its original sense. It is much more appropriate to use the word "delivery" in all these cases. What is the delivery of a publication? Evidently the number delivered—not merely printed. With direct mail, the same term applies with the same definiteness. What was the delivery of the circular? From such a definite term, no confusion can result. The delivery of a window display, of a poster, or a radio broadcast is equally definite and understandable. The delivery in each case is the number of people to whom a message was delivered.

But owing to the strong force of habit, there is small chance of the word "circulation" being discarded for another term, no matter how much more appropriate the other word may be.

Quality of Circulation

The foregoing considerations do not ignore the fact that similar media differ greatly on the quality of the service they perform. For example, two magazines may have approximately the same circulation. One of these is filled with such interesting material that every buyer is a consistent reader; the other may find its way into the wastebasket in the original wrapper for sheer lack of interest to induce the recipient to open it. The same condition may prevail with two different newspapers. While one may be read regularly and with a considerable degree of thoroughness, the other may be valued for some one feature, such as the comic page or a favored column or market reports, and have little other interest. Again, with radio advertising, one broadcasting station may have a reputation for presenting such good programs that it will have many more regular listeners than another station which is far less popular. Again this is the difference in the quality of the service and is not necessarily the difference in the size of the circulation. This difference in quality can be described by saying that selling a medium means convincing the advertiser that the quality of delivery is satisfactory. Bill distributors may cover the same territory, leaving circulars at the same houses, but if one puts the circulars under the door and the other throws them on the front porch, there is a difference in the quality of the service.

It is evident that comparing two like media is comparatively simple and may be demonstrated with a degree of accuracy, but to compare the efficiency of two unlike media, such as radio and magazines or newspapers and outdoor advertising is much more difficult. No method has yet been developed for a scientific measurement of comparative values of different kinds of advertising media. There is no way to demonstrate in advance whether a newspaper or a local broadcasting station is more effective. It is still a matter of trial and error. A similar amount of money may be invested in each medium, then the results watched closely to decide which is better for some particular time, place and product. This is sure to be inconclusive, however, because the nature of the message must of necessity be different for each medium. If the copy is much superior in one instance, it is the copy and not the medium that should be credited with the better result. It is difficult to compare in advance copy that is unlike in character; difficult to the point of impossibility. A sample market may be used to test the copy, and that requires skill and experience.

The same copy in two different newspapers may be used to test results for those newspapers. To use the same copy in a magazine and a newspaper where the size of the page is different, the kind of paper is unlike, and the frequency of issue in one is much greater than the other, will not necessarily produce comparable results.

The author does not maintain that a convincing test of two unlike media is impossible, but it is so difficult and there are so many variable factors that it requires the experience of an expert to make an authentic comparison. Space does not permit a full discussion of this subject here, but the reader may find a comprehensive discussion in "Advertising Media."

Rules Governing Media Selection

The selection of an advertising medium involves a combination of both the message and the means of sending it to prospective purchasers. The following factors are important in making this decision:

1. The nature of the message. Is it long or short? Does it involve a picture, map or diagram? Is it something

that should be presented in a manner that can be reviewed and analyzed? Is it of such a nature that a striking picture will convey the most appealing aspects as in advertising many food products?

2. Is the time element important? If one must have the sales message before the public in a few hours, the choice is much more closely limited than in a continuous campaign which runs for weeks or even months.

3. What would be the cost of preparing and sending the required number of messages by each of these media? This does not mean merely the cost of reaching every one of so many individuals in a given district but of reaching each of the possible buyers. With some products, everyone is a possible buyer. Chewing gum, cigarettes, confections and similar goods are of this nature. Then the greatest economy requires the use of media that will present the message to the greatest number of people the greatest number of times, at the least cost. If, on the other hand, there is only one or two buyers in a thousand people, a more restricted medium may be preferred.

4. What is the prestige of the medium? The cheaply printed handbill or homemade display card creates no confidence. It is a cheap means of announcement. On the other hand, beautiful pictures in color, presented by a medium that is known to be responsible, tend to create confidence in the product even though the product is wholly new to readers.

5. The amount of money available to carry on the campaign may also be an influential factor. Indeed, it may be the determining factor. The manufacturer might like to advertise much more extensively and would find a different form of advertising more economical and effective, yet if the funds available provide only for a few circular letters, he must be governed accordingly. The same principle holds when much larger amounts are involved.

Example of Media Selection

As an example of media selection, suppose you had a beautiful summer home that you wanted to sell. If you could convey an impression of the expansiveness of the lawn, the coolness of the breeze, and the shade of the trees, together with the boating facilities and spacious drives, it would be part of the sales message. It would be the introductory part, which would arouse interest and create desire. Furthermore, if the picture or pictures showed people enjoying the comforts and luxuries that the estate provided, in addition to presenting the actual property, it might make the estate seem even more attractive. To place these pictures before possible buyers would be the service of an advertising medium. It is not the intent of the message up to this point to close a sale, for with a property of such evident value probably many steps will intervene between the point where prospects become interested in the property and the point at which they finally decide to buy. Meanwhile, many other things must be considered. The "prospect," or, if there are more than one, "prospects," will want to know: the distance from transportation; the provisions for light, gas, sewage, heating equipment; the type of neighborhood; the cost of upkeep; the possible increase in value; the assessed value; the price asked; and the terms of payment. Probably many other inquiries will be made concerning the property.

If a large investment is involved, it might be expedient to attract many possible buyers, as there probably will be only one in several thousands who may be actively interested in buying the property. In arousing the interests of hundreds or even thousands of people in such a property, there might be an endless amount of correspondence if the inquiries of each one were to be answered by individual letters. So the seller would do well to prepare the answers to anticipated questions in printed form and send these as at least a partial answer to inquiries made by the prospective purchasers. This, also, would be an advertising medium.

It would be of restricted circulation, going only to prospects
who had evinced sufficient interest to make inquiries.
However, it would be an advertising medium and would
deliver a sales message in a dignified and impressive way.
It would make the estate seem more important than merely
sending a mimeographed sheet.

Another Example from Real Estate

Instead of a summer home, suppose you had a large office
building that you wanted to rent. Now your interest in
publicity of necessity becomes much more extended. First
of all, you decide to what particular business or profession
you can best appeal: publishers, transportation companies,
importers, physicians, dentists, lawyers, architects. Having
decided this, your first concern is in reaching as many of the
members of the profession as you think might be interested.
Lists are easily available, and a well-printed booklet, if
generously distributed, would probably bring a number of
inquiries. But it is a well-known fact that professional men,
particularly those who depend upon the general public for
clients, like physicians and dentists, prefer to have their
offices in a well-known building. There are many reasons for
this, one of the chief of which is that the building is easily
remembered, and as a headquarters for offices, adds prestige
to its occupants. A first-class building pre-empted by the
members of a profession will attract patients for its renters.
To make a building well known to the public requires much
more than merely sending circulars to prospective tenants,
or the incidental publicity in newspapers. Attractive pictures of the building, with the name prominently displayed
and perhaps some directions, such as a map of streetcar
and bus routes, showing how it can be most conveniently
reached from different parts of the city, might constitute an
effective campaign. If the campaign is successful, it would
be valuable to tenants and would make the space for rental
more valuable. Space could be more easily rented. This
second purpose of the campaign is more difficult than the

first and probably much more expensive, and the returns are hard to trace, as they would all be indirect. Or rather, being indirect, results would be much more difficult to trace.

Again, the same basic questions arise. How could the sales message be carried most convincingly and with the least expense? It is conceivable that two media might be used, one to reach the prospective tenants and another to popularize the building with the general public. There is also the possibility of using mass media for both. Showing a good picture of the building and writing the copy in such a way that it would invite inquiries from tenants might bring satisfactory returns. Doctors, dentists, lawyers, architects and a host of businessmen use public conveyances and would see car card and painted bulletin advertising. Realizing that a suitable office building is being extensively publicized makes it seem attractive to prospective clients. Another thing should be considered. A painted bulletin would be so impersonal that the solicitation could not be considered unethical. There is an unwritten code that frowns upon one landlord enticing tenants away from another. The more direct the overture to a prospective tenant, the more likelihood of trampling the code of real estate ethics. Conversely, the more indirect, the less danger of criticism.

These two illustrations, both from the field of real estate, bring out a few of the numerous questions that are involved in most cases concerning the selection of media.

Classification of Advertising Media

Although there are more different media in advertising than one could recount in many pages, all of these can be grouped into four separate divisions, each with distinctive characteristics. The four are: mass media or signs, publications, direct advertising, and radio.

Publications include both magazines and newspapers. The striking characteristics of publications are: they are issued at regular intervals; are sold to the public rather than given away; and they go to approximately the same readers month after month and even year after year. In so far as the advertiser is concerned, he looks at these lists as being fixed. He must take them in their entirety, or not use them at all. Also, his message must conform to the size and shape of the page, and is limited to the color or colors chosen by the publisher.

With these media, the Audit Bureau of Circulations checks circulation. It is an organization made up of advertising agencies, advertisers and publishers. By constitutional limitation, a majority of the directors must be advertisers, although both of the other two classes of members may be more numerous. "Net circulation," according to the Audit Bureau, "is the number of copies that are sold for at least fifty per cent of their advertised price."

Direct advertising is so well known and understood that it needs little discussion. Its first outstanding feature is that the advertiser controls the audience that he appeals to. He makes out his own lists and varies them according to his requirements. Second, the advertiser varies the form of his message to suit the time and place and circumstances. It may be a post card or a 2,500-page catalogue. It may be printed on paper, cloth, leather or metal. It may be a simple message or a form of utility, either a blotter or envelope opener. Third, the advertiser also controls the frequency of sending his messages. He may send out one broadside and only one. He may have a follow-up system which runs through a cycle of letters, circulars, booklets, catalogues, etc.; or it may be a continuous performance, such as mailing a house organ once a month, or more often.

Mass media or signs are of many different forms, such as electrical spectaculars, painted bulletins, posters, identification and point of purchase signs, store signs, window displays, bus, streetcar, elevated and subway cards and posters, and the vast number of miscellaneous exhibits, such as airplane streamers, skywriting, wagon signs and many more. Being a mass medium, signs are valued according to the number of people that may see them or the number of sales messages they may deliver. The media are not selective, except to the extent that they may be used in designated districts preferred by the advertiser. Electrical spectaculars, painted bulletins and posters constitute what is known as the "outdoor advertising industry." (For rates and evaluation, see Chapters 5 to 7.) So much space is devoted to this medium elsewhere that it

A twenty-four-sheet poster of unusual attractiveness. It was given first place in the seventh annual exhibition of Outdoor Advertising Art for 1936.

will be passed over here with a mere mention of its basic characteristics. It is the one medium that can be depended on adequately to reach both consumers and distributors and consequently needs little or no "merchandising."

Publication Classifications

Magazines are variously classed by their size, by their literary content, and by the frequency of issue. Not only that, but all these classifications are jumbled together in such an otherwise scholarly publication as *Printers' Ink*. There are approximately two thousand different magazines that are published regularly. A practical classification of these can be given in terms of the literary content, as is shown by the following comprehensive grouping, where content is made the basis of classification. This differs from other classifications, no two of which are alike.

Newspapers:[1]

1. Daily morning, daily evening, Sunday.
2. Weekly publications—the country press.
3. Foreign-language publications.

Magazines:

1. General.
2. Women's.
3. Class.
4. Business.
    a. Trade (or distributors).
    b. Industrial.
    c. Administration, executive, or management.
    d. Technical and professional.
5. Religious and fraternal.
6. Agricultural.
    a. National.
    b. Local.
    c. Special.

Directories and miscellaneous.

This classification, it will be noted, has one weakness in that it uses the word "class" to describe a type of magazine, when, as a matter of fact, each magazine, except those designated as "general," appeal to a particular class. The term, however, is used so commonly in advertising circles that there is little danger of its being misunderstood. Such magazines as *Town and Country, Esquire* and *House and Garden* fall in this group.

In periods of issue, magazines are weekly, biweekly, monthly and quarterly. Those that are published semi-annually or annually are considered rather as yearbooks or directories.

Strong and Weak Points of Magazines

The features of magazines which advertisers value are that for the most part they are carefully edited, and that

[1] Hugh E. Agnew, "Advertising Media," D. Van Nostrand Company, Inc.

they are authoritative and, therefore, inspire confidence in the editorial content, which tends to stimulate confidence in the advertising. Most of them are well printed and are sufficiently well bound so that they withstand several readings. A large number of magazines, perhaps a majority, are read by more than one person. Being well printed, magazines permit the use of high-grade illustrations. With most, the use of color is possible, but it is usually available for large space only. Magazines also are long-lived, each one surviving its predecessor by a considerable space of time. Data on magazines are fairly accurate, and their circulation has been studied more thoroughly than that of any other medium, except outdoor advertising. Advertising rates are fixed and the list of advertisers, with their expenditures in the different magazines, is easily ascertained.

Magazine readers fall into groups of definite interests. This again has the exception of the general magazines. Each major interest of life is represented by one or more magazines. Women's styles are presented with authority by most of the leading women's magazines and especially by such as *Harper's Bazaar* and *Vogue*. Outdoor sports are represented by such magazines as *Yachting, Spur* and *Field and Stream*. Religion, vocations, education, politics and even avocations have their "organs" or group mouthpieces.

One of the restrictions of magazine advertising is that it is rigid. Copy has to be supplied from 1 to 6 months in advance of publication.

Another limitation of magazine advertising is that a very large part of the population does not read magazines with any degree of regularity, if at all. In contrast, nearly one per cent of the families of the country regularly subscribe for twelve or more magazines each. One family in a hundred may seem like a very small part, but when it is considered there are thirty million families in the country, 1 per cent means that 300,000 families have a minimum of twelve magazines coming into the home regularly. Another three and one-half per cent of the homes have from nine to eleven magazines. An advertiser cannot be sure that he is not having a very high degree of duplication in any magazine schedules that he may choose, for up to date the studies of magazine duplication have not been very highly conclusive.

The advertising rates vary beyond reason. One of the nationals charges less than $2 per page a thousand for black and white space. The usual rate for the general magazines runs about $3 per page a thousand, again for black and white. As the reading audience becomes more selective, the rates per thousand copies advance. Some of the magazines charge as high as $15 to $20 a page per thousand. Fractional pages are sold at proportional rates; but some magazines require a slight increase for broken pages. Many give an exact proportional rate down to one-eighth page, smaller space being sold by the agate line. An agate line is a space one-fourteenth of an inch high across a column.

Business Publications

Business publications are lumped in with magazines in the logic of reducing the classification to its lowest minimum. The magazines that go to businessmen have comparatively little in common with magazines that go into the home. They do not offer entertainment features and are in no sense recreational reading. They frequently have rates that are very high as compared with the general magazines. Ten to twenty-five dollars a page a thousand is not uncommon. Fifty dollars a page a thousand is by no means unknown. That means 5 cents a page for each one who buys the magazine. Oftentimes the circulation is small, but the value of any business publication as an advertising medium is not gauged according to the size of the circulation, but rather to the extent to which it covers an industry or specific group of buying interests. Obviously, if an advertiser is interested in reaching those engaged in the petroleum industry, he will value the degree of coverage far above any reasonable rate per thousand. To double the circulation provides no more customers. But to cut down the number would omit valuable prospects of far greater potential value than any possible saving in cost. Again, if a magazine goes to eight hundred manufacturers of an article like straw hats, it represents the whole market for materials to manufacturers. Increasing circulation to eight thousand would not enhance its value to the advertiser.

The business magazine is a primary medium for those who sell directly to the industry represented, and only to the industry, such as automatic machines, equipment and material. For the general advertiser, it is an excellent supplementary medium for every one of the media which is used to reach consumers. In other words, business magazines supplement general magazines, newspapers, outdoor advertising and radio by advising the distributors of the consumer campaign. This is one phase of what is called "merchandising" advertising. If a dealer is advised well in advance of a coming poster that will be effective with his customers, he can take advantage of that campaign in placing his store advertising, in making window displays and perhaps otherwise.

Trade publications are read chiefly by those who distribute merchandise. Industrial magazines cover different industries, and are supposed to have something of interest for all engaged in the industry represented. The magazines published in the interests of management or administration are not restricted to any one industry, but concern themselves with problems that are supposed to be common to many if not all industries. The same is true of technical and professional publications. An example is a very attractive magazine which devotes all its space to packages. This is of interest to many people in different industries. The same is true of a magazine called *Credits and Collections*. There are nearly 1,600 business publications in these four groups.

Newspapers

Newspapers are divided into morning, evening, Sunday and the country press, nearly all of which is weekly. There

are a few biweekly and a few semiweekly newspapers, but
these are of such minor importance that they may be passed
over.

Newspapers are highly localized and provide the most
flexible service of any medium, except direct mail. There
are in the United States and Canada 2,200 dailies in English, and 156 in other languages. The evening papers have a
combined circulation of 25,694,981; and the morning papers,
15,599,215; Sunday papers, 31,401,892, with somewhat
more than 11,000 country newspapers which are published
once a week. The total number of newspapers seems to be
declining rather than increasing. It is commonly said that
everybody reads the newspapers, and the exceptions are
only enough to prove the rule. Most families, especially
those in the metropolitan districts, have at least one morning and one evening paper, while many other families
receive regularly at least three newspapers daily. These are
in addition to the Sunday paper.

As an advertising medium, the newspapers probably rank
first in the total volume of business. The amount of newspaper advertising is variously estimated at $500,000,000
to $700,000,000 a year. Students of advertising estimate
that about one-fourth of this is manufacturers', or national,
and three-fourths local or retail. No study has ever been
made that is at all exhaustive to show the actual amount.
The country press represents so many different publications, and their rates are so difficult to get, that no one has
measured their receipts. All of these weeklies carry local
and foreign, or manufacturers' advertising, and many also
have the advertising that comes with the "patent-inside."
This means that one side of the sheets was printed by a
syndicate before they were sent to the local publisher who
printed the other side. All the advertising that appears in
the patent-inside is placed by the syndicate and the syndicate gets the receipts.

With the regular daily press, which constitutes the
"newspaper advertising" as it is regarded in advertising

agencies, there is perhaps twice as much local, or retail, advertising as there is advertising placed through agencies. Practically all the general advertising comes from advertising agencies. It is also handled by the newspaper representatives, who require an extra 8 to 25 per cent for their services. To make up for the expense levied by the advertising agency and the newspaper representative, the foreign rate is made from 25 to 50 per cent higher than the local rate.

Newspaper Rates

Newspapers commonly give a discount for volume of advertising. Sometimes this is a graduated scale of five or six steps, running up to 10 or 15 per cent for 100,000 lines used within a year. There is also a discount for the regularity of advertising and for those who place copy every week or oftener. Then there are a large number of discounts that are given for different commodities. The "book" rate is much less than the "financial" rate. Those seeking employment can buy space at a much lower rate than those looking for employees. There may be as many as thirty different classifications of commodities and services which take different rates in the metropolitan newspapers. This is regardless of whether the advertising originates with retailers or national advertisers.

The basic newspaper rate is founded on a space called the "agate line," or more often the "line." But, as there are so many different rates and as newspapers have no standard for making rates, a new term has been coined which is called the "milline" rate. The purpose of the milline rate is to show the difference in newspaper rates in comparing different circulations. The milline is the cost per agate line per million copies. But as the basic line rate varies considerably, such publications as the "Standard Rate and Data Service" give a maximil and minimil rate. These terms indicate the maximum rate per agate line per million circulation, and the minimum rate per agate line per million circulation. The milline rate is computed by multiplying the agate line rate by a million and dividing by the amount of the circulation. The quotient is the milline rate. The same formula is used to calculate the maximil and the minimil rate. For these, the maximum agate line rate is used for the maximil and the minimum line rate for the minimil. The run of paper (R.O.P.) line rate is commonly used in computing the milline rate.

In addition to the different discount rates offered by the newspapers, there is also a long list of premium rates. In most of the large daily papers, space on pages 2 and 3 and 4 and 5 is charged at a much higher rate than the R.O.P. rate. Favored position, top of column, or first following reading matter, or alongside and following reading matter are also charged at premium rate. However, there is no uniformity with different papers in the amount of premium that is charged. Rates also vary widely. One large tabloid has a milline rate of approximately $1. The "regulars" in metropolitan districts run from $2 to $6 a milline. Rates in papers of smaller circulation are usually higher; from $4 to $12 per milline.

Newspaper Advertising Summary

The advantages and weaknesses of newspapers as an advertising medium are summarized in "Advertising Media"[1] on pages 234 to 239, and that summary has been condensed to the following, giving the advantages first:

1. Practically everybody can be reached by newspaper advertising.
2. Newspapers have a diversity of appeal, that is, they are so inclusive in their subject matter that they are supposed to have something of interest to each member of the family.
3. Newspapers can handle copy very expeditiously which makes it possible to adapt the copy to weather conditions or other influences which might affect the sale of the advertised product.

[1] *Ibid.*

4. Frequency of issue is an advantage for many advertisers, especially for retail stores.
5. Newspapers give quick results. The store knows the results of its advertising in the daily papers each night when it closes.
6. Newspapers permit of local, sectional or national campaigns.
7. Many newspapers offer a marketing service which is sometimes valuable to advertisers.

The weaknesses of the newspaper, on the other hand, follow:

1. Being of a low-grade paper, they do not permit of high-grade illustrations. Consequently, most of the illustrations are line drawings. This, of course, does not refer to rotogravure sections or to the newspapers which print one or more sections in color.
2. Newspapers are read very hurriedly. To read a metropolitan paper of twenty-four pages thoroughly would require hours of time, while, as a matter of fact, twenty minutes is about the average that is devoted to each issue of a newspaper.
3. Newspapers are not selective in their readers. The great proportion of the population has little choice. There may be one morning and one evening paper; in a very large number of cities with 25,000 population or less, there is only one daily paper.
4. For a campaign that is really national, newspapers are expensive. A very large number of papers are necessary if even a small percentage of the people in each district are to be reached.
5. The machinery through which newspaper space is sold is cumbersome and expensive to the advertiser. That has already been discussed.
6. Since national advertisers are charged a higher rate than local advertisers, many of the former are at a disadvantage. For example, the chain stores may place

their advertising for coffee at the local rate while the national advertiser would have to pay the national rate. This might happen not only with the same classification of goods but with exactly the same items. A rate 50 per cent higher might be exacted from the national advertiser than from the chain which places its copy through the local unit.

The Radio as a Medium

Radio, unlike other media, claims circulation that is potential rather than actual. Thus total radio "circulation" includes every radio-equipped home in the United States, if the set is in working order. This total circulation, as of Jan. 1, 1937, is estimated at 24,269,000. The author would count only those tuned in to a program as circulation. The Joint Committee on Radio Research estimated a total of 22,869,000 radio families as of Jan. 1, 1936. To this is added approximately 1,400,000 new homes supplied with sets during 1936, as reported by the Radio Manufacturer's Association. Circulation coverage differs throughout the United States, varying from as high as 92 per cent for New York State to 36 per cent for Mississippi. The United States total is estimated at 73 per cent. Some large cities are estimated to have a circulation coverage of as much as 98 per cent.

A single radio station claims as many of these radio homes as are located in its listening area. The extent of this area depends on the power and equipment of the station. Thus a 500-watt station would effectively cover a small area, probably not over a radius of 6 to 30 miles, while a 50,000-watt station might effectively cover a radius of 60 to 300 miles. Large stations in thickly populated areas claim circulation in the millions.

The advertising value of a radio station, however, should by no means be judged by power alone. Other important factors are its popularity in the community, whether local newspapers carry its programs, the type of advertising accepted, and its ability to produce results.

Stations may be independently operated or they may be units of a network (regional or national). The three big networks are National Broadcasting Company, with the combined Red and Blue Networks of 112 stations; Columbia Broadcasting System with 97 stations; and Mutual Broadcasting System with several high-powered stations in large cities.

Time is sold in units of quarter-, half- or whole hours. Many of the small stations sell 1-, 3-, and 5-minute periods. Rates vary from as low as $30 for a half-hour on a small local station to $750 on a large station. A nighttime hour on a popular national network, 90 stations, costs $16,932. Daytime rates are approximately half nighttime rates (6:00 P.M. to 11:00 P.M.) because of the more limited daytime "circulation." Other hours, if programs are given, are sold at about one third the nighttime rates.

The stations of a network are connected by specially leased wires which make it possible for a program to be staged in a single studio and telephoned to each station on the chain and then broadcast locally. This allows the chains to produce more pretentious shows with greater "stars," since the cost can be spread over the total number of stations.

Advertisers on independent stations, on the other hand, must charge the talent cost to the broadcast of the single station. Small independent stations are often handicapped because of this cost and also because of the scarcity of talent in their localities. This is in part overcome by electrically transcribed programs. Programs thus recorded can be shipped to stations and broadcast at any specified time. The improvements in recording devices within the last few years have given this type of program wide listener acceptance. Many advertisers thus stage a pretentious show in the studio, have it transcribed, have a hundred records struck off and shipped to that number of small (or large) independent stations. This is called "spot" broadcasting in contrast to network broadcasting. Most stations today accept recorded programs. A few large stations, however, will accept only live talent shows for broadcasting.

So far as listener popularity of a radio program is concerned, the entertainment value is not so important a factor as the way the program is merchandised. Merchandising a radio program is "selling" it to the potential listeners and the dealers by using other media, such as newspapers, magazines, outdoor advertising, etc., to call the public's attention to the program and the advantages of listening to it. The rapid growth of radio advertising is largely due to the publicity given it in other advertising media. That is unique in advertising circles. It is a grave question if it is wise to divert the reader's attention, when he is reading an advertisement, from the product offered for sale to an entertainment.

Streetcar Cards

This medium was organized, standardized and finally monopolized by Barron G. Collier, but with the coming of buses and the consequent discontinuance of surface line and interurban streetcars, other companies have acquired a substantial interest in this medium. There was a time when the streetcars collected 112 fares daily for each one hundred residents of cities having car lines. Just how this has changed with the change to buses, available statistics do not show.

The car-card service is sold in four different units: (1) Double runs, that is, two cards for each car. This provides that one be placed in each end of the car and on opposite sides. Otherwise special positions are not supposed to be sold except for the large cards in the ends of the cars. (2) Full run, one card for each car. (3) Half run, one card for each two cars. (4) Quarter run, one card for each four cars. Beginning in 1934, a double-card service was inaugurated, which provided for a card of 42 inches in length. The usual cards are 11 by 21 inches.

The basic rate provides a charge of 50 cents for each thousand riders, with the advertiser supplying the cards. This works out for 50 cents to $3 a month for each card, depending on the number of passengers. Bus rates and taxi rates for the display of cards which change automatically are slightly higher.

Primary and Supplementary Media

The student would readily conclude from the above that the four primary media are outdoor advertising, newspapers, magazines and radio. This primary or major classification holds true whether the campaign or advertising program is national, sectional or local in scope.

The secondary or supplementary media are large in number and represent a wide variety of uses, primarily to supplement and strengthen the major media used as the principal force in the campaign or program.

The following is a list of the generally recognized supplementary media:

Business publications, including technical, professional, occupational and trade papers and magazines.

Car cards, used in street cars, buses, subways, elevated and suburban railroad line cars, ferries, taxis, and express and delivery trucks.

Direct mail, including letters, circulars, broadsides, booklets, calendars, blotters, catalogues and house organs.

Directories, such as the *Telephone Red Book, Polk's City Directory*, trade and professional directories, *Thomas' Register of American Manufacturers, Daily News Almanac and Year Book*, etc.

Motion pictures and stereopticon slides, for presentation in schools, in conventions, to company staffs and to meetings of distributors and dealers.

Novelties, such as billfolds, card cases, pencils, cigarette lighters, clip matches, and many others. These carry the trade-mark, product name, or name of the manufacturer, dealer or distributor for presentation to distributors' and dealers' salesmen and to consumers.

Premiums, such as household articles and utensils, cutlery, jewelry and toilet articles, exchanged for coupons given at the time of purchase or package labels or box tops of goods or merchandise being promoted.

Press agentry and stunts, including parades, publicity stories, telephone calls, telegrams, street banners, sandwich men, testimonials, athletic and sport team sponsoring and skywriting.

Sampling and demonstration, in or through stores, house to house, on the street, at fairs, industry shows and exhibits, for coupons or package inserts, and by mail.

Show window and store displays, using merchandise, lithographed cut-outs, cartons, over-sized package reproductions, show cards, hangers, counter stands, display containers, panel screens, transparencies, decalcomanias and electric flashing and mechanical action displays.

Theater programs, consisting primarily of the programs published and distributed to patrons of legitimate theaters when attending a theatrical production or other stage performance for which the particular program is furnished.

Direct mail is used as a part of practically every campaign. Circular letters, catalogues and notices of one kind or another are almost universally required to keep the advertiser in touch with his distributors and dealers.

In using secondary or supplementary media, it is important that they be carefully selected with a specific objective part to play in the advertising plan or campaign; otherwise they may represent a heavy expense without commensurate return.

There are some individual advertising solicitors who specialize in supplementary media who really have little to offer that will be resultful in a business way. They operate primarily on some other appeal than promoting sales for their customers. For this reason, it is best to leave the decision as to the use of this classification of media to the judgment of the advertising agency so that there will be no interference with the major advertising program.

CHAPTER 5

Selling Outdoor Advertising[1]

Selling Necessary

Outdoor advertising must be sold the same as most services. The real work of the salesman for the outdoor medium is to help the advertiser analyze the sales resistance and then apply outdoor advertising to reduce that resistance. Sometimes the salesman can bring an analysis to the advertiser that will be new and thought provoking, or the salesman may merely talk matters over with the advertiser and explain to him the effectiveness of outdoor advertising in acquainting the public with the merits of a product and encouraging the dealer not only to stock the product but to give it active support. The one who is selling space, art and copy, plus a knowledge of markets has a valuable service to offer, and the selling consists primarily in assisting the advertiser to apply the selling force of outdoor advertising to his product. He offers coöperation in planned advertising.

Not logically can all classifications of nationally advertised products use outdoor advertising. The nature of each product, its distribution, and its economic advertising possibilities determine whether outdoor advertising can be soundly used. Some of the leading classifications of nationally advertised products using the medium are as follows:

[1] Much of the material for this chapter was contributed by **Mr. C.O.** Bridwell, vice-president of Outdoor Advertising Incorporated.

Agricultural products	Food products
Amusement and community	Gasoline and oils
Associations and chain stores	Health products
Automobile tires and acces-	Home appliances and fur-
sories	nishings
Automobiles and trucks	Hotels
Beverages	Insurance
Building materials	Jewelry
Business equipment	Publications
Cleaning and laundry prod-	Radio and musical
ucts	Sporting goods
Confections	Tobaccos
Dairy products	Toilet preparations
Dress and wearing apparel	Transportation
Finance	

These classifications can be said to represent the major possibilities for outdoor advertising. Some advertisers

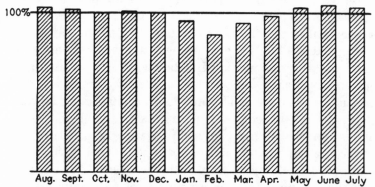

A careful study of seasonal traffic fluctuation in twenty-eight cities, scattered over a large part of the United States, gave results indicated. This was for 1936, and the study was under the direction of the Traffic Audit Bureau.

should run a continuous campaign, every day and every month in the year. With others, their campaigns are necessarily seasonal. However, it should be noted that the seasonableness rests with the product and not with the medium. Fur coats can best be sold in the fall and winter; Palm Beach suits in the spring and summer. The outdoor advertising medium is one that has come to be independent of seasons, as shown by the charts on page 92. It is no disparagement to say that outdoor advertising is not adapted to every need of the advertiser. The very thought of trying to rent a room, secure a servant or get a job by means of outdoor advertising indicates what a ridiculous extreme would be reached by recommending the medium for every and for all purposes.

Attributes of Outdoor Advertising

A picture conveys at a glance an idea that may require many words to portray. Outdoor advertising lends itself readily to the use of this power of pictures.

Color motivates attention and impression, both necessary to successful advertising. Color is vital to appetite appeal and to the complete presentation of all merchandise. Outdoor advertising is the only major medium where unlimited use of color is optional without extra cost.

Impression copy is an affirmative appeal to the desires, ambitions and other emotions of the prospective consumer. Impression copy carries conviction through color, pictures and a few words. Outdoor advertising is impression advertising.

Remembrance is based on continuity and repetition in advertising. An outstanding characteristic of successful advertisers is their continuous appeal by advertising to their market. Outdoor advertising is economically geared for continuity and repetition.

Changed conditions of American life have radically changed the advertising situation. The increased mobility of the people, due principally to the automobile and new highways, has greatly extended the boundaries of retail trading areas. Communities formerly rural have been converted into the truly suburban classification. This moving population is the "outdoor market" which is reached only by advertising out of doors.

Poster advertising is sold by market units. The advertiser uses only those towns, cities, markets or territories where he has distribution or where his selling conditions are best. Painted displays may be used to cover entire markets at strategic points of heavy circulation and buying power or sections within a market, such as racial centers, school or theater districts, along routes of travel to and from the suburbs, etc. By concentrating outdoor advertising in the territories of greatest market value, the advertiser obtains the maximum effectiveness from his appropriation.

Reduced to its simplest element, efficiency in advertising is the ability to influence the greatest number of sales for the least number of dollars. In operation, it means conveying an advertising message in an effective manner to the greatest number of consumers (circulation), the greatest number of times. The NAC figures, attested to by the Traffic Audit Bureau, reveal low costs per thousand circulation.

It is the everlasting iteration of a pleasing and forceful suggestion that establishes familiarity for a product, conveys an impression which endures, and achieves that widespread public belief which leads to automatic mass sales.

The advertiser's salesmen, distributors and dealers see outdoor advertising in the course of their daily travels about town. It keys up their enthusiasm for the products advertised.

The dealer in particular is influenced by this advertising which he sees himself, right in his own neighborhood. He knows it is on display every day of the week, always at work building up familiarity for the products he sells and bringing people into his store.

Coverage

With rare exceptions, the advertiser aims to send his message to as many people as can be reasonably expected to buy his product. In other words, he wants to cover his

market. There was a time when daring advertisers took
generous space to announce the advent of their product
and then depended on this advertising to get distribution.
That method may yet be used occasionally, but it would
be an exceptional condition that would make it a profitable
procedure.

Coverage means:

1. The distribution of a sales message
    (*a*) to those who might be possible customers,
    (*b*) and to all who help to influence buyers. Some-
        times with a high-priced article it is necessary
        to establish a reputation, even among those who
        will not be buyers, before the product will sell.
2. The presentation of the message in a way that will be
    impressive.
3. Reaching buyers with at least as great frequency as
    they make purchases. That, with many products, is
    not sufficient. Oftentimes, as with a watch, one's
    advice is asked by probable purchasers. So even where
    purchases are made at long intervals, it is advantage-
    ous to an advertiser to keep his customers advised
    of the good service he gives and the reasons his
    product is desirable.

Coverage naturally is expected to be accomplished in the
most economical means without sacrificing any of the
foregoing. Outdoor advertising provides a coverage of
the whole population, except perpetual shut-ins and prison
inmates. All who walk or ride on our streets and sidewalks
or are passengers on our railways and buses are covered by
this medium. Not only does the coverage provide a high
degree of frequency, but, also, as we have already seen,
offers prestige in space and a variety of colors limited only
by the perfection of the printing and lithographic arts. The
outdoor medium also offers a very high degree of selectivity.
The elite of the nation visit such resorts as Atlantic City
where from the famous Boardwalk they can be advised of
your product. On the other hand, the painted bulletins and

walls can be so distributed as to cover any designated location, such as the Queen Anne Hill district of Seattle, the Lincoln Highway or U.S. No. 1, while posters can be restricted to the village of Amboy, or cover every metropolitan city of the country.

Painted walls have spoken in Italian to the residents of Little Italy in New York, in Swedish to the Swedes of Minnehaha on the far side of Lake Nocomis in Minneapolis, in Polish to the Poles in the Pilsen district in Chicago, and in French to the wide stretches of Montreal. It has also presented the same message at the same time to 16,000 cities, towns, villages and hamlets in the United States and Canada. This means that national advertising is a multiplicity of local campaigns run simultaneously.

Not only does the outdoor medium offer all the flexibility of a chess board, but it offers service of a great deal of exclusiveness for the advertiser. There is only a limited number of intensive showings, or even representative showings, that can be offered in any town, city or market, including the metropolitan cities. The magazine publisher can insert a few more pages to take care of all the advertising offered. Indeed, in the past, some of the popular magazines have had as many as two hundred pages in an issue. This was induced by the offering of a liberal amount of advertising, much of which was for similar products. We are all familiar with the newspapers that run from forty to sixty pages daily to hundreds of pages on Sunday. Again, it is the call for advertising space, including many competitors, which makes these large issues common. It is true that the radio cannot put on an entertainment for two competitors at the same time, but they may follow each other with the minimum lapse of time. In addition, there are three major broadcasting outfits, and scores of lesser ones, which will provide ample opportunity for a competing advertiser to seek the same audience at the same time. With the outdoor medium, this is impossible. Very few districts have a competing service with duplicate coverage. When an advertiser has employed an intensive showing, he has taken up so great a part of the plant's available service that there will seldom be an opportunity for any great number of other campaigns of equal intensity, and then only in the metropolitan markets. The full story of outdoor advertising coverage can best be appreciated by the traveler who comes to greet identical poster panels as friends scattered from one end of the country to the other. For completeness of coverage, for flexibility in time and territory, for low cost, what other medium can offer so much?

Classifications of Outdoor Advertising Sales

There are three classifications of outdoor advertising sales, namely, national, coöperative and local.

The term "national" is applied to the outdoor advertising of any product or service which is the subject of national or sectional distribution. The term "coöperative" is applied to the outdoor advertising of any product or service which is the subject of national or sectional distribution for which payment is made in part by the manufacturer, his distributors or his retail outlets.

The term "local" is applied to the outdoor advertising of any retail or manufacturing business, product or service, the distribution of which is confined within the metropolitan zone or recognized retail trading area in which the advertising is to be done.

There are two general divisions of sales. One is for national and sectional advertisers, and the other is for local advertisers whose market does not exceed a contiguous local territory.

Local Selling

Most of the plant owners have a local selling force. In the smaller plants, either the owner himself or the manager of the plant acts as salesman. In the larger plants, a local sales force is regularly employed. Their duties are to sell local merchants the service of the poster, painted display and electric spectacular facilities.

In considering local sales to merchants, it is well to bear in mind that in principle it does not differ from national selling. Interest must be created, space recommended must

City and suburban streamliner type of bulletin. Hotels have the problem of meeting incoming visitors, and the outdoor medium gives them an opportunity, both on highways and along railways.

be approved and copy must be written. In the majority of cases, the plant owner's own organization creates and produces the copy.

To find the most economical and effective way of reproducing the message is also part of the local selling job. The hand-painted poster is used for very small runs of posters; the silk stencil process is used for a somewhat larger quantity, and the lithographed posters for the larger runs.

The volume of local outdoor advertising is generally about 25 per cent of the plant owner's business. The other 75 per cent comes from national sources. The number of salesmen employed in selling local and national advertising is in about the same proportion, but reversed. That is, there are about three times as many men employed in selling local advertising as in selling national advertising.

In the use of painted bulletins or wall displays by local advertisers, the plant owner's organization usually writes

An effective store bulletin used by Lachman Brothers of Los Angeles.

the copy and always makes the technical design layouts which the painter uses in executing the copy on the wall or bulletin. Where an electrical effect or special mechanical device of any kind is added, the plant owner actually constructs these for installation in the display.

Local salesmen, generally speaking, are employed on a salary basis. In lesser degree, some salesmen are employed on a commission basis, and in larger companies on a combination salary and bonus plan. They devote their time to developing sales and also to keeping the advertising serviced, so that the advertiser is assured of a continuing interest from a selling point of view throughout the term of his advertising display.

A Formal Local Sales Presentation

Instead of going in and "putting up an argument" with the prospect, most salesmen carefully prepare a written discussion of the proposition they have to offer. The following is a reproduction of such a presentation for the New York City market, submitted in 1936. In the original form, it was neatly typed on sheets bearing the signature of the operator, together with a decorative border on two sides. These sheets were appropriately bound in a folder, on the front cover of which was the statement: "A plan prepared expressly for Obido." The title page bore the following notice only:

> "A Plan for Increasing the
> Sale of Obido in Metro-
> politan New York by the
> Use of Poster Advertising."

Then followed the presentation as given below:

A Formula

for investing Obido advertising dollars in the New York market in relation to the possibilities of return.

The City of New York, as a market for a bleach and disinfectant, such as Obido, should be divided into Boroughs, and each Borough be considered as a separate market.

Since Obido is a product, designed especially for home use, principally as a bleach, and of secondary importance in the home as a disinfectant, the Boroughs of New York should be considered separately as a market for Obido on the basis of the amount of home washing and home cleaning that is done by reason of the character of the homes in each area.

> The City of New York
> as a market for a
> Bleaching Material.

Considered as a whole, the City of New York is a home laundry market and ought to be one of the most profitable markets in America for a bleach that is used in laundry work done at home.

This fact is very strongly suggested by the Laundrymen's Association. Their statistical department gives us the following information as to the annual expenditures for public laundry service per capita in cities of the United States.

Los Angeles	14.03
Chicago	13.27
Washington	9.63
St. Louis	9.32
New York City	8.44

According to the Laundrymen's Association the non-use of public laundries indicates the amount of washing done at home. The above table, therefore, would suggest that the City of New York is a relatively rich market, per capita, for the manufacturer of a bleaching compound. In the City of New York (all Boroughs) there are known to be 44,280 electric washing machines, and it is reasonable to suppose that the distribution of these machines would indicate the extent to which laundry work is done at home in the various Boroughs. This distribution is indicated below.

Borough	Families	Washers	Per cent of total
Richmond	35,020	5,000	14.28
Queens	286,280	18,280	6.39
Brooklyn	657,980	12,920	1.96
Bronx	329,400	5,040	1.53
Manhattan	494,620	3,040	.62

Within the City of New York a comparison of public laundry expenditures also indicates that certain Boroughs are relatively much better markets for cleaning materials than others. The following table shows the annual expenditure, per family, for public laundry service.

Borough	Families	Expenditure
Queens	286,280	$21.06
Richmond	35,020	26.44
Bronx	329,400	28.55
Brooklyn	657,980	35.38
Manhattan	494,620	44.36

These figures form the basis for our belief that Queens is probably the best market for home laundry materials in the country.

The Heller Committee for Research in Social Economics thoroughly investigated the buying habits of families of each class, during 1934, and are authorities for the statement that the average family consumes two large bottles of bleaching material in one year.

The Chicago Standard Budget for Dependent Families establishes one small bottle per month as an absolute necessity for poor families.

The facts, on the average family consumption in New York City, approximate these estimates but do not tally with them.

In the belief that New York City might show deviations from studies made in other sections of the country, we have conducted our own investigation, in various sections of three Boroughs of New York, and have interviewed chain grocery officials on the subject.

All agree that people in the City of New York have greatly increased their use of bleach and of disinfectant within the past one or two years. We were amazed to learn that the consumption of some individual families of washing material reached two gallons each week.

All of the grocerymen interviewed agreed that the absolute minimum figure which could be used was an average of one small bottle each month by each family, of a preparation of equal strength to Obido.

We consider this last estimate to be sufficiently conservative to form the basis of a chart of relative costs of exploitation by poster advertising in each market. The following chart is based on the continuous use of a quarter showing of posters in each market (naturally the cost would be the same for twice the number, during six months of each year).

Name of borough	Monthly cost	Monthly market (in bottles)	Market for advertising dollar
Brooklyn.............	$1,012.00	657,980	648
Queens..............	556.60	286,280	510
Bronx...............	750.00	329,400	438
Manhattan...........	1,250.00	494,620	396
Richmond...........	167.40	35,020	210

We have already pointed out that some Boroughs are better than others as markets for materials used in home laundry. The above tabulation should be interpreted in the light of other information already given.

However, we have here a workable formula for investing Obido dollars in this market. The following table shows how we would recommend that Obido enter this market with poster advertising. The Brooklyn poster showing should be used first, as most likely to prove profitable. The Queens showing should then be used and so on down the list as the Obido advertising budget permits. The right-hand column of figures indicates the total cost of the campaign per month as the various Boroughs are added.

Name of borough	Number of families	Poster allotment		Cost of minimum showing	Cumulative totals
		Illum.	Nonillum.		
Brooklyn.....	657,980	20	40	$1,012.00	$1,012.00
Queens.......	286,280	11	22	556.60	1,568.60
Bronx........	329,400	10	25	750.00	2,318.60
Manhattan...	494,620	15	20	1,250.00[1]	3,568.60
Richmond[2]...	35,020	3	8	167.40	3,736.00

[1] A saving of $250 below this figure can be made by buying Manhattan in conjunction with the Bronx. The combination allotment is 20-18-37 for $1,750.

[2] Richmond (Staten Island) is operated by The Richmond Poster Advertising Company, 64 Hanna Street, Tompkinsville, S.I.

These estimates of cost do not indicate the effectiveness of a poster advertising campaign in the City of New York. The cost of covering the entire territory for one month ($3,736) does not suggest the power of such a campaign. There is little doubt that the entire campaign can be delivered at an average of less than 9¢

per thousand, net effective circulation. In other words, the campaign would deliver a daily effective circulation of approximately 2,000,000 impressions in New York City. This is a daily circulation which is equivalent to the combined circulation of the morning newspapers, and is greater than the combined circulation of all evening papers.

We believe that a poster advertising campaign such as this one would be the best possible investment of Obido advertising dollars in this market. So far as we know, there is no other method by which the metropolitan New York market can be attacked Borough by Borough, and the campaign confined to the area of greatest profit possibility.

Maps which show how posters in this amount are distributed in New York City are attached. Requests for further information on this market should be directed to:

> The General Outdoor Advertising Co., Inc.
> 894 Fulton Street,
> Brooklyn, New York.

Coöperative Campaigns

The campaign in which both the manufacturer and distributor participate is commonly called a coöperative campaign. The term "vertical coöperative" is currently used to describe this coöperative effort to distinguish it from such campaigns as "Say it with flowers" and "Save the surface," where competitors join to raise funds for advertising. Where the distributor is assessed so much for advertising purposes to be handled by the manufacturer, as has been common in the automobile industry, it is not in the strict sense a coöperative campaign. Rather, it is an advertising levy in which there is no coöperation.

The advertising in a coöperative campaign may be supervised and directed by the manufacturer or by the distributor; the former is to be preferred. The arrangements are usually one of the following:

1. The manufacturer supplies the posters imprinted with the dealers' names or the painted display designs and pays part of the space cost. A fifty-fifty arrangement is common.

2. The advertiser furnishes posters or the painted display designs for the distributor to put up and allows some predetermined percentage of the distributor's purchases to defray the advertising costs.

This is an excellent example of a coöperative display, which gives the distributor the full value without detracting from the selling effect.

3. The advertiser merely supplies the posters or painted display designs for his distributor or dealers and requires them to pay space and imprinting costs. This is really a "dealer help" campaign and not coöperative.

Where the distributor manages the campaign and contributes a share of the costs with the manufacturer, there are also three different possibilities in supervision:

1. The distributor takes full charge of the advertising and charges up an agreed part to the manufacturer. This form of coöperative campaign is usually not satisfactory to the manufacturer.

The above are miniatures of posters which are sent to dealers. From these a selection can be made, or all may be used by a large dealer who can afford to make an advertising investment. The various terms upon which coöperative advertising is done are stated in the text.

2. The distributor selects certain types of advertising that are recommended by the manufacturer and buys space, as he sees fit, charging the manufacturer the predetermined portion.
3. The distributor is simply given an advertising allowance for which he does not account. This is tantamount to granting a discount equal to the allowance.

In coöperative campaigns, Outdoor Advertising Incorporated requests the plant operators' salesmen to contact and present the plan of campaign and the designs to the distributor, his salesmen and dealers.

The recommendations of Outdoor Advertising Incorporated for coöperative campaigns are as follows:

1. That nothing less than a fifty-fifty space basis, or better, be recommended to a manufacturer.
2. That at least one-fifth of the space design be allowed for dealer's imprints—preferably more, and that the use of overlay strips on posters be discouraged.
3. That posterette reproductions of the designs, size 10¾ by 24 inches, in full color should be used in merchandising in the campaign.
4. That the advertiser's sales force should have a presentation of the outdoor medium, including designs.
5. Plant owners should be requested to give O.A.I. the details of unusual sales on coöperative accounts so that information may be made available to plant owners in other territories.

Contacting the Trade

It must be kept in mind that with competition as keen as it is in the present day from the standpoint of actually selling merchandise, each manufacturer is faced with the problem of developing the proper outlets for the sale of his product. These may take the form of exclusive distributors and dealers, or branch offices and dealers, or dealers direct.

The factory, because of its problem in developing and maintaining sales, is anxious to lend every assistance to a deserving jobber or distributor in any given territory so that nothing will be left undone that would increase volume.

In planning a national advertising campaign, most concerns present their plans to the representatives of the distributing outlets for two purposes: first, to secure their approval for the plan adopted; second, which is more important, to obtain active coöperation. The success or failure of many national selling programs is in direct proportion to the amount and quality of sales coöperation given to the advertising campaign. In other words, the advertising is a sales tool of the manufacturer placed in the hands of the distributing or jobbing outlet.

Sales conditions are not the same the country over. This accounts for the fact that most concerns do not have complete national distribution. In those territories where a given manufacturer is selling his product, we may find many different conditions, when comparing one territory with another; therefore, it is not possible to use exactly the same methods in solving the sales problems in every territory, although naturally a general plan must be formulated. Probably the best informed authority as to the sales conditions pertaining to a product in any territory is the wholesale distributor handling that product. He is in a position to know what the potential market is and what the competitive problems are, and has a good opinion as to what should be done to correct negative conditions and lower sales resistance toward the item for sale.

If the wholesale distributor, for example, is selling enough volume of the merchandise to produce a substantial profit for the manufacturer, it is assured that any recommendation made by such distributor will receive the proper sort of consideration at the headquarters of the advertiser. Obviously, the factory wishes to foster the profitable relationship with the distributor to keep the sales volume moving.

To sum up the situation so far as the advertiser is concerned, he is finding it more and more necessary each day to respect the opinions of his wholesale outlets as to the type of advertising that should be used to create an increased volume of business.

Contacts Are Valuable to Plant Owners

These conditions make it most important that outdoor advertising plant operators establish and maintain contact in their operating territory with the wholesale distributing and retailing outlets of advertiser clients and prospective clients.

Through such contacts, systematically maintained, the advertiser is assured that his outlets will be fully informed regarding his plan for using outdoor advertising, and the plant owner has an opportunity to sell his medium and the character and scope of his services.

This activity is valuable to advertisers and their advertising agencies in coordinating the entire sales, merchandising and advertising program. It is of great assistance to the national sales representative of the medium in developing the most effective use of outdoor advertising. This contact work often is of definite and direct value to the plant owner in holding, expanding, extending or renewing contracts for space for the market or markets in which he operates.

The contact work should begin upon receipt of the contract. The wholesale and important retail outlets should be informed of all the details of the campaign as communicated to the plant owner by the national sales representative and the source of business. When the plant owner has assigned the space to the contract, it should be graphically portrayed on a traffic flow map of the market and shown to the important outlets so they will know what type of coverage is to be provided.

When the poster or paint copy is received, the outlets should be invited to the plant owner's place of business to see it, so their local sales and promotion efforts can be tied up with the copy appeals. When the posters or paint copy are on display, every reasonable attempt should be made to have the important outlet representatives see the entire display.

In the case of distributors, wholesale jobbers, etc., opportunity should be sought to make a presentation of the medium, the campaign, and the plant service to their salesmen in group meetings at the beginning of the campaign. These salesmen should be urged to request the retailers to give the product prominent store, counter and window display in coöperation with the campaign.

Then a continuing interest should be evidenced throughout the campaign by contacts and inquiries regarding sales volume results, etc. The plant owner should periodically give a report to the source of the business and his national sales representative of his contacts and the reactions received.

Selling National Outdoor Campaigns

The chief difference between a local and a district campaign is that the former includes just one trading center or one principal trading center with its satellites. A district campaign may include three or four or even more trading centers with their surroundings. A regional campaign would comprise a considerable section of the country, for example, the Pacific Coast States. No advertising agent participates in the strictly local campaign, as a rule. It is too simple and too little is involved to call for the services of an advertising agent. That is also true of most of the district campaigns, but as the district to be covered gets larger and loses its homogeneity of population and complicated problems of distribution enter the campaign, then an advertising agent's broader knowledge of advertising problems makes his advice essential.

There are comparatively few national advertisers in the sense that their products are sold everywhere. Many manufacturers have distribution for their products in cities of

25,000 population and over. A much smaller number are represented in cities of 5,000 and over. But those who have their products on sale in every town and hamlet are few indeed. Some five-cent candies, cigarettes, chewing gum and, possibly, some laundry and toilet soaps and a few food products have truly national distribution. There may be a few others. Two popular-priced automobiles have representatives in practically all cities of 2,500 or more population. More commonly will the national advertiser be interested in certain States or in wholesale districts, and his outdoor advertising will be so developed as to support the business that he already has. In opening a new territory, the distribution of goods will usually precede the placing of advertising. One good reason for this is that when goods are actually in stock, the advertising may become effective at once. If the advertising precedes the display of goods by too long a time, people lose interest after being told that the item requested is not in stock. So great is the confidence of the trade in outdoor advertising that it will usually stock any item which is to be given the immediate support of the outdoor medium.

The salesman who is working on a national account will determine well in advance of the time that he makes his actual presentation to the advertiser just what kind of campaign would be best suited and most effective for that advertiser—paint, posters, spectaculars or some combination of them. He will study previous campaigns as well as the current advertising. He will secure a large amount of data pertaining to markets, such as is prepared by Outdoor Advertising Incorporated, and given by them in such publications of their research department as "Metropolitan Markets" and "Main Street Plan." The coverage of outdoor advertising in comparison with other media will be carefully tabulated and oftentimes graphically presented. Preparing a presentation for an outdoor advertising account may require weeks of work before the salesman feels that he is in a position to call on the advertiser at all. But when he does finally complete his study and presents it, the chances are that he will have much that is new and intensely interesting for the advertiser, which frequently includes new merchandising ideas. After the market has been carefully considered, then, and not until then, are the advantages and disadvantages of competitive media searchingly reviewed.

When to Sell Posters

The three standard classifications of outdoor advertising, namely, posters, painted displays, and electrical spectaculars, have distinct characteristics which, in general, determine the form or forms of the medium to be used.

The following outline explains the conditions and circumstances which generally govern the selection of each of these classifications.

Poster advertising, twenty-four-sheet posters, should be recommended when general coverage, general distribution, and repetition are the main factors for consideration, such as:

1. The product is sold by a large number of thoroughly distributed retail outlets; that is, it is an article of general consumption and popular price.
2. The product is consumed in a short period of time and requires frequent replacement; in other words, it has a rapid turnover.
3. The product has a small unit cost.
4. The product is of large unit cost using exclusive or few dealers and is of wide public interest.

The term of the poster campaign should be governed by the following considerations:

1. If the product is consumed frequently and at a constant rate throughout the year, then the campaign should be on a 12-month basis, and the objective to be accomplished should be divided into twelve copy

messages containing a major factor of continuity in basic sales appeal and copy theme, and also a major factor of variety or change in color and illustration to maintain attention value.

2. If the product is seasonable, then the term of the campaign should be equal to and be continuous during the months of the season or seasons in which the article is consumed, and the objectives should be reached by dividing the copy into as many strong selling statements as there are months involved. Continuity in this case can be secured through use of color and illustration. If the number of months involved in the season or seasons is more than three, continuity should not be sacrificed.

3. If the season is not more than three months, the copy may be made specifically applicable to each month, but even where the subject changes, the continuity of copy and display should not be broken. In other words, the series should be closely related.

Three Intensities of Showings

Poster advertising coverage is available in three intensities, known as intensive, representative, and minimum showings. Normally, the ratio of intensity of the showings in number of posters is $3:2:1$.

In selling poster advertising, the coverage showing intensity most appropriate to fill the needs of a given advertising situation is recommended to the advertiser by a salesman from Outdoor Advertising Incorporated, or by his advertising agency. Each showing is equal in size, coverage and advertising value to every other showing of the same intensity in a given town. Each city or town is sold individually except where a number of towns are grouped as a market, in which case the market is sold as a unit. Posting is sold for a minimum period of 1 month. Paper is usually posted on the first or fifteenth of the month, but in some larger plants there are four or five posting dates.

In laying out these showings, scientific methods are applied to find the coverage requirements of the market. Counts are made of circulation on the main thoroughfares. Locations of shopping centers, theaters, churches, recreation centers are also ascertained. From these factors, the preferred routes of travel are divided into posting zones. Each zone is then allotted one panel for a minimum showing, two panels for a representative showing and three panels for an intensive showing. Each zone contains a norm of 3 miles of important street length. Hence, the number of zones determines the number of panels in a showing and insures the right coverage in the different sections of the city and on the major routes of travel. The intensity of coverage known as the representative showing is more frequently used. Illustrations of showings are found on the inserts facing page 116.

Recapitulations as of July, 1937, of the resident population, number of cities and towns, number of posters and the cost per month of a representative showing by States and for the United States and by population groups during 1938 are shown on a following page.

The distribution of poster advertising to provide coverage of the market is governed by the following factors:

1. Buying power.
2. Wholesale and retail outlets.
3. All forms of transportation.
4. Consuming but nonbuying public.
5. Points of continuing attraction and interest to residents and visitors.
6. Type and character of the community.
7. Space position (see pages 180–182).
8. Quantity and quality of circulation.
9. Repetition.

The inserts give a traffic-flow map of Detroit, Mich., on which has been indicated the location of the posters in a representative coverage allotment for that city. In cities and markets of over 50,000 resident population, such locations as have a heavy night circulation are illuminated from sundown until midnight.

The Sales of Three-sheet Posters

Three-sheet poster advertising should be recommended when the coverage desired is limited to neighborhood shop-

This shows the effectiveness of a three-sheet poster when placed on the wall of a building where the product is sold. It is well called "point of purchase advertising."

ping districts in the urban market centers having heavy pedestrian traffic. It is essentially a point-of-purchase reminder medium. The three-sheet poster is used principally to reinforce other forms of advertising in connection with food and drug products. They are located on the side walls of retail outlets or on other buildings in or near the neighborhood retail centers.

The three-sheet poster is sold in showings or groups which vary in size in cities of the same population due to local physical conditions and the number and size of neighborhood retail centers. Three-sheet posters are of much more limited sales than the twenty-four-sheet panels. Prices range from $2.50 to $4.

The cost of twenty-four-sheet and three-sheet posters varies, depending on the design, the method of reproduction, the number of printings required and the quantity of posters to be produced (see page 122).

When to Sell Painted Display

Painted display advertising should be recommended when specific coverage, restricted distribution or dominant impression are the main factors for consideration, such as:

1. If the product is sold through an exclusive dealer or a small number of appointed dealers and is of substantial unit cost, its purchase and replacement occurring infrequently, preferred position painted display located in dominant positions in heavy traffic zones of strategic value should be used. This might be called standard practice to which there are some exceptions. Occasionally a firm prefers paint to posters, when either might be used profitably.

2. If the product is sold in a limited section of the market (one or more neighborhoods), then either store bulletins or neighborhood walls or a combination of both should be used.

3. If prestige, stability or institutional factors control consideration, then boulevard and highway or central business district bulletins in combination should be recommended.

The term of the painted display campaign should be governed by the following considerations:

1. Painted display as a primary medium should not be used for a term less than one year.

2. It is most effective when three or four paints per year are used.

City and suburban bulletin, illuminated, at Los Angeles.

3. Repaints with same copy should be discouraged. Change of copy improves the effectiveness of painted display.

4. The dates on which change of copy occur should follow as nearly as possible any special or seasonal appeal that may be made in behalf of the product as determined by investigation and the basic sales appeal decided upon. In other words, change of copy dates every 3 or 4 months should not be arbitrarily decided upon. The copy should fit the merchandising and advertising problem of the advertiser.

Painted display is the most flexible of all forms of space advertising. Each unit is selected to serve a specific need. A single unit may be used or a number necessary to cover a market or any particular section thereof may be selected.

Types of Painted Display

There are six different types of painted displays, which are described as follows:

1. Preferred positions are principally located in the downtown area. They dominate points of very heavy circulation. The size varies as required by perspective and space availability. The structural design and embellishment are standard in type, or streamlined.

2. City and suburban bulletins are principally located on the important streets and boulevards in the city and suburban area having heavy circulation. The size is standardized at $12\frac{1}{2}$ feet high by 47 feet long, and the structural design and embellishment are standard in type.

3. Store bulletins are located at eye level on the side walls of stores and buildings in downtown and neighborhood retail centers and at transportation depots and transfer points where the pedestrian circulation is especially heavy. The size is standard in height, namely, 9 feet $10\frac{1}{4}$ inches, but the length varies

RECAPITULATION BY STATES, REPRESENTATIVE SHOWING

State	Population	No. of towns	No. of posters	Cost 1 month
Alabama	1,006,034	356	548	$5,183.30
Arizona	247,375	34	76	903.60
Arkansas	651,447	436	564	5,108.10
California	4,760,351	387	1,022	16,097.90
Colorado	596,298	132	227	2,645.85
Connecticut	1,531,275	71	362	6,008.40
Delaware	162,970	37	68	921.20
District of Columbia	517,593	1	42	820.00
Florida	834,728	194	403	5,183.80
Georgia	1,260,470	593	826	7,757.55
Idaho	231,941	166	216	2,021.60
Illinois	6,369,780	956	1,665	19,458.15
Indiana	2,341,441	652	1,063	11,606.00
Iowa	1,477,338	750	1,016	10,704.06
Kansas	936,419	573	756	7,395.92
Kentucky	1,066,553	389	592	5,440.60
Louisiana	1,087,338	337	489	5,083.60
Maine	523,234	118	223	3,130.20
Maryland	1,058,777	153	261	3,309.50
Massachusetts	4,095,656	108	593	10,910.90
Michigan	3,543,143	548	1,001	12,320.51
Minnesota	1,560,642	549	757	7,807.35
Mississippi	533,044	285	400	3,736.20
Missouri	2,254,439	603	926	10,262.55
Montana	200,007	37	94	1,122.60
Nebraska	696,526	378	476	4,734.40
Nevada	71,991	41	54	531.25
New Hampshire	356,807	79	153	1,701.60
New Jersey	3,595,091	208	789	13,577.50
New Mexico	174,582	75	116	1,186.00
New York	11,061,483	695	1,809	27,934.66
North Carolina	1,099,310	350	559	5,767.90
North Dakota	157,596	74	107	931.00
Ohio	4,825,446	729	1,429	18,042.91
Oklahoma	1,247,072	501	763	7,540.15
Oregon	574,889	135	226	2,898.40
Pennsylvania	7,210,157	1,259	2,255	27,321.99
Rhode Island	657,147	25	147	2,006.30
South Carolina	641,792	234	380	3,436.05
South Dakota	214,238	145	179	1,680.50
Tennessee	1,126,627	429	627	6,203.30
Texas	3,213,738	1,184	1,783	19,079.92
Utah	314,639	56	116	1,436.90
Vermont	172,106	43	79	1,016.40
Virginia	962,574	220	409	4,604.40
Washington	1,037,123	189	340	4,530.95
West Virginia	825,107	367	518	5,583.50
Wisconsin	1,913,598	672	981	10,437.77
Wyoming	117,255	40	66	607.30
Total	81,104,669	16,593	28,551	$337,730.49

An illuminated city and suburban bulletin for a transcontinental railway. This display was at Milwaukee.

Metropolitan highway and railway bulletin.

according to perspective and space availability. The structural design and embellishment are standard in type.

4. Highway and railroad bulletins are located to face traffic on principal United States and State highways and along the main railroad lines where circulation justifies. The size is standardized at 12½ feet high by 42 feet long, and the structural design and embellishment are standard in type.

City painted wall. An eye-catching display in New York.

5. Metropolitan bulletins are located so as to show to circulation city bound over heavily traveled United States and State highways and main line and suburban railroads where a larger unit is needed because of the problems of space availability and perspective. The size is standardized at 18 feet high by 72 feet long. The structural design and embellishment are standard in type.

6. Painted walls are principally the side walls of buildings in the downtown and neighborhood retail centers. The size varies as required by visibility and

space availability. The wall space is surrounded with a painted standardized border design.

Painted display units in cities of population of 50,000 and over range in price from $50 to $500 a month. The price range depends upon the quantity and quality of circulation, the character of the location, its space position dominance, the size of the structure, the speed of travel, the length of approach and the number of times the display is to be painted each year.

RECAPITULATION BY POPULATION GROUPS—REPRESENTATIVE SHOWING

Group	Population	No. of towns	No. of posters	Cost 1 month
100,000 and over........	43,102,593	120	4,535	$92,302.96
50,000 to 99,999.........	6,793,150	103	1,463	24,159.26
25,000 to 49,999.........	6,069,974	176	1,642	23,700.51
10,000 to 24,999.........	7,156,663	477	2,514	27,246.02
5,000 to 9,999...........	4,905,655	716	2,193	21,247.16
2,500 to 4,999...........	4,218,961	1,207	2,230	21,003.11
1,000 to 2,499...........	4,620,713	3,051	3,206	29,788.13
Under 1,000.............	4,237,060	10,743	10,768	98,283.34
Total.................	81,104,769	16,593	28,551	$337,730.49

COST OF CAMPAIGN FOR PAINTED WALLS IN CITIES
OF DIFFERENT SIZES

Cities and towns population	No. of walls	Cost per wall	Cost for coverage per month
1,000 to 2,500	1	$6.00	$ 6.00
2,500 to 5,000	2	6.00	12.00
5,000 to 7,500	3	6.00	18.00
7,500 to 10,000	4	6.50	26.00
10,000 to 15,000	5	7.00	35.00
15,000 to 25,000	7	7.50	52.50
25,000 to 35,000	9	8.00	72.00
35,000 to 50,000	12	8.50	102.00

Spectacular Displays

Electric and bulletin spectacular displays have been used to accomplish many different advertising purposes. They can be soundly recommended under proper market, distribution and sales conditions to:

1. Introduce a new product.
2. Establish or confirm leadership of a well-known product.

A spectacular bulletin which appeared on Broadway, New York City, and in metropolitan centers throughout the country.

3. Give emphasis to or climax and enhance all other advertising of a product.
4. Nationalize local advertising of a product.

The influence is great on consumers, jobbers, retailers and the advertiser's organization. Electric and bulletin spectacular displays are principally located so as to dominate only the points of greatest circulation concentration in the metropolitan centers of night life. The size is controlled by considerations of perspective, visibility, space availability and the advertising copy design.

An electrical spectacular which appeared at the intersection of Randolph Street and Michigan Boulevard, Chicago. For daylight display see page 264.

Some famous spectaculars, together with locations, are shown on this page and on pages 123, 144 and 145.

CHAPTER 6

Mechanics of Selling
Outdoor Advertising[1]

Recognizing Agencies

Each plant operator has the right to sell his service in the way that seems best to him and on contracts that are satisfactory to himself and the buyer. With local advertisers, the process is very simple. The operator of the plant, or a salesman representing him, calls on local advertisers who may be induced to employ the outdoor advertising medium.

However, if each plant operator attempted to solicit business from each national advertiser who places posters in many different cities, towns and States, endless confusion would result. Conceivably over 1,000 different plant operators would call on each national advertiser, if that plan were followed. In the interest of efficiency, agencies for handling national accounts have been established. They are discussed in the following paragraphs. Chief among these are the recognized advertising agencies.

The Outdoor Advertising Association of America, Inc., acts as a source of recommendation of advertising agencies which qualify under and conform to a reasonable standard of requirement not unlike qualifications necessary to secure

[1] The material from which this chapter was written was supplied in part by Frank T. Hopkins, president of the National Outdoor Advertising Bureau, Inc., and in part by Dr. Miller McClintock, director of the Traffic Audit Bureau, Inc.

recognition from the American Newspaper Publishers' Association, the Periodical Publishers Association, Associated Business Papers, Agricultural Publishers' Association in connection with newspapers, magazines, trade papers, and agricultural publications.

To secure and retain the recommendation of the Association as a source of national business, an agency must:

1. Possess and maintain a credit rating commensurate with the scope of its operations and must furnish credit statements when and as required by the Association.

2. Establish an outdoor advertising department with adequate personnel possessing a sufficient technical knowledge to represent its clients effectively in presenting and servicing the medium of outdoor advertising.

3. Maintain or employ an art department informed in the special technique of outdoor advertising design as applied to poster advertising, painted display advertising and electric and spectacular display advertising.

4. Prepare or cause to be prepared at its expense the necessary specifications, blue prints, solar prints and pencil layouts when distributing painted display or electric and spectacular display copy to members.

5. Procure the special forms necessary to the efficient placement of outdoor advertising business.

   It is understood that the terms and conditions set forth in sublet contracts and in written or verbal instructions in relation thereto shall not be in conflict with the terms of the Agreement of Recommendation, especially as they relate to equality of treatment and the Association standard of service as outlined in paragraph 5 of the "Requirements of Association Members."

6. Possess and maintain adequate knowledge of poster advertising, painted display, electric and spectacular

advertising, including the circulation, advertising and price values in all such forms of outdoor advertising.

7. Install and maintain currently adequate statistical records of poster advertising facilities and rates.

8. Not represent to any advertiser that it can purchase outdoor advertising in any form at prices and terms more favorable than those available to any other recommended source of national business.

9. Make prompt payment for services rendered by members of the Association within 30 days of the expiration of each month's service covered by contract.

It is understood that if payment is not made within 60 days of expiration of a given month's service, the subject source of business shall be considered delinquent and no agency differential shall be allowed on any business executed for the subject source of business until the delinquency has been liquidated. And, further, that if the period of delinquency extends for more than 90 days beyond the expiration of any month's service, the recommendation of the Association of the subject source of business shall be withdrawn.

10. Not request members of the Association to accept commitments for space subject to less than 60 days notice of cancellation or deferment of posting date, unless the space allotted to such commitment can be sold to another advertiser by the member.

11. Not request members to post posters or to execute painted display copy which is critical of the laws of the United States or any State or which induces a violation of Federal or State laws or which is offensive to the moral standards of the community at the time the copy is offered for display, or which is false, misleading or deceptive.

The Association will give consideration to any copy submitted to its headquarters office to determine

whether or not copy may be in violation of the foregoing standard.

(NAME OF SOURCE OF BUSINESS) ADDRESS					

POSTER ADVERTISING CONTRACT

To

Date. . . . . .

Contract No. . . . .
(To Appear on all Location Lists and Invoices)

Shipping Address

Please post — paper for this Company as specified hereunder

TOWN, CITY, OR MARKET	NO. OF 24 SHEETS	COST PER MONTH	DATE TO POST	POSTING PERIOD	CONDITIONS OF CONTRACT
					1. This contract shall be carried out by you in accordance with the Service Rules of the Outdoor Advertising Association of America, Inc.
					2. If posters have not been received ten days prior to posting date or if there is a shortage in the number received, advise us promptly.
					3. This contract is subject to an agency differential of 16⅔%.
					4. You hereby agree to indemnify us and save us harmless from all loss or damage resulting from accidents to or injuries suffered by an employee or other person and against any loss or damage to property for which we shall or might be or become liable and/or for which a claim shall be made against us.

(NAME OF SOURCE OF BUSINESS)

By

This is the original order which the source of business sends to the plant which
is to give the service. Obviously one order goes to each plant, and if several
hundred plants are to do the posting, the clerical work becomes extensive.

12. Make arrangements with members for verification
   and evaluation of outdoor advertising under contract
   in their respective territories as far in advance as
   possible to conserve the time of all concerned.

Complaints with respect to the service delivered in relation to the provisions of the governing contract

(NAME OF SOURCE OF BUSINESS)
ADDRESS

POSTER ADVERTISING CONTRACT

Date ....

Contract No. .   ... .
(*To Appear on all Location Lists and Invoices*)

Shipping Address

... .

To

Please post

paper for this Company as specified hereunder

TOWN, CITY, OR MARKET	NO. OF 24 SHEETS	COST PER MONTH	DATE TO POST	POSTING PERIOD	CONDITIONS OF CONTRACT
					1. This contract shall be carried out by you in accordance with the Service Rules of the Outdoor Advertising Association of America, Inc.
					2. If posters have not been received ten days prior to posting date or if there is a shortage in the number received, advise us promptly.
					3. This contract is subject to an agency differential of 16⅔%.
					4. You hereby agree to indemnify us and save us harmless from all loss or damage resulting from accidents to or injuries suffered by an employee or other person and against any loss or damage to property for which we shall or might be or become liable and/or for which a claim shall be made against us.

ACCEPTANCE OF CONTRACT   *Date*   ... .

The above contract is hereby accepted.

....
(**Plantowner's Signature**)

This is the form on which the plant operator acknowledges the original order. This and the order are printed in manifold form, the original order, the acknowledgment from the plant operator and the copy retained by the one placing the order.

shall be called to the attention of the member at the time the verification and evaluation are made.

It is understood that if service shortcomings are not corrected promptly by the member, the source of business shall file formal complaint with this Association.

The recommendation of the Association may be withdrawn at any time for nonconformity with the foregoing requirements.

There are more than thirty-five agencies which have individually qualified with the foregoing requirements and have been recommended to plant operators by the Association. There are, in addition, approximately 225 agencies which place business through the National Outdoor Advertising Bureau, Inc., which has the Association's recommendation. For specimen standard contract see Appendix.

Printing Posters

The national advertisers have their posters printed either by placing an order direct with the lithographers or placing it through their advertising agents. The copy and design for the poster are commonly prepared by the advertising agent or by the agent in consultation and coöperation with Outdoor Advertising Incorporated. This institution has a very fine art department and has been responsible for a large number of outstanding poster designs.

The mechanical preparation and distribution of posters will be considered in another paragraph, particularly those that are used in national campaigns. In local campaigns, whether twenty-four-sheet or three-sheet posters are used, the method of reproduction varies depending upon the design and the number of printings required and also, of course, upon the number to be used.

The tables on pages 132 and 133 give the current approximate costs by methods of reproduction for the average design.

Poster Lithographers

There are about twenty-five lithographers in the United States equipped to manufacture twenty-four-sheet posters.

(Space for Name Plate)

REPORT OF SERVICE

Order No. _____

Date _____

Received From _____

Product _____

Design _____

No. Posters _____ Date Posted _____

Territory _____

LOCATIONS	LOCATIONS

A

(Space for Name Plate)

INVOICE

Order No. _____

Date _____

To _____

Product _____

Design _____

Total Number of Posters _____

Total Amount of this Invoice $ _____

TERRITORY	POSTING PERIOD		NO. OF POSTERS IN SHOWING	AMOUNT
	FROM	TO		$

B

These two forms are used. Form *A* notifies the advertiser that the posters are on the panels and gives locations. Form *B* is used in billing the service.

The most efficient process is that in which the design to be reproduced is transferred to lithographic plates by hand drawing or photography.

Formerly, the poster design was reproduced by the use of wood blocks or lithographic stones upon which the design had been drawn or etched. This evolution in process has made possible more faithful reproduction of design and

BY LITHOGRAPHY

24 sheets, priced for each poster[1]

Quantity	30 printings	40 printings	50 printings	60 printings
500	$1.40	$1.65	$1.90	$2.15
1,000	1.00	1.15	1.30	1.45
2,000	0.80	0.90	1.00	1.10
5,000	0.67	0.75	0.81	0.90
10,000	0.62	0.70	0.75	0.83

3 sheets, priced for quantities named

Number of printings	500	1,000	1,500	2,500	5,000
9	$270.00	$340.00	$400.00	$512.50	$800.00
10	295.00	365.00	435.00	550.00	850.00
11	320.00	400.00	465.00	600.00	900.00
12	345.00	425.00	485.00	625.00	950.00
13	360.00	440.00	517.50	662.50	1,000.00
14	380.00	470.00	547.50	700.00	1,050.00
15	405.00	510.00	585.00	745.00	1,130.00

[1] These figures are based on the use of 55- to 60-pound paper and fadeless inks.

color tone. Posters are produced on rotary lithographic presses, either offset or direct, depending upon the nature of the design. The inks and poster paper used in the manufacture of posters are of prime importance, as they must withstand the posting process and exposure to the weather. The progressive movement in lithographic processes, equipment and materials used is largely due to the work of the Lithographic Technical Foundation, a research institution founded and financially sponsored by the Lithographers National Association, its members and others directly and indirectly interested.

The poster lithographers coöperated with the Outdoor Advertising Association of America, Inc., in establishing

BY SCREEN PROCESS

24 sheets, priced for each poster

Printings per poster	10	20	30	40	50	100	125	150	200
10	$5.00	$3.15	$2.55	$2.30	$2.10	$1.65	$1.55	$1.50	$1.35
20	8.75	5.60	4.50	3.90	3.60	2.65	2.45	2.25	2.05
30	11.50	7.60	6.25	5.25	4.60	3.50	3.23	2.98	2.67
50	16.30	10.90	8.80	7.40	6.60	4.98	4.65	4.20	3.70

3 sheets, priced for each poster

Printings per poster	25	50	75	100	150	200	300	400	500
2	0.85	0.60	0.50	0.45	0.40	0.35	0.30	0.27	0.24
3	1.10	0.75	0.65	0.60	0.50	0.45	0.40	0.35	0.30
4	1.40	0.90	0.80	0.70	0.58	0.52	0.46	0.40	0.35
5	1.70	1.05	0.95	0.80	0.65	0.59	0.52	0.45	0.40
6	2.00	1.20	1.05	0.90	0.73	0.66	0.58	0.50	0.45
7	2.25	1.35	1.15	1.00	0.80	0.73	0.64	0.55	0.50
8	2.50	1.50	1.25	1.10	0.88	0.80	0.70	0.60	0.55
9	2.75	1.65	1.35	1.20	0.95	0.85	0.75	0.65	0.60
10	3.00	1.80	1.45	1.30	1.00	0.90	0.80	0.70	0.65
11	3.20	1.90	1.55	1.35	1.05	0.95	0.85	0.75	0.70
12	3.40	2.00	1.65	1.40	1.10	1.00	0.90	0.80	0.75

the present standard 24-sheet poster as to specifications and layout arrangement.

The functions of a twenty-four-sheet poster lithographer are:

1. To determine from the artist's sketch to be reproduced the layout arrangement and the number of printings, as well as the cost thereof, based on the number of posters required.

2. To sell his services to the advertiser or his agent.
3. To manufacture and collate the posters.
4. To ship the posters to plant operators in accordance with shipping instructions furnished by the source of business which places the contract.
5. To bill the advertiser or his agent for the posters and shipping charges and collect therefor.

Mechanics of the Schedules

With the local campaigns, where the posters are made by the silk-screen process or by any other process that offers a satisfactory result for a small number, selecting the territory to be covered and the intensity of coverage offer no problem. The advertiser knows his market intimately, and is familiar with the traffic conditions and the sources of that traffic. But in the national campaigns, which almost universally use lithographed posters, selecting and deciding upon the exact markets or territory to be covered is infinitely more difficult. The bookkeeping is more complicated than in other major media, as the poster showing in each town, city or market is dealt with as a separate account, which requires a vast amount of detailed work. It is in this difficult work that the National Outdoor Advertising Bureau is helpful to a large number of agencies. This institution renders all the service incident to advertiser-agency contracts, including:

1. The furnishing of statistical information and estimates of coverage allotments, rates, specifications, and costs of poster, painted display and electric spectaculars to its agency members.
2. The placing of sublet contracts for space with outdoor advertising plant operators in accordance with the governing advertiser-agency contract.
3. The preparation and furnishing to lithographers of shipping instructions and labels to cover the shipment of posters to plant operators and the preparation and

furnishing to plant operators of working copy for painted display and electric spectaculars.

4. The securing, receiving and recording of reports of service rendered under sublet contracts by plant operators and advising the related agency-member accordingly.

5. The billing of the agency-member for service rendered under the governing advertiser-agency contract, collecting monies due, and paying the related plant operators for service rendered under the sublet contracts.

6. The traveling of field representatives throughout the country for personal contact with plant operators in the interest of good will and understanding and for first-hand verification of service delivered.

Plant operators pay $16\frac{2}{3}$ per cent commission to the Bureau on business billed. The Bureau compensates the agency-member out of this commission, after deducting the cost of handling.

It should be borne in mind that by no means all of the agencies place their outdoor advertising business through the Bureau, but with the exception that they work directly with the advertiser, their functions are the same as those of the Bureau, above outlined, and they receive the same commission on business billed.

The following routine, as given by Frank T. Hopkins, president of the National Outdoor Advertising Bureau, Inc., is enlightening, as it covers in such complete detail the mechanics of distribution and collection.

When the Bureau issues its sublet contracts to plants, it furnishes carbon copies to the agency on a special form for loose-leaf binders. Thereafter, reports of all changes, corrections or special arrangements are made to the agency for notation upon these record sheets, and the agency at all times has a complete running record of the exact status of the order in every city or town.

As the posters go on display, bills and location lists are rendered by the plant operators. Posters are sold in standard showings which require a specific number of posters, but when showings are billed each poster panel must be identified according to its location. These bills and location lists are checked against contract records and audited.

When all bills and lists for a particular account have been received, recorded and approved, one statement is rendered to the agency, and the agency makes payment by one check. This procedure may be varied to suit the needs of a particular agency or advertiser. Bills may be rendered by States, by trading areas, according to the advertiser's own territorial divisions, etc.

Payments are made by the Bureau direct to the plant operators for all services rendered. In making these payments, a large number of accounts may be grouped together and paid by one check. In 1936, the Bureau issued 26,041 checks to plants in payment for space. If the same accounts had been handled individually, more than 500,000 checks would have been required to cover exactly the same billing.

This simple illustration will give some idea of the saving through this coöperative method. The same principle applies to many of the other operations and these savings are of benefit alike to the advertiser, the agency and the plant owner.

Mechanics of Handling Contracts

In many ways, the same principles that are involved in placing orders for poster displays apply to the placing of orders for painted displays, electric spectacular signs and various types of bulletin-spectacular units. However, there are some important differences. Painted bulletins, painted walls and all of the various types of special units other than posters are priced and sold by the individual unit and usually under contract for one year or more. Each unit or location must be selected and approved in advance of the placing of an order.

As in the case of posting, the agency may furnish the original design. From this design, the Bureau makes up all the special painting instructions that go out with orders to plants. These include reproductions of the design, blue prints of all different layouts, color samples and specifications, etc.

Field Service

There is no uniform contract or practice applying to electric spectacular signs. Each is treated individually, and Outdoor Advertising Incorporated or the Bureau gives all the special advice and information that its members call for concerning the purposes of this part of the campaign. Both work with the agency in the actual negotiations. One of the most important activities of the Bureau is conducted by the Field Service Department. During the past year, this Department has consisted of thirty people, twenty of whom are travelers. These men travel continuously throughout every section of the country, the majority of them in Bureau-owned automobiles. They call upon plant operators and check all current displays, both paint and posting.

They select painted displays for new accounts, call upon dealer outlets and render all the personal service and coöperation necessary to the handling of an advertising contract.

No attempt is made to verify the service on every single unit, but such a comprehensive cross section of checking is made that the agency and advertiser can place business with complete confidence. Summaries of each checking report are passed along to the agency as a part of the routine service.

Extent of National Outdoor Advertising Bureau's Operations

In 1936, the Bureau placed orders for and rendered service upon the accounts of about 275 different national advertisers. These accounts were produced through 140 advertising agents. The showings of different advertisers ranged all the way from a single unit in one city to many thousands of units covering all cities, towns and main highways throughout the country.

From the plant owner's standpoint, the Bureau justifies itself in much the same way that it does in respect to the agency and advertiser. The plant owner knows the financial standing and responsibility of the Bureau and has complete confidence in it.

The Bureau's relationship to its members and clients is exactly as confidential as that of the agency and client. In 1936, the Bureau volume exceeded that of 1935 by 40 per cent and was the greatest of any year since the Bureau was organized.

Showings as Found in Cities of Different Sizes

Reference has been made to showings with the standard designations of intensive, representative, and minimum. In order to make this important subject so clear and definite that there can be no misunderstanding, it is reviewed here. The basic idea is that such an arrangement of poster panels should be made that each advertiser buying a representative showing in a given city shall get the same amount of circulation and coverage as every other advertiser who buys a representative showing.

To accomplish this, the plant operator adopts an informal zoning system for each city. These zones are really display districts. An intensive showing may mean three panels for each zone; a representative showing, two panels for each zone; and a minimum showing, one panel for each zone.

The Traffic Audit Bureau has provided the advertiser and his advertising agency with a very complete index of the size of showings in communities from small to large. The representative or middle-sized showing is that which is most commonly used and has, therefore, been taken as the basis for statistical computations by the Traffic Audit

Bureau. In communities of under 2,000 population, the normal representative showing allotment is composed of one unilluminated panel. These towns are so small that one well-located panel is able to give complete coverage. In cities of from 6,000 to 8,000, the average representative showing has three unilluminated panels. In cities of from 40,000 to 50,000 population, ten unilluminated panels constitute the average representative showing allotment.

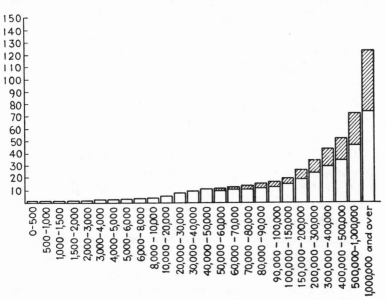

The average number of panels for population centers of different sizes, ranging from small towns to cosmopolitan centers. The white part of the bars indicates the number of unilluminated panels; the shaded portion indicates the number illuminated.

Illuminated panels are quite regularly added to the allotment in all cities of above 50,000 population. Thus, the average representative showing in a city of 100,000 to 150,000 population is composed of six illuminated panels and fourteen unilluminated panels. In cities of from 400,000 to 500,000 population, the typical representative showing allotment is seventeen illuminated panels and thirty-two unilluminated panels.

Ratio of Population to Showings

One interesting ratio revealed by the Traffic Audit Bureau's work is the ratio of the population in the market to each panel in a representative-showing allotment. In markets of under 1,000 population, the range is from 250 to 750 resident persons for each panel in a representative showing. If this allotment ratio were maintained through the larger markets, the number of panels in a representative showing allotment would become excessively great. Indeed, such a fixed ratio would be entirely unnecessary, for in the larger markets the circulation pattern is of such a character that increasing proportions of the entire population are concentrated upon a comparatively few routes of travel. Thus, a single panel exposed to such a circulation route is capable of providing many times the daily circulation of a poster panel in a smaller market. In cities of from 50,000 to 60,000 population there are 4,500 resident persons per average panel in a representative showing. In cities of from 400,000 to 500,000 there are 8,700 persons per average panel. In cities of over a million population there are 18,000 persons per average panel.

The total number of people who are daily exposed to outdoor advertising reaches almost astronomical proportions. This, of course, is due to the fact that outdoor advertising is so built and distributed throughout the market that it is exposed to the great daily movements of buying power along the principal routes of travel and under conditions where there is a high degree of repetition. The average poster panel in a market of less than 1,000 population is passed daily by more than 2,000 persons. (Since an individual may pass a given panel more than once a day, "persons," as used here, means what might be termed the number of "persons-passings.")

In cities of from 40,000 to 50,000 population, more than 9,000 persons pass the average panel each day, and in cities of from 400,000 to 500,000 population more than

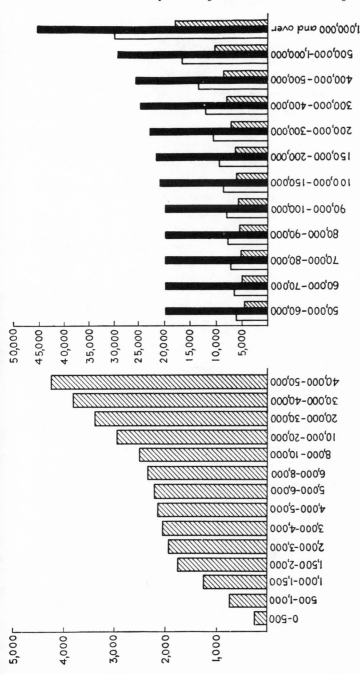

In the left-hand side of the chart, the bars indicate the number of people who see each panel, graded according to the size of the cities. In the right-hand side of the chart, the black bar indicates the number of people who see each illuminated panel. The shaded bars show the number who see each of the unilluminated panels. The white bar is a weighted average of the two. In small cities there are more unilluminated than illuminated panels in each showing, hence the weighted average of the two is closer to the unilluminated than to the illuminated panels. This remains true for cities up to a half million or less.

20,000 persons pass the average panel each day. At this point it is interesting to note that in this last class of market 34,800 persons pass the average illuminated panel during the 18-hour day of from 6:00 A.M. to midnight, and more than 12,000 persons pass the average unilluminated panel in the 12-hour day from 6:00 A.M. to 6:00 P.M. According to the procedure of the Traffic Bureau, the total number of people passing an outdoor advertising structure is designated as gross circulation. In many respects, outdoor advertising would be justified in claiming this total number of people as its circulation base. They are in a very real sense in physical proximity and exposure to a message which is displayed. The entire procedure of the Traffic Bureau has been predicated, however, upon ultraconservative principles. The vast amount of circulation that results from sources not counted is rated only as plus."

Effective Circulation as Influenced by Size of City

The relationship between gross and effective circulation can be illustrated by an analysis of the circulation figures for a representative showing as produced by the Traffic Bureau. In average towns of from 500 to 1,000 population, the gross circulation is 2,750, whereas the effective circulation is 1,400, or 50 per cent. In cities of from 40,000 to 50,000 population, the gross circulation per day is 76,220 and the effective circulation is 38,050. In cities of from 100,000 to 150,000 population, the gross circulation is 253,740 per day, and the effective circulation is 121,420. In cities of from 500,000 to 1,000,000 population, the gross circulation is 1,795,830 per day, and the effective circulation is only 768,780, or substantially less than 50 per cent.

The current audit analysis shows that the highest panel ratings are to be found in the very smallest markets, that is, those of less than 500 population. The average plant in this group has a panel efficiency of 92 per cent. This very high rating results naturally from the greater amount of open land found in these smaller towns. Markets of from

500 to 40,000 population have an average panel efficiency ranging from 83 to 91 per cent. This somewhat lower rating arises from the increasingly crowded building conditions along the principal routes of travel. Cities of over 40,000 population have average panel rating of from 76 to 80 per cent. No average population group shows less than 70 per cent average panel efficiency. This is especially significant when it is realized that the space-position rating table of the Traffic Audit Bureau is very severe in its evaluations.

By Population Groups

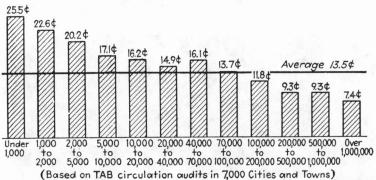

(Based on TAB circulation audits in 7,000 Cities and Towns)

Cost per thousand, net circulation, based on Traffic Adult Bureau's adults in 7,000 cities and towns.

It is no surprise to the media analyst in advertising agencies to find that the circulation unit cost of outdoor advertising is comparatively high in small markets and comparatively low in large markets. This is simply due to the fact that high unit costs always prevail where services are bought in comparatively small quantities. This is typically illustrated in milline rates in newspapers, just as it is in cost per thousand NAC in outdoor advertising. In towns of under 500 population, poster advertising averages 26 cents per one thousand daily NAC. This cost falls sharply in larger towns. The great portion of the industry, representing markets of from 5,000 to 300,000

ELECTRIC SPECTACULAR

Name:	Wrigley
Description:	Times Square, Broadway, 7th Avenue between 44th and 45th Streets, east side, facing west
Circulation:	1,091,000 daily
Dimensions:	75 feet high by 200 feet long
Number of electric bulbs:	29,508
Number of feet of neon tubing:	1,084
Colors:	Ultramarine blue and, of course, sea green predominate in the spectacular. Vermilion is also strong, appearing in varying degrees in the design of each fish. Other colors include black, yellow, metallic green, and white—all the colors that a vivid sunset reflects on green waters, or that Mr. Beebe discovers at the bottom of a tropical sea. Colors were achieved through the use of frosted or capped lamps and variously colored neon. The famous little Spearman matches the water, and the circle in which he sits carries out the ultramarine motif.
Action:	In direct contrast to the other quick-flashing spectaculars which line Broadway, this display is keyed to a slow-motion tempo. Gigantic multi-colored fish appear to glide about at different speeds among waves of sea green light. Actually the fish are permanently fastened to the spider-like steel framework, the illusion of movement being created by the flickering lights on the fishes' scales, the waving fins and the running movement of the waves. In the center of the scene, the traditional "Spearman" calls attention to the messages by moving his arms and pointing his fingers.

Animating the brilliant tropical display which is spread across this steel network are intricate flashing mechanisms rivalling the ingenuity of stage-lighting devices, and of a magnitude never before attempted on an outdoor electrical picture.

population, has a price range of from 19 to 9 cents per one thousand NAC. All average markets of over 300,000 population have a cost of less than 9 cents, the lowest naturally being in the larger metropolitan centers where the average plant produces NAC at a rate of 7.4 cents per thousand.

Traffic and Trade[1]

Changes in the Amount and Methods of Travel

During the past fifteen years, people have been "going places and doing things," farther and faster than ever before in our history. This "modern tempo" was the result of fundamental changes in American transportation brought about by the creation of numerous small-payment, install-ment-buying plans. By means of this process, it became possible for any person to become the operator of a self-propelled vehicle—the automobile.

These changes may be best illustrated by comparative statistics. In 1920, the passenger mileage of steam railways rose to a peak of nearly fifty billion miles and declined to eighteen billion five hundred million miles in 1935. Pas-senger mileage of electric railways fell from fifty billion miles in 1925 to below thirty billion miles in 1933. Com-mon-carrier bus mileage rose from about five billion miles at the close of the war to a total of more than eleven billion miles in 1935; and, most startling of all, the passenger mileage of the private automobile rose from approximately thirty billion miles at the close of the war to a total of more than four hundred billion miles in 1930. The accom-

[1] Much of the material for this chapter was supplied by John Paver, research engineer, who has become one of the leading authorities on highway traffic.

REVENUE TRAFFIC: RAILWAYS, PIPE LINE CARRIERS, INLAND WATERWAYS, AIR LINES AND INTERCITY BUSES IN THE UNITED STATES

Calendar Years 1926 to 1935

Years	All railways		Pipe line carriers		Total ton-miles of freight carried on inland waterways of the U. S. (000)	Domestic and foreign air lines (American operated)		Intercity bus traffic	
	Ton-miles (000)	Passenger-miles (000)	Miles of line operated	Oil transported (barrels)		Passengers carried	Passenger-miles	Passengers carried (000)	Passenger-miles (000)
1926	447,443,627	35,672,729	72,846	¹	99,580,384	5,782	¹	255,000	4,375,000
1927	432,013,979	33,797,754	76,070	¹	93,289,899	8,679	¹	285,000	4,900,000
1928	436,086,747	31,717,566	81,676	¹	96,514,434	49,571	¹	321,000	5,535,000
1929	450,189,394	31,164,739	85,796	¹	105,982,780	173,405	¹	422,000	6,797,000
1930	385,815,376	26,875,642	88,728		86,453,072	417,505	103,747,249	428,000	7,080,000
1931	311,072,637	21,933,345	93,090	488,690,545	57,767,740	522,345	119,968,577	395,000	6,725,000
1932	235,308,521	16,997,426	92,782	532,995,783	32,638,788	540,681	146,552,587	357,000	6,300,000
1933	250,651,190	16,368,043	93,724	566,641,194	55,300,566	568,940	198,800,079	328,780	6,433,000
1934	270,291,541	18,068,635	93,070	592,595,404	57,690,056	561,370	225,267,559	378,200	11,287,000
1935	283,637,058	18,509,497	92,037	766,588,403	68,096,389	860,761	360,569,431	651,999	¹

¹ Not available.

SOURCES: "Statistics of Railways in the United States," Interstate Commerce Commission.
"Annual Report of the Chief of Engineers," United States Army.
Air Commerce Bulletin, United States Department of Commerce.
Bus Transportation.

panying tabulation gives some of the striking changes in transportation in the decade of 1926 to 1936.

There are approximately 350,000 filling stations in the United States. Nearly every town has a tourist camp. The United States Department of Commerce has estimated that the tourist industry is about 3 per cent of the national income. In 1929, the amount spent by tourists was over $500,000,000, and it has increased rapidly since.

This phenomenal growth created new and vital problems which neither this nor any other country ever before experienced. These problems caused by traffic began to affect our municipalities and retail business. Traffic assumed a new and vital meaning.

Despite the expenditure of billions to build new roads and widen old ones, our country found it impossible to police its highways, untangle its street-corner jams and locate parking space for its motorists.

Progressive American business responded to this new tempo and hastened to adjust its methods to take better advantage of these moving markets. We are learning to utilize this mobile force to appeal to these "people on wheels." Guesswork and rule-of-thumb have given way to the slide rule and scientific analysis of basic traffic facts.

With improved roads, automobiles took the place of horse and buggy and speed of travel jumped from 5 or 6 miles per hour to 40 or 50. A peculiar phenomenon of this increased speed was that the time consumed in going to market was not so much reduced as the distance traveled to favorite places of trade was increased. Ten miles and return was a day's engagement over ungraded dirt roads with horses and wagon. But the farmer who thought 10 miles was a long way to market now regards 40 or 50 miles as only a moderate distance to go to larger and better marts of trade.

The consequence is a general improvement in the secondary trading centers at the expense of village stores, which were unable to compete with those more fortunately situated in larger markets.

Four Studies in the Relation of Traffic to Trade

Alert manufacturers, especially those who advertise their products, soon became aware of the profound changes. The new modes of travel and increased buying power that came at the same time made the people of the country not only a vaster market but a much better market.

In studying the new conditions, the Association of National Advertisers propounded the following four questions:

1. What effect does this basic change in buying power mobility have upon distribution methods?
2. Do daily movements of population, or buying power in motion, form basic trading areas and can they be charted with a sufficient degree of economy and accuracy to be usable?
3. Do these fundamental movements conform to rules or norms which can be analyzed?
4. Do the characteristics of these movements afford a guide to improved marketing methods?

Because of the importance of mass advertising in the solution of these questions, the Association of National Advertisers sought the coöperation of the Outdoor Advertising Association of America and the American Association of Advertising Agencies. Assurances of support were given. As a result, the two associations joined in a coöperative effort. A preliminary survey indicated that there was available widespread information regarding patterns of trade activity. But this information was not coördinated and had no common denominator.

The Bureau for Street Traffic Research in Harvard University, under the direction of Dr. Miller McClintock, had, for a number of years, been making intensive studies, in coöperation with public and civic agencies, of the various engineering, administrative and economic aspects of the street and highway traffic problems. Dr. McClintock was asked by the sponsoring group to organize and direct, as a part of the Bureau's activity, a comprehensive study of the relationship between daily population movements and trade activities. This was the beginning of the Traffic Audit Bureau, which has become such an important factor in outdoor advertising.

The original studies strongly indicated that adequate facts would reveal that traffic patterns could be used: (1) as a basis for the accurate determination of the limits of basic retail trading areas; (2) for the distribution of advertising and the placement of retail trade outlets. There was also reason to believe that an adequate quantitative and qualitative analysis of traffic flow would serve as a guide to the determination of the trade potentials of trade locations.

The findings of this project can be found in the volume "Traffic and Trade," by John Paver and Miller McClintock, the first work of its kind on the subject.

Researches based upon the original studies were directed to the analysis of traffic flow or buying power as a means to determine trade potentials of markets, portions of markets and the proper locations of retail trade outlets. Retail sales potential of any given location or any given trading areas can be gauged by analyzing the traffic habits of that location.

A further project of the Traffic and Trade Researches is being sponsored by the Advertising Research Foundation —a coöperative organization founded by the Association of National Advertisers and the American Association of Advertising Agencies. The Foundation has sought, with coöperation of the Lithographers National Association, Window Advertising Incorporated and other suppliers of window display materials, to determine the advertising and selling value of window display space and window display under normal conditions. The report was completed early in 1937.

Traffic Patterns

Composite traffic streams of various classes of traffic make definite and stable patterns. The shape and character of the pattern results primarily from the distribution of resident population, the character of activity, and the physical facilities which have been provided for movement. Gradual changes come about in community life or in physical conditions over periods of time. Business centers grow in importance, or they decline. A new location of a large store or important market may change the traffic for several blocks.

The flow map of any urban area shows that traffic streams are disseminated as they go from the center of the city outward. This is true because population density is distributed in the same manner. Where light density or population exists, there usually is found light volume of traffic, and, likewise where there is heavy density there is usually heavy traffic.

Traffic flow is not homogeneous. The various classes of traffic, pedestrian, automobile, truck and mass transportation vary with the location, size and physical characteristics of the city and at different points in the same city. Weather conditions also exert an influence.

In the central business district of a city of 50,000 population, the vehicular traffic predominates, while in the large metropolitan city of 2,000,000, the mass transportation traffic dominates.

In almost every city, the central business district contains a combination of all classes of traffic, while in the residential areas, the volume of vehicular traffic is usually greatest. On certain routes, large streetcar volume is found; on others, large truck or bus volume. Pedestrian traffic is principally in the business, shopping or recreational areas.

Traffic as Influenced by Time

As has been previously stated, traffic is the daily habitual movement of people. In the morning in any community, men, women and children leave their homes. They walk, they ride in automobiles, streetcars, buses, and, in many large cities, in railroad trains or by rapid transit. They are on the move; to work, to play, to study, and most important of all, to buy.

The morning rush hour is almost entirely made up of those going to work and to school. Later in the morning, the movement increases, owing to the morning shopping and business activity. The traffic in both large and small communities gradually increases in the afternoon as a result of combined business, shopping, and recreational activities, and reaches a peak with the homeward rush of the employed. During the evening meal, the tide has a definite ebb. Between 7:00 P.M. and 9:00 P.M., it gradually increases to an evening peak. This volume of traffic flow is almost entirely made up of those people who are following recreational or social pursuits, going to and from the theater and social gatherings. After the evening recreational period is over, the tide of traffic flow recedes very rapidly and the movement of people out of doors after midnight is almost negligible.

The flow of vehicular and pedestrian traffic is quite different from that of mass-transportation traffic. Mass-transportation traffic volume is composed for the most part of what may be called "necessity riders," that is, those who are forced by employment to travel at particular hours. This is the reason for the very high peak of work-bound traffic during the morning hours and the even higher peak of home-bound traffic, composed of those returning home from work, school, places of amusement and from buying and shopping in the late afternoon.

Traffic Flow by Days of the Week

The time distribution of vehicular and pedestrian traffic flow by days of the week, is shown on the charts on a later page. The volume of movement on the working days of the week is similar—Monday to Friday, inclusive.

On Saturdays and Sundays, the volumes vary. On Saturday, the traffic volume increases owing to the necessity of shopping for two days (Saturday and Sunday) and the desire for recreation during the leisure periods of the day.

On Sunday, the volume decreases, because there is no need to travel to work. However, there are generally volumes of traffic on the highways and in recreational areas. In those areas, such as financial districts, where the traffic is extremely heavy during the weekdays, there is practically none on Sunday.

The variation of the hourly distribution of vehicular traffic flow for the average weekday, the average Saturday, and the average Sunday is shown by the charts on pages 155 and 157.

On Saturday, traffic flow is nearly constant from 9:00 A.M. until 9:00 P.M. On Sunday, there is little traffic flow in the early hours from seven to nine and practically none in the financial, industrial and warehousing districts. The traffic flow increases gradually from 9:00 A.M. to a peak between 5:00 P.M. and 6:00 P.M., causing heavy volume on boulevards, highways, and arteries leading to churches, theaters, and recreational places. Total traffic on Sunday over an entire area is usually less than on weekdays. From 6:00 P.M. there is a gradual decline.

Over a decade ago, there were wide variations in traffic flow during the four seasons of the year, but the development of hard roads and efficient snow removal has had a tendency to eliminate these seasonal variations, which are least in large centers where a large volume of traffic must move regardless of weather conditions and upon the principal highways where seasonal variations are also small. Where the vehicular traffic reaches its peak in the summer months, the mass transportation traffic is at its minimum; while in the winter months the mass transportation traffic reaches its maximum and the vehicular traffic is at its minimum.

Distribution of Retail Trade

The relation between traffic and trade occurs in varying degrees of intensity. The sale of convenience goods is almost directly in proportion to traffic—especially pedes-

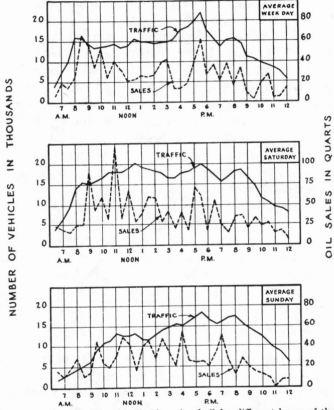

The above charts show graphically the sale of oil for different hours of the day compared with the number of passing automobiles. Note the variations in the curves for different days of the week. (*Charts are from "Traffic and Trade" by Paver and McClintock.*)

trian traffic. An exception, or what seems to be an exception, is a comparison of different hours of the day. If the pedestrian traffic is made up primarily of people going to or from work, 100 passers-by will not buy as much as the same number of people, say from three to four in the afternoon, who are primarily out to shop. But even then there is a direct relationship between the number of passers-by and sales. Double the traffic, and sales will double in either of the given examples. Or reduce the traffic by 50 per cent in either case, and sales will decrease approximately by the same amount. With shopping items, the relation of traffic to sales has not been so closely established. There are three principal shopping or trading districts in each city. They are: (1) the central business district; (2) the outlying business centers, or secondary business districts; (3) the neighborhood business districts and the outlying areas which contain isolated stores.

The central business district represents the heart of the city and consequently is the heart of the retail business and the focus of traffic. Stores comprising this district usually do a larger volume of business than those in any other area within the city. In this area the concentration of multistory buildings excludes residential occupancy. Here are found large department stores, women's and men's clothing stores, furniture stores, shoe stores, jewelry stores and all other outlets for shopping goods. Of course, there will also be cigar stands and other stores handling convenience goods. But while the stores in the main shopping center dominate the shopping goods market, convenience goods—especially foods—may be sold in greater quantities elsewhere.

The central business district, the retail heart of the market, not only draws consumers from all parts of the city but from suburbs and towns lying in the surrounding territory. The extent of the trading area of the city is measured by the distance customers regularly come to buy in the central business district. Transportation facilities of the city are focused on this district. This naturally causes congestion of traffic on the streets of this area, particularly at the rush hours. When this congestion reaches such a point of inconvenience that people prefer to go elsewhere rather than contend with it, outlying business centers or secondary business districts begin to spring up.

The outlying business centers, or secondary business districts, represent in miniature the same condition of retail structure which characterizes the central business

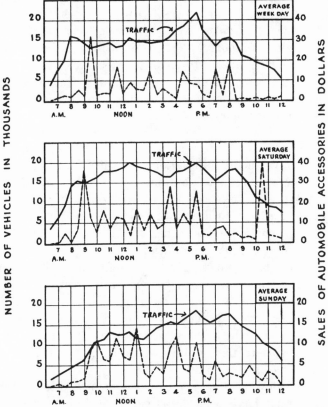

The above charts show the sales curves of some automobile accessories for different hours of the day compared with the passing of automobiles. It is interesting to compare the different sales as shown in the curve. (*Charts are from "Traffic and Trade" by Paver and McClintock.*)

district. In the large cities of the country, one finds these secondary business districts strung along great transportation routes for many blocks. In these secondary shopping areas, interspersed with the convenience goods stores, are a sprinkling of shopping goods stores.

Neighborhood business districts spring up to satisfy the demands of the consumers living in the immediate neighborhood, and are usually located within easy walking distance of a residential community. A small food store may exist primarily to supply the residents of one or two apartment houses. The volume of sales of these stores is relatively small. Other types of trading centers are usually spread over the entire residential portion of the city. Often, there are outlying areas in which isolated stores are located. One or two stores may be located at a particular intersection, but without exception these stores are found in residential areas and cater entirely to the convenience goods needs of the area.

Trading Areas

There have been a number of different ways of evaluating and giving approximate boundaries to trading areas. Trade in this sense means sales for retail stores. In order for a manufacturer to allocate his advertising in such a way as to give proportional assistance to his various outlets, he must have a definite evaluation of the different trading districts of the country. This also holds in employing and routing salesmen. It is not necessarily the number of outlets that determines the number of salesmen, but it is the location, the difficulty in reaching them and the frequency with which these outlets should be called upon. This depends in part upon the importance of each as a distributor of merchandise.

In the following paragraphs will be reviewed the different methods that have been employed to establish and evaluate trading areas of the country. Those that have been sufficiently well developed to appear in print and to be available to general students of marketing and the departments of marketing in colleges and universities will be considered. One of the first of these was a study of what was called the "hundred thousand group" of American cities. That meant that the cities containing a hundred thousand or more population were given attention. These were supposed to represent the chief retail districts of the United States, of which there were ninety-six. This study

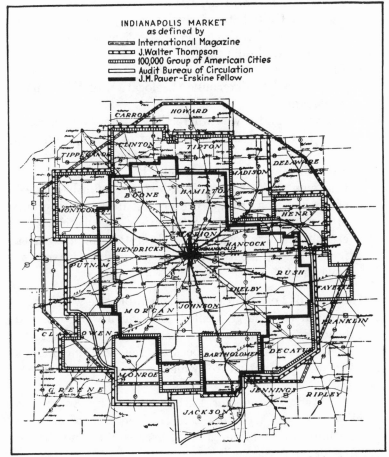

The trading area of Indianapolis according to five different methods of computing limits.

was sponsored by a newspaper in each city, which was supposed to supply the information on the different kinds of stores and wholesalers and a limited amount of other information of a similar nature.

The J. Walter Thompson Company, in 1931, used the following methods to establish the trading areas of the United States, as indicated in "Population and Its Distribution":

1. The locations of all department stores of substantial size of the United States which were reported in any one or more of the three department store directories were indicated on a map.
2. The financial rating of the stores thus located was investigated to determine the location of those most important.
3. The cities and towns where these stores were located were identified. The surrounding or nearby counties more easily accessible to each of these cities than to any other were grouped about the trading center. In this way, 683 trading areas were established, each composed of a trading center and its satellite group of surrounding or nearby counties. The district thus established was regarded as the retail shopping area from which a department store would draw its out-of-town trade.

There are 642 other cities of considerable size which were situated near these larger centers and which were regarded as subcenters. In a few cases, a small city was found to be an important trade center because the area included a considerable population to which a larger city was not accessible.

The "Market Guide for 1931," put out by *Editor and Publisher*, defines a trading area as "the area of greatest population concentration, greatest accessibility and strongest newspaper coverage."

The International Magazine Company, in determining the shopping centers as published in "Consumer Trading Areas," used the following guide:

1. The principal trading areas were selected by a study of population.

2. Geographical characteristics were noted.
3. Sources of wealth, such as mining, agriculture, or manufacturing were estimated.
4. Transportation facilities were enumerated.
5. Trade outlets: the number and kind of stores were recorded.

About each of these 632 central points, boundaries were fixed by the factors which influence the trend of buying habits.

In 1923, Batten, Barton, Durstine, and Osborn, Inc., studied the newspaper circulation as a basis for defining the areas shown in "Trade Areas for Budgetary Control Purposes." The analysis of this data indicated that 745 areas should be created. They contained one or more counties, each of which received more than half of its daily newspaper circulation from one of the 745 points of publication. During the next 5 years, these areas were combined into 187 large areas according to local jobber, retailer and chain store activities.

The Crowell Publishing Company for several years issued a study entitled "National Advertisers and National Markets." This was a summary of the data given by the United States Census for each of the 3,070 counties in the country. It gave the income of each of these counties from fisheries, mining, agricultural products and manufactured products. The counties were also printed in color, indicating their value as markets, which was determined in each case by the total income of the county.

The Bureau of the Census Studies Trading Areas

The growth of our large American cities has been one of the outstanding phenomena of this century. Near every large city there are small surrounding centers, towns and suburbs which, with the large city, constitute an urban or populated area where the population is in most cases uniformly distributed. These areas are usually linked together as social, economic and physical units, but politically they are separated.

The United States Bureau of the Census gives us a well-rounded statement concerning metropolitan districts:

In many cases the number of inhabitants enumerated within the municipal boundaries of a city gives an inadequate idea of the population grouped about one urban center. In fact, in only a few of the large cities do the municipal boundaries closely define the urban area.

Immediately beyond the political limits of many cities, and connected with them by rapid transportation system, are densely populated suburban districts which industrially and socially are parts of the cities themselves, differing only in the matter of governmental organization.

This idea was expressed by the United States Bureau of the Census in 1909, in connection with the census of manufacturing, and used in the census of 1910 for the first presentation of population data for metropolitan districts.

In 1920, the Bureau used the following method of defining metropolitan districts:

1. Each city of 200,000 population, not falling within the area surrounding a still larger city, was selected as the heart or nucleus of the district.
2. Every minor civil division having a density of 150 persons per square mile, lying in whole or in part within 10 miles of the city limits of the central city, and all civil divisions regardless of density of population, the greater part of whose population or area lies within 10 miles of the city limits of the central city, were included as part of the metropolitan district.

In 1930, the Bureau in coöperation with the United States Chamber of Commerce invited the local chambers to assist in determining the boundary limits of metropolitan districts. A similar method to that of 1920 was used in 1930, but revised. In this census, metropolitan districts included, in addition to the central city or cities of 100,000 population and surrounding area, all adjacent and contiguous minor civil divisions having a density of population

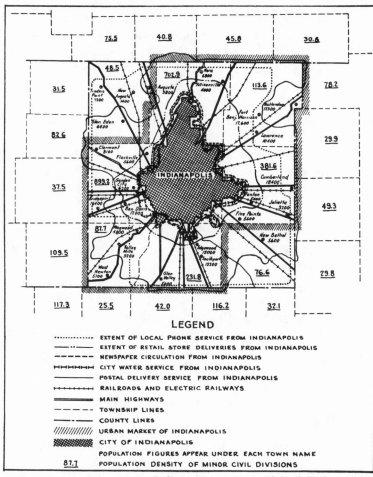

A theoretical trading area for Indianapolis, as it would look if the various boundaries were to be presented. For advertising and marketing purposes a simpler map is more practical.

not less than 150 inhabitants per square mile and also, as a rule, those civil divisions of less density that are directly contiguous to the central city or are entirely or nearly surrounded by minor civil divisions that have the required density. No mileage limitation was applied in the 1930 study.

The Civic Development Department of the Chamber of Commerce of the United States, in the spring of 1927 suggested to chambers of commerce in cities of 50,000 population that they coöperate with the United States Bureau of the Census in establishing metropolitan districts by preparing maps of the area. Many of them saw the advantage of having their metropolitan area officially designated and published by the Bureau; however, there was considerable difficulty in securing the data in a uniform procedure.

Local chambers of commerce were asked to select a base map which included all of the metropolitan area with the addition of several miles of territory lying beyond. The map was to show:

1. Corporate limits of city.
2. Any state lines which touch or intersect the surrounding territory.
3. County lines or lines of other similar political unit.
4. Political township lines or lines of other similar political units and the names of these units.
5. Cities, towns and villages within the proposed metropolitan area and in adjacent nearby territory.
6. Railroad and electric railway lines.
7. Principal highways.
8. Water courses, rivers, streams, lakes, etc.
9. Graphic scale.

On the base map, the local chambers were asked also to place the boundaries of each of the control factors enumerated below, using a different symbol for each factor used:

1. Commuters.
2. Deliveries from retail stores located in the central city.

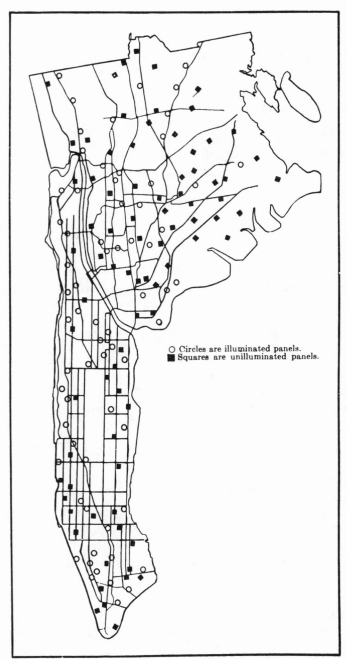

O Circles are illuminated panels.
■ Squares are unilluminated panels.

A representative showing of illuminated and unilluminated panels for Manhattan and the Bronx, given with reference to the chief arteries of traffic.

3. Power and light from central city.
4. Phone service from central city. By indicating on the base map a line which will include the area served by telephones operating from the central city as a base.
5. City water. All the territory served by the water supply system of the central city.
6. Newspaper delivery. For evening newspapers delivered from house to house.
7. Postal service. Delivery by city mail carriers and the rural deliveries from the central city.
8. Sanitary service. The house connections with city sewer system.

It is evident that as each of these factors would usually require a different boundary line the resulting map would be so complicated and confused that it would be useless. The trouble was that the plan was conceived by a geographer rather than by a marketing man.

Primary Retail Trading Area Defined by Traffic Flow

Traffic stabilization has been found to be closely associated with the decrease in population density usually found at the outskirts of urban markets. This has suggested that the point of traffic stabilization may be used to define the limit of the urban market. By the application of this principle for all routes leading into and out of Indianapolis, the boundary of the Indianapolis urban market was established. It is recognized that in going out of one city toward another, the traffic grows less for a time, then, as the second city is approached, increases again. The place where increased travel is noted is the traffic divide: the natural or normal division in the movement of buying power between two competitive markets.

To substantiate the theory that traffic flow patterns may be used as a means of bounding urban markets and retail trading areas, various other indices have been studied and compared. These various indices are: (1) the distribu-

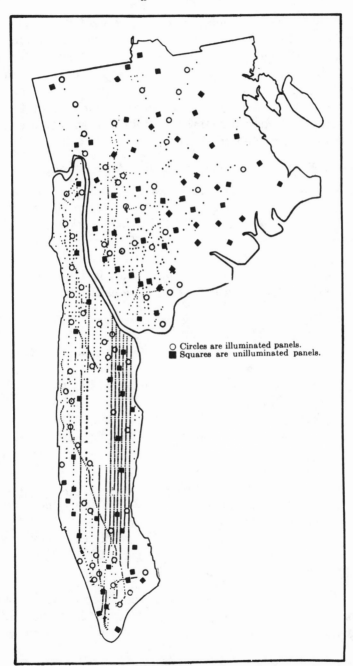

A representative showing of illuminated and unilluminated panels for Manhattan and the Bronx, given with relation to the retail drugstores of these two Boroughs.

tion of resident population of minor civil divisions; (2) consumer interviews to determine the area from which the consumer comes to shop or buy in the trading center; (3) the origin or registration address of consumer automobiles and trucks parked in various parts of the trading center, or the address of those automobiles and trucks moving past counting stations established at the entrances and exits of populated areas.

Field Work in Establishing Trading Area Boundaries

Personal consumer interviews were made in the region surrounding the urban market to determine the extent of the sphere of influence of the urban market or trading center and of the buying habits of the population of the area. These interviews revealed the extent of the area from which the consumer comes to buy or shop in the trading center. The questions asked were as follows:

1. In what city or town does the family shop or buy regularly? Occasionally?
2. What is the distance of your residence from the trade center regularly used?
3. In what city or town does the family buy the following commodities:

Automobiles	Children's clothing	Gifts
Auto accessories	Radios and musical	Electrical
Men's clothing	instruments	appliances
Women's clothing	Novelties	Dry goods
	Jewelry	Amusements

4. The family shops or buys in the town most often named because of—

Greater variety?	Friends and acquaintances?
Better quality?	Other attractions?
Greater accessibility?	

The interviews were taken in the areas in the vicinity of the low point of population density and the traffic divides. In each area, a portion of the interviews were

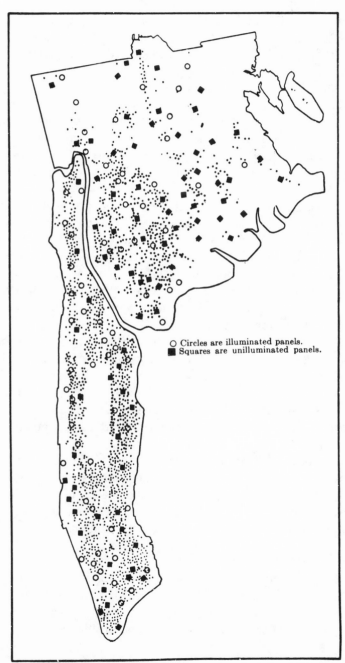

Circles are illuminated panels.
Squares are unilluminated panels.

A representative showing of illuminated and unilluminated panels for Manhattan and the Bronx, given with reference to the location of independent retail grocery stores in those two Boroughs.

made in the high-, low- and medium-class residential sections and in the local trade centers. As was to be expected, the majority of the answers indicated that buying habits were reflected in street traffic.

The boundary line was determined by indicating the breaking point between trading centers where trade started to flow in the opposite direction, as described above. This point was adjusted to the nearest boundary line of the minor civil division and representing the area of primary retail trade influence of the urban market or trade center.

In various markets studied, the license plates of parked cars and trucks, both in garages and on the streets of the central business district, were recorded over a series of days and the origin or place of residence of the owner of the vehicle secured. These residences were spotted on a map of the area. In some instances, the license plates of vehicles passing counting stations were also recorded and their origin determined.

The number of automobiles or trucks coming from any particular town or township was compared with the population and with the number of vehicles registered for the town or township. The result of the comparison of these figures established a percentage which indicated the normal daily attraction of the large urban center to the surrounding towns or townships.

By means of this study, the extent of the influence or pull of the trading center was determined. In a general way, these counts substantiated the theory of traffic as a trading index, and also tended to confirm the accuracy of the conclusion drawn from the questionnaires.

Method of Measuring Traffic Flow

In measuring stream flow or the ocean tide, use is made of technically designed meters, which constantly record the rise and fall, the hourly, daily, weekly and monthly variations. The normal practice of traffic engineers in

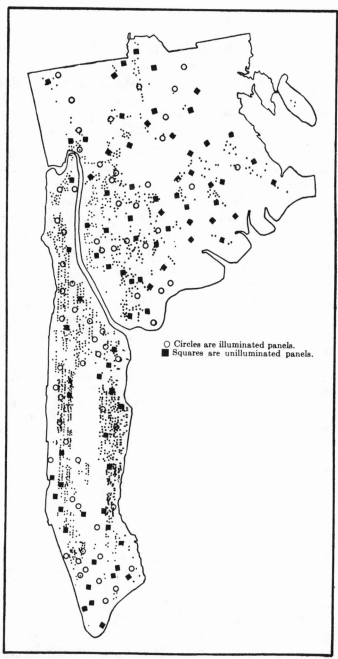

○ Circles are illuminated panels.
■ Squares are unilluminated panels.

A representative showing of illuminated and unilluminated panels for Manhattan and the Bronx, given with reference to location of chain grocery stores in those two Boroughs.

making traffic volume studies is to count passing traffic at strategically located counting stations. Naturally, these methods limit the continuous collection of traffic data because of the excessive cost involved.

The short count method of determining traffic volume (described in Chapter 8) was based upon the fact that there is a high degree of stability and regularity during certain periods of the day. This scientifically designed method of sampling makes it possible to obtain great masses of traffic information through short counts in given hours. These short counts are converted into 12- or 18-hour totals, thus offering great economy and efficiency.[1]

These traffic appraisals have been of great value to the operators of outdoor advertising plants. In locating the most important traffic arteries, and showing the boundaries of the urban center, as a trading point, the survey shows definitely the most strategic points for placing poster panels and painted bulletins. Also, the traffic count by hours indicates with unerring accuracy the panels and bulletins that should be illuminated and at what hours traffic justifies illumination.

[1] At the time this is written, the alert members of the Traffic Bureau are trying out such devices as the electric eye, developed by the International Business Machines Corporation, and a portable "Traficounter" invented by John Paver and J.M. Sills. If these can be adapted to traffic counting, they will greatly facilitate gathering and recording both pedestrian and vehicular traffic.

CHAPTER 8

The Traffic Audit
Bureau, Inc.[1]

Nature of the Traffic Audit Bureau

The verification of circulation is generally considered to
be an essential element in buying or selling the service of
any advertising medium. There are several principles which
must be followed in such a verification activity: (1) pro-
cedures and methods must be absolutely uniform; (2) the
audit must be of a character to reveal actual values; (3) to
insure these two the investigation must be conducted under
the joint control of buyers and sellers so that there will be
complete confidence in the accuracy and integrity of the
audit.

The circulation of outdoor advertising is audited and
verified by the Traffic Audit Bureau, Inc. This is an international, nonprofit service corporation which functions for
outdoor advertising very much as the Audit Bureau of
Circulations serves the various publications. The Traffic
Bureau, as we shall call it, sets forth in the "Standard
Procedure for the Circulation Evaluation of Outdoor
Advertising," a uniform procedure which is followed by
outdoor advertising plants of the United States and

[1] The material for this chapter was furnished by Dr. Miller McClintock,
auditor of the Traffic Audit Bureau, Inc., and director of the Bureau for
Street Traffic Research in Harvard University. No one has contributed more
than Dr. McClintock to establishing a uniform method of evaluating the
circulation of outdoor advertising.

Canada. The Traffic Bureau meets requirements of joint control. It is governed by a board of nineteen directors, nine of whom represent national advertisers, five represent national advertising agents and five represent the organized outdoor industry.

The Traffic Bureau was organized to meet a conscious need for accurate and uniform circulation data in outdoor advertising—a need as old as the industry itself. It was felt both by the operators of plants and by the buyers of space. For many years, various forms of circulation analysis had been attempted.

They naturally varied from elementary to complex and with wide degrees of accuracy. Advertisers also had attempted either through organizations or, more frequently, through their advertising agencies to develop some reasonable means for measuring the circulation of the outdoor medium. It was apparent that such efforts were doomed to failure, and by 1931 this failure was generally admitted. This was not because of lack of accuracy but because no one was willing to accept the results produced by an interested party, whether a buyer or seller. Another inherent handicap of the early studies in circulation measurement lay in the fact that no one technical method could gain sufficient dominance to win the acceptance of all other groups. There was no uniformity. The greatest technical progress which had been made in this field was through the Barney Link studies in the University of Wisconsin conducted under the supervision of several different members of the faculty.[1] The remedies finally

[1] The studies, conducted under the Barney Link Fellowship at the University of Wisconsin, were under the supervision of a committee of which Professor James G. Moore was chairman. Other members of the committee were Professors K.L. Hatch and A.W. Hopkins.

Professor W.A. Sumner and F.A. Aust were ex officio members of the committee because of their direct relationship to the lines of the work undertaken.

At various times, Professors E.H. Gardner, D.R. Fellows and V.A.C. Henmon served on the committee.

applied by united effort were found partially in the development of a technique for traffic engineering and partially in a new standard for the evaluation of outdoor advertising circulation.

Close figuring forced by the depression hastened the adoption of these remedies. The users of outdoor advertising, including those who had the greatest success, felt, as they never had before, the lack of definite, accurate circulation measurements.

Traffic and Trade Researches

In 1931, the outdoor committee of the Association of National Advertisers (generally referred to as A.N.A.), under the chairmanship of Turner Jones, Vice-President of the Coca-Cola Company, took definite action looking toward the establishment of a circulation authority for outdoor advertising. Among other groups considered for the conduct of the initial research was the Bureau for Street Traffic Research in Harvard University. This agency, largely supported by the interests of the automobile industry, for a period of approximately ten years, had been conducting comprehensive studies of the traffic congestion and safety problem in various American cities. Under the able management of Dr. Miller McClintock, it had discovered many fundamental principles for the collection and analysis of traffic data.

The A.N.A. committee decided that the Harvard Bureau was best equipped by personnel and experience to conduct the necessary investigation. This was soon broadened to include all traffic and trade factors as well as the specific problem of outdoor advertising circulation. The researches inaugurated were given the title of "The Traffic and Trade Researches." The scope of these studies, which are still continuing, is indicated in the publication entitled "Traffic and Trade."[1]

[1] J. Paver and M. McClintock, McGraw-Hill Book Company, Inc., 1935.

These studies have been extended to include the "Window Display Research" of the Advertising Research Foundation and other traffic and trade studies sponsored by that organization. The window-display study is producing results comparable in importance to the surveys and analyses made for outdoor advertising by the trade and traffic studies of the Audit Bureau.

The comprehensive study of auditing outdoor advertising was sponsored by a tripartite committee representing the Association of National Advertisers, the American Association of Advertising Agencies, and the Outdoor Advertising Association of America, Inc. In the spring of 1932, a study was started as an independent activity having no connection with the Bureau for Street Traffic Research in Harvard University. The investigation led to the formation of "Standard Procedure for the Circulation Evaluation of Outdoor Advertising" and to a specific plan for organizing a controlling authority. As a result, the Traffic Audit Bureau was formally incorporated as a nonprofit membership corporation under the laws of the State of New York in May, 1934. Stuart Peabody served as president until 1936, when Harrison Atwood was elected, and he, in turn, served until 1938 when the present incumbent, J. W. Dineen, was elected.

The Traffic Audit Bureau has three classes of members: corporate members, plant members and service members. The corporate members are nineteen in number, nine being appointed by the Association of National Advertisers, five by the American Association of Advertising Agencies and five by the Outdoor Advertising Association of America. Appointments are for a 2-year period, one-half being appointed each year. These corporate members form the board of directors of the Traffic Bureau and have exclusive authority over its management.

The actual administrative functions of the Traffic Audit Bureau are assigned by the board of directors to an officer designated as "auditor" who, under the direction of the board, is responsible for all executive action. Dr. Miller McClintock, the present auditor, has been the only one to serve in this capacity.

Plant and Service Members

Any operator of an outdoor advertising plant, consisting of structures of generally recognized standard character, may become a plant member upon simple application and the payment of a $2 annual fee. This membership entitles the holder to receive a copy of the "Standard Procedure" and the regular editions of "Standard Circulation Values of Outdoor Advertising."

The qualifying phrase prescribed for membership, "structures of generally recognized character," requires further explanation. The poster panel in the United States and Canada was generally standardized in the so-called "five-year plan" beginning in 1925. This marked a substantial advancement in the poster medium, as it created a uniformity of structure more readily bought and sold on a national basis. At the present time, the Traffic Bureau has a total of 1,094 plant members.

The third class of membership in the Traffic Bureau is "Service Membership." It is composed of advertisers, agencies, solicitors or others who may use the medium. Any person or firm may become a service member of the Traffic Bureau by the pre-payment of an annual fee of $100. This entitles him to receive the regular publications of "Standard Circulation Values of Outdoor Advertising" and other statistical publications as issued. In actual practice, service memberships are not sold. The bylaws provide service memberships for the members of the Association of National Advertisers, the American Association of Advertising Agencies, and such advertisers, agencies and solicitors as are not members of either of these associations but who may be nominated for service membership by the Outdoor Advertising Association of America, Inc. or by the Poster Advertising Association of Canada.

At the present time, the Traffic Audit Bureau has more than 1,600 service members. The list includes nearly every important advertising agency and advertiser.

Audit Service Growth

Actual audit service is extended to plant members who sign a uniform contract. This requires the plant member to provide the Traffic Bureau annually with a plant member's statement in accordance with the Standard Procedure and containing all of the necessary data prescribed by the Procedure. The plant member also agrees to pay each year a prescribed fee for the audit of his poster panels or painted bulletins. This fee is set annually by the board of directors and is designed to provide an operating income for the organization. Should surpluses result, the bylaws provide that the unused money must be returned to the plant members or used for the reduction of future audit fees. Current fees are at the rate of 50 cents per poster panel per year and $1.00 per painted bulletin per year.

When the Traffic Bureau was organized by the three sponsoring associations in the summer of 1933, its objectives were little more than ideals. Subsequent growth has justified the practical idealism of the founders. The best measure of this growth is the number of outdoor advertising plants annually audited since 1933. The first publication in 1934, less than a year after organization, contained the audited records of 261 plants. By the end of the second year, the annual publication contained 2,095. The third publication, issued in the summer of 1936, contained 4,928 plants. The last annual edition contains 7,312 plants.

Following is a table indicating the distribution of audited properties in the 1936 edition according to the sizes of the communities in which the plants are located. (By June, 1938, the total number of cities and towns had reached 7,023.)

Population	Number of towns audited	Number of towns in service	Percentage covered
Under 1,000...................	2,802	10,933	25.6
1,000–2,500....................	990	3,141	31.5
2,500–5,000....................	451	1,249	36.1
5,000–10,000...................	285	755	37.7
10,000–25,000..................	179	492	36.4
25,000–50,000..................	79	172	45.9
50,000–100,000.................	62	107	57.9
100,000 and over...............	80	117	68.4
Total.......................	4,928	16,966	29.0

Population covered by industry................	80,564,000
Population covered by 1935–1936 audit.........	50,866,207
Percentage covered by 1935–1936............	63.1
Number illuminated panels audited............	30,882
Number unilluminated panels audited..........	102,780
Total number panels audited...............	133,662

It will be observed that the present audit coverage is much more complete for plants in larger communities. This results in a much more comprehensive audit than would be indicated by a mere listing of the number of plants covered. Accurate computations show that there are now 257,000 poster panels in the United States. The audits in 1936 covered 134,000 of these panels, and the last annual audit covered 185,000 panels. The population represented in the 1936 audit plants was in excess of 65 per cent of the total population covered by the poster medium. In terms of annual money appropriated for poster advertising, the audits probably represented in excess of 75 per cent. The continuous and rapid growth in auditing gives reason to believe that the Traffic Bureau will provide coverage for the entire medium in the near future.

Routine Procedure of the Audit

The plant member's initial step in the preparation of his statement is to make an actual traffic count of the principal routes of travel in each plant. This count must provide circulation data for each poster panel or painted bulletin

Form A   Preserve this record for Audit Purposes
                              FIELD RECORD

CITY___*Jeffersonville*___ STATE. *Illinois*
COUNTING
STATION___*Main St 100 ft N of First*___

DATE *Nov. 13, 1934*___

Place a cross (X) on the line, (A, B, C, D or M,) on which the count was taken. Write in the names of all streets.

If the intersection is not a simple one draw a new diagram in this space

PEDESTRIAN CIRCULATION

½ HOUR PERIOD From — To	NO. OF PED'NS	18 HOURS Factor	Circulation	12 HOURS Factor	Circulation
MORNING 9:15 to 9:45	60				
AFTERNOON 2:45 to 3:15	85	11	1,595	8	1,160
SUM OF COUNTS	145				

AUTOMOBILE-TRUCK CIRCULATION

½ HOUR PERIOD From — To	NO. OF AUTOS	18 HOURS Factor	Circulation	12 HOURS Factor	Circulation
Morning 9:15 to 9:45	120				
AFTERNOON 2:45 to 3:15	160	27	7,560	19	5,320
SUM OF COUNTS	280				

LINE	STREET CAR—BUS		
Main St #17		2,090	1,463

REMARKS_____

COUNTED BY___*Joe Hodson*___

Fig. *A.*—This chart is self-explanatory, except for the term "Factor." That is a numerical relationship, worked out after long study between a specific half-hour and 12 hours or 18 hours. This "Factor" is simply the multiplier by which the half-hour traffic is multiplied to convert it into a full day of 12 or 18 hours as desired.

in the plant. The actual counting is by means of a so-called "short-count" method (see Figs. *A* and *B*). This method was originally developed in principle for traffic engineering studies and through the Barney Link studies at the Uni-

Fig. *B.*—This is a tally sheet used for each location. This is not an actual sheet which has been filled in, but rather an example, showing both pencil and meter methods of recording.

versity of Wisconsin. The method was refined and adapted to standard practices by the Traffic and Trade studies at Harvard University. It consists of a sample count taken for a designated period in midmorning and another in midafternoon. These two sample counts are combined and converted by the use of a constant multiplying factor into 12-hour totals, 6:00 A.M. to 6:00 P.M., and 18-hour totals, 6:00 A.M. to 12:00 P.M. The former total is used for un-illuminated structures and the 18-hour total for illuminated structures. The gross traffic thus collected for each outdoor advertising location is classified in three groups: pedestrian traffic, automobile traffic, and mass-transportation traffic.

The short-count method produces a reasonable range of error for any particular location, but the constant multiplying factors have been so arranged as to compensate for these errors, so that over any series of locations the gross traffic obtained by the method shows a negative error, as against actual traffic, of not more than 10 per cent.

Effective Circulation

The next step is the conversion of gross circulation to effective circulation for each location. All of the location data are collected in a "Summary Record of Traffic Data" and depreciation factors applied (see Fig. *C*). These depreciation factors are based upon widespread research which indicates that under varying conditions certain portions of the number of persons passing did not have a reasonable physical opportunity to see a display location. These depreciations were based upon the minimum conditions. According to the rules, effective circulation at any location is composed of 50 per cent of the gross pedestrian traffic, 50 per cent of the gross automobile passenger traffic and 25 per cent of the gross mass transportation. Thus, effective circulation at any location never exceeds 50 per cent of the gross traffic. Effective circulation may be defined as "the least number of people that have a reasonable physical opportunity to see an outdoor advertising display location."

The consideration of circulation per se may be left at this point for the time being. Effective circulation, described above, is one part of the final circulation evaluation of each outdoor advertising display. The other part of the formula deals with space measurements. This is entirely in accord with the practice in the circulation evaluation of news-

Form C

Preserve this record for Audit Purposes

SUMMARY RECORD OF TRAFFIC DATA

Date_____Nov. 16, 1934_____City_____Jeffersonville_____State__Illinois,_____

List Counting Points, double spaced, in geographical sequence from North to South and West to East along arteries of traffic, arranged alphabetically. All circulation figures to be recorded in thousands to one place decimal.

COUNTING STATION	18 HOUR TRAFFIC					12 HOUR TRAFFIC				
	Pedestrian	Auto-Truck	St. Car-Bus	Gross Circulation	Effective Circulation	Pedestrian	Auto-Truck	St. Car-Bus	Gross Circulation	Effective Circulation
Main St. 100' N. of First	1.6	7.6	2.1	11.3	5.1	1.2	5.3	1.5	8.0	3.9
" " 50' S. of First	1.8	8.9	3.0	13.7	6.0	1.3	5.9	2.1	9.3	4.1
" " 75' N. of Second	1.5	6.5	3.0	11.0	4.6	1.1	4.6	2.1	7.8	3.4
" " 75' S. of Second	1.0	3.4	3.0	7.4	2.9	.7	2.4	2.1	5.2	2.1
1st St. W. of Main St.	10.0	20.6	15.6	46.2	19.2	7.0	18.4	10.9	36.3	15.4
" " E. of Main St.	8.0	15.0	7.3	30.3	13.3	5.6	10.5	5.1	21.2	9.3
" " W. of C St.	5.0	6.0	4.0	15.0	6.5	3.5	4.2	2.8	10.5	4.6
" " E. of C St.	4.0	5.0	3.0	12.0	5.2	2.8	3.5	2.1	8.4	3.7
Vine St. W. of F St.	2.0	4.0		6.0	3.0	1.4	2.8		4.2	2.1

Fig. C.—The counting stations are listed and the circulation given for each in thousands and tenths of thousands (hundreds) for each classification of traffic.

papers which results in a milline measurement in which *mil* represents circulation and *line* represents a unit measurement of advertising space, that is, the agate line.

Just as all pages of a given publication are of equivalent size, so twenty-four-sheet poster panels are now standardized to an equal size of 12 feet in height and 25 feet in length. At this point, however, the analogy ends.

Three Basic Circulation Factors

There are three basic factors which control the space-position value of a standard poster panel in relation to its effective circulation. These factors are: (1) the clear, unobstructed distance through which approaching traffic may see the face of the panel; (2) the speed of the traffic stream to which the panel is exposed; and (3) the angularity of the panel to its traffic stream. The clear approach distance governs the degree of opportunity which approaching traffic has to see the face of the panel and any copy which may be displayed upon it. This factor is like that of the time exposure in a camera which controls the opportunity for the photographic impression to record itself. The second factor is a related one for, obviously, if traffic is fast a greater approach distance is required to afford the same length of exposure. The angularity of the panel, the third factor, is of equal importance in judging the circulation effectiveness of the panel. There are two principal elements in angularity; (a) a parallel classification and (b) an angled classification. A panel built parallel to the line of traffic flow is foreshortened to the eye of the individual in the approaching traffic stream. Though its physical size is unchanged, this foreshortening makes its actual size in the eye of the approaching individual much less. On the other hand, a panel which is built at right angles to the traffic flow or at an angle of 45 degrees is one which can be seen in its full physical size and dominance and without distortion of any copy which may be placed upon it.

These three factors of space-position value, approach distance, speed and angularity, are combined by the procedure of the Traffic Audit Bureau into what is known as the "Space-Position Valuation Table" shown herewith (see Fig. *D*). By means of this table, any conceivable poster panel may be given its space-position rating. The application of this table to each specific poster panel in the outdoor advertising plant is the next step undertaken by the plant member in the preparation of his annual Plant

SPACE POSITION VALUATION TABLE Code and Scale of Value for Poster Panels								
		TYPES OF PANELS						
APPROACH		Angled Single (AS) Angled nearest the Line of Travel (AE)		All Other Angled (A)		Parallel Single (PS) Parallel End of a Group (PE)		All Other Parallel (P)	
FAST TRAVEL	SLOW TRAVEL	CODE	VALUE	CODE	VALUE	CODE	VALUE	CODE	VALUE
LONG APPROACH Over 350 feet / Over 250 feet		1AS 1AE	10 or (100%)	1A	9 or (90%)	1PS 1PE	8 or (80%)	1P	7 or (70%)
MEDIUM APPROACH 200 to 350 feet / 150 to 250 feet		2AS 2AE	8 or (80%)	2A	7 or (70%)	2PS 2PE	6 or (60%)	2P	5 or (50%)
SHORT APPROACH 100 to 200 feet / 75 to 150 feet		3AS 3AE	6 or (60%)	3A	5 or (50%)	3PS 3PE	4 or (40%)	3P	3 or (30%)
FLASH APPROACH Under 100 feet / Under 75 feet		AF	4 or (40%) 3 or (30%) 2 or (20%) 1 or (10%) 0 or (0%)	AF	3 or (30%) 2 or (20%) 1 or (10%) 0 or (0%)	PF	2 or (20%) 1 or (10%) 0 or (0%)	PF	1 or (10%) 0 or (0%)

Fig. *D.*—This is a comprehensive summary chart giving the technical data for a panel evaluation as worked out by the Traffic Audit Bureau. Note that the abbreviations are explained in the panels at the top of the chart. Also by comparing the ratings, it is easy to follow the method used for evaluation. For example, 1PS means a single panel, parallel with the traffic. Value is graded according to the angle with traffic and the length of the approach. A single panel, at an angle to the line of traffic, is valued 10; others are proportionately lower, as shown.

Member's Statement. Each panel is given its space-position rating ranging from 100 per cent to zero, and this rating is entered in the plant member's statement opposite the description of each panel (see Fig. *E*). The space position actually answers the question, "How well can this panel be seen?"

The plant member has now produced for each panel the two necessary elements for an accurate evaluation. On one hand, he had the effective circulation and, on the other, the efficiency of the panel in relation to this circulation.

Form E

Preserve this record for Audit Purposes

POSTER PLANT MEMBER'S STATEMENT

Date **Nov. 20, 1934** City **Jeffersonville** State **Illinois**

LOCATION		Panel			Circulation		Space Position		Net Advertising Circulation	
No	DESCRIPTION	No.	Ill.	Unill.	Gross	Effective	Code	Value	Each Street	Total
	Main St. W. L. 200' N. of 1st St.	1	x		11.3	5.1	1PE	8		4.08
		2	x		11.3	5.1	1PE	8		4.08
	Main St. and 4th St. S. E. Main	1		x	5.0	2.5	2A	7	1.75	
	4th				3.0	1.5	1AE	10	1.50	3.25
	Main	2		x	5.0	2.5	1AE	10	2.50	
	4th				3.0	1.5	1A	9	1.35	3.85
	(NOTE: Illuminated panels and Unilluminated panels should be listed on separate sheets.)									
PAGE TOTALS										

Fig. *E*.—Note that under the heading "Space Position" there are two columns: "Code" and "Value." In the first line "1PE" means: "1" the approach is the best; "PE" that it is parallel with traffic and at the end of the group. Yet its value is put at "8" or 80 per cent. Parallel boards are practically never given a perfect rating. Other ratings are worked out similarly. See Fig. *G*.

The next step, therefore, is the simple combination of the two factors. The effective circulation of each panel is multiplied by the space-position value of each panel and the result is the net advertising circulation (NAC) of the panel. Just as *effective circulation* answers the question, "How many people have a reasonable, physical opportunity to see this outdoor advertising location?" so the final measurement (NAC) answers the question, "How many people have a reasonable, physical opportunity to see this panel and how well?"

Analysis of Plant Member's Statement

When the plant member has completed his plant evaluation in accordance with the above procedure, he next recapitulates the values produced in what is known as the "Analysis of Plant Member's Statement" (see Fig. *F*). This record includes all the essential data regarding the physical inventory of the plant, information regarding rate and allotment and all of the analyzed data relating to the circulation evaluation of the plant. Poster advertising is, of course, sold in groups of panels which are known as "showings." These are of three sizes according to the number of panels included; minimum showings, representative showings (usually containing twice as many panels as the minimum showing) and intensive showings (containing three times as many panels as a minimum showing).

The representative showing is used by the Audit Bureau for all of its statistical reports, as this showing is the one most commonly bought and sold. The "Analysis of Plant Member's Statement" shows, among other significant factors, the net advertising circulation (NAC) per day produced by the average representative showing and the exact computed cost per thousand of this circulation. Aside from its use in the Traffic Bureau for auditing purposes, the analysis statement has become an invaluable plant-control record. Many plant operators follow the practice of keeping their plant member's statement up to date at all times, showing new construction, take-downs, and conversions. An analysis of plant member's statement may be prepared each month, and thus the operator has an exact knowledge of the rating of his property at all times. Each proposed new location is carefully analyzed for its circulation and the space-position value of the panel or panels which might be constructed. Thus, the operator has a precise control over developing values and can intelligently engage in long-term planning looking toward the production of increasing advertising values.

The plant member's statement and its analysis correspond to the publisher's statement prepared by the individual publisher for the Audit Bureau of Circulations. It is the operator's claim, prepared in accordance with the uniform instructions of the standard procedure, as to what his property is able to produce in terms of measured circulation. It is apparent that the statement, based entirely upon the operator's claims, would have little authority. This is not because plant operators would engage in fraudulent practices but because buyers in all forms of commercial transactions consider it their natural right to test the quantity and the quality of the merchandise or service offered to them. This is the basic reason behind all auditing practice.

The Traffic Bureau represents neutrally the interest of both buyer and seller. Serving both, it has no objective other than the production of accurate and authoritative data.

Auditing of Reports

There must be an annual audit of the circulation statement for each plant. This statement covers each panel both for posters and for painted bulletins. The report first goes to the Traffic Audit Bureau, New York City, where it is examined for completeness and accuracy in entering the fundamental data. The computations are then verified.

After this initial audit and the corrections of all errors, a field investigation and audit is made. This is done by a field auditor from the Traffic Bureau. The magnitude of this work is apparent when one considers that the Bureau now passes on the circulation reports of nearly 8,000 poster plants. These plants are scattered throughout the United States and Canada, and each must be visited by a qualified auditor.

The work of the field auditor starts in the office of the plant member where the books are first given consideration. One of the purposes of this is to check all the locations which the plant member's statement covers.

The auditor does not attempt to make a traffic count for every location, unless there is evidence of gross errors or misrepresentation by the plant member. That very seldom happens. However, a few locations are taken and a traffic count made. The purpose of this is to verify the accuracy with which the previous count was made. As the plant owner does not know in advance which locations will be rechecked, he has the same incentive for accuracy with each panel. The field audit will also discover any discrepancies in the report, as changing conditions may have affected locations. The opening of a new bridge or the repaving of a road and the like might require new traffic counts.

The auditor also checks up on the individual poster panels to secure an even balance in the different showings for the city. The principal reason for establishing showings, or at least one of the reasons, was to guarantee each advertiser equal service with all other advertisers.

The plant audit tends to make the plant member more careful in his reports than he otherwise might be. It also assures every advertiser that he will receive the full service which is represented by his listing.

Examination of Coverage

Poster panels are, of course, not sold as individual units but, as previously explained, in showings composed of a stipulated allotment or number of panels. To give full representation to the advertiser's message throughout the

Form F.

ANALYSIS OF POSTER PLANT MEMBER'S STATEMENT

JEFFERSONVILLE POSTER ADV. CO.
PLANT NAME

Jeffersonville, Illinois
MAILING ADDRESS

Joe Hodson
MANAGER

JEFFERSONVILLE
CITY

ILLINOIS
STATE

POPULATION COVERED BY PLANT 54,300
From Selective Values: Population Covered

Cost Per Month $216.36

Date of Last Audit 12/16/55   Date of Current Audit 12/17/34   Cost per Day $7.21

Number of Panels in Plant (1) — Illuminated (a) 54, Unilluminated (b) 152, Total (c) 206

Number of Locations in Plant (2) — 104

Average Number of Panels per Location (3) — 1.98

Gross Circulation (4) — all Illuminated panels (a) 968.7, Unilluminated (b) 841.0, Total Plant (c) 1809.7

Average Gross Circulation (5) — per Illuminated panel (a) 17.94, Unilluminated (b) 5.57, Panel (c) 8.78

Effective Circulation (6) — all Illuminated panels (a) 475.1, Unilluminated (b) 430.1, Total Plant (c) 905.2

Average Effective Circulation (7) — per Illuminated panel (a) 8.80, Unilluminated (b) 2.82, Panel (c) 4.39

Net Advertising Circulation (8) — all Illuminated panels (a) 365.98, Unilluminated (b) 376.19, Total Plant (c) 742.17

Average Net Advertising Circulation (9) — per Illuminated panel (a) 6.78, Unilluminated (b) 2.47, Panel (c) 3.60

Number of Panels in a Representative Showing (10) — Illuminated (a) 4, Unilluminated (b) 8, Total (c) 12

Number of Representative Showings in Plant (11) — 13

Gross Circulation per Average Representative Showing (12) — 116.32

Effective Circulation per Average Representative Showing (13) — 57.76

Average Space Position Value per Panel (14) — 0.81

Net Advertising Circulation Ratios (15) — N A C per Average Representative Showing (a) 46.88, N A C to Gross Circulation (b) 0.41, N A C per Representative Showing to Population Covered (c) 0.92

Cost per 1000 N A C of Representative Showing (16) — 15¢

Plant has established posting zones, and maintains equalized showings (17) — Yes

FIG. F.—On this sheet the plant's facilities are listed with costs and circulation.

market, the panels composing the showing must be distributed territorially in such a manner as to give what is known as "coverage."

The Audit Bureau recognizes that a fundamental value in poster advertising is its coverage of all essential portions of a market. That means the distribution of displays along the principal routes of travel in each part of the market in such a manner that there will be adequate repetition but that undue repetition will be avoided. This condition is considered satisfactory in any market if all of the principal routes of travel have been zoned so that, as a norm, there are three to four miles of such route in each zone, and the displays are so distributed that two poster panels are located in each zone for each representative showing.

The field auditor makes a careful observation of the distribution of the plant throughout the community, and, if there is conformity to the principle stated above, the plant is certified for coverage.

The Traffic Bureau audits painted display as well as poster advertising plants. No special discussion of this field of auditing is presented here, because it is similar to that followed for the poster medium. The formula, however, is somewhat more complicated, owing to the fact that a painted bulletin is normally sold as a single unit and that painted displays have a considerable range in size, whereas poster panels are standardized to one size. After the circulation and space-position value of the painted bulletin have been determined, the so-called SQQ formula is applied to the net circulation thus obtained. This SQQ formula provides a definite percentage rating for size, quantity of circulation and quality of circulation. This results in a final figure which is an index number and is known as "rated value."

Summary of the Traffic Audit Bureau's Activities

Periodically the audited reports are prepared and arranged alphabetically according to states and within

TRAFFIC AUDIT REPORTS OF POSTER ADVERTISING PLANTS

CITY	PLANT MEMBER	Date of Audit	Population Covered	No. of Panels Ill.	No. of Panels Unill.	Cost Per Month	Average Gross Circulation PER DAY	Average Net Advertising Circulation PER DAY	Average Rate per 1000 NAC in Cents
PENNSYLVANIA									
PENFIELD	Du Bois Poster Adv. Co.	10-36	350		1	$ 9.60	1,700	540	59.3
PENNSBURG	Perkiomen Ad Co., Inc.	10-36	1,494		1	9.35	1,660	790	39.2
PENNS CREEK	O. O. Orner Outdoor Adv. Co.	10-36	275		1	9.60	1,100	490	65.3
PENNSDALE	Williamsport Outdoor Adv. Co.	1-37	120		1	9.36	1,450	740	41.9
PERKASIE	Lehigh Advertising Co.	10-36	3,463		2	22.00	2,160	1,060	68.9
PERKIOMENVILLE	Perkiomen Ad Co., Inc.	10-36	75		1	9.35	1,500	760	40.8
PERRYVILLE	Wilson Poster Adv. Co.	11-36	226		1	9.60	1,750	880	36.4
PETROLIA	Wilson Poster Adv. Co.	11-36	469		1	9.60	5,850	2,770	11.6
PHILADELPHIA	General Outdoor Adv. Co.	11-37	1,950,961	44	66	2,320.00	3,282,840	1,111,000	7.0
PHILADELPHIA (Philadelphia and Upper Darby Township)	The Penn State Adv. Co., Inc.	10-37	1,997,587	36	74	1,926.00	2,984,240	953,500	6.7
PHILIPSBURG	Altoona Adv. Service	10-37	3,600		2	18.70	6,380	2,960	20.9
PHOENIXVILLE	Hen. Johnston, Inc.	12-36	12,029		4	38.40	13,360	5,360	23.9
PILLOW	O. O. Orner Outdoor Adv. Co.	10-36	350		1	9.60	1,000	330	97.0
PINE GROVE	Hen. Johnston, Inc.	12-36	2,257		1	9.60	3,100	1,550	20.6
PINE GROVE MILLS	O. O. Orner Outdoor Adv. Co.	10-36	362		1	9.60	730	360	88.9
PITTSBURGH DISTRICT	Pittsburgh Outdoor Adv. Co.	9-37	922,275	38	62	2,175.00	2,216,240	798,580	9.1
PITTSFIELD	Reed Poster Adv. Co.	11-36	313		1	9.60	2,560	1,090	29.4
PITTSTON DISTRICT	Rees Poster Adv. Co.	1-37	55,243	2	10	170.00	92,560	35,500	16.0
PLAINFIELD	Adams Advertising, Inc.	10-36	250		1	9.60	2,400	1,160	27.6
PLEASANT GAP	O. O. Orner Outdoor Adv. Co.	10-36	426		1	9.60	2,500	860	37.2
PLEASANT VALLEY	Altoona Adv. Service	10-37	2,800		1	9.35	2,400	1,120	27.7
PLEASANTVILLE	Oil City Andrews Adv. Co.	12-36	627		1	9.90	1,600	660	50.0
PLUMER	Oil City Andrews Adv. Co.	12-36	110		1	9.90	1,780	920	35.9
PLYMOUTH MEETING	General Outdoor Adv Co.	8-37	1,200		1	10.00	6,900	3,350	9.9
POINT MARION	Allegheny Poster Adv. Co.	11-36	2,039		1	10.20	1,800	730	46.6
POLK	Wilson Poster Adv. Co.	11-36	3,337		2	19.20	4,860	2,340	27.4
POMEROY	General Outdoor Adv. Co.	8-37	319		1	10.00	2,100	800	41.3
PORTAGE	Johnstown Poster Adv. Co.	12-36	4,432		2	19.20	7,560	3,100	20.6
PORT ALLEGHENY	F. R. Holmes P. A. Co.	11-36	2,193		1	9.60	2,240	870	36.8
PORT CARBON	Hen. Johnston, Inc.	12-36	3,225		1	10.00	6,480	2,150	15.3
PORT CLINTON	Hen. Johnston, Inc.	12-36	406		1	9.60	5,200	2,410	13.3
PORTERSVILLE	Dunmyre Poster Adv. Co.	11-36	185		1	9.60	7,540	3,540	9.0
PORTLAND	Slate City Poster Adv. Co.	9-36	551		1	12.00	8,070	3,470	11.5
PORT MATILDA	Altoona Adv. Service	10-37	508		1	9.35	3,500	1,750	17.7
PORT TREVORTON	O. O. Orner Outdoor Adv. Co.	10-36	475		1	9.60	3,860	1,880	17.0
POTTERS MILLS	O. C. Orner Outdoor Adv. Co.	10-36	339		1	9.60	1,450	730	43.8
POTTSTOWN DISTRICT	Hen. Johnston, Inc.	12-36	22,530		5	48.00	23,800	11,150	14.3
POTTSVILLE DISTRICT	Hen. Johnston, Inc.	8-37	26,669	1	5	78.00	52,090	23,730	11.0
POWELL	Elmira Andrews Adv. Co.	12-36	500		1	9.90	1,020	500	66.0
PROMPTON	Rees Outdoor Adv. Co.	1-37	220		1	9.60	1,900	600	53.3
PROSPECT	Dunmyre Poster Adv. Co.	11-36	455		1	9.60	6,080	2,910	11.0
PROSPECT PARK	General Outdoor Adv. Co.	8-37	4,623		1	10.00	12,450	5,400	6.1
PUNXSUTAWNEY	Indiana Poster Adv. Co.	11-36	9,266		4	38.40	15,880	5,680	22.5
PURITAN	Johnstown Poster Adv. Co.	12-36	466		1	9.60	1,300	650	49.2
QUAKERTOWN	Lehigh Advertising Co.	10-36	4,883		2	24.00	6,440	3,160	25.3

Fig. *G.*

the states by cities and towns, and printed in "Standard Circulation Values of Outdoor Advertising." It shows the name of the plant operator, the population covered, the number of panels in each representative showing and the cost per month for a representative showing. For each representative showing, it sets forth the average gross circulation per day and the average net advertising circulation per day. The cost per thousand net advertising circulation (NAC) is computed for each plant. For a typical page see Fig. *G*. This publication is sent to each plant member of the Traffic Bureau and to each service member. Thus, the audited data are made available to the members of the outdoor advertising industry and to advertisers and agencies who are buyers or potential buyers of the medium.

Since the Traffic Bureau has been in existence for only five years, it is apparent that its full effects could not have made themselves felt. It is obvious that it has already had a profound effect upon the entire industry. As earlier indicated, the Traffic Bureau was brought into existence because the advertisers of the country demanded more information concerning the circulation of the outdoor industry. They needed a uniform and accurate evaluation of circulation comparable to that afforded in the publication field by the Audit Bureau of Circulations. This the Traffic Bureau has achieved. This makes it possible for the buyer to evaluate outdoor advertising accurately in relation to other advertising media. It also makes it possible to select those plants which, through their favorable locations or the special abilities of their operators, are offering superior service, and to avoid those operators who are below standard.

The effects of the Traffic Audit Bureau within the industry itself are perhaps even more pronounced. It has put a sound economic urge behind the natural desire of plant operators increasingly to build good plants. This economic urge arises from the fact that an operator can definitely see what plant improvement will bring in sales.

CERTIFICATE OF POSTER PLANT AUDIT BY THE TRAFFIC AUDIT BUREAU, INC.

City	Market	Population Covered	No. of Panels in Plant	Number of Panels Ill.	Number of Panels Unill.	Cost Per Month	Average Gross Circulation Per Day	Average Space Position Value Per Panel	Average Net Advertising Circulation Per Day	Average Rate per 1000 (NAC) in Cents
						REPRESENTATIVE SHOWING				
Illinois										
Jeffersonville		54,500	206	4	8	$216.36	116,320	8.1	46,880	15.
Davies		9,347	44	4		40.00	17,280	8.8	7,680	17.5
Caldersburg		2,000	8	1		9.25	4,500	7.4	1,700	18.2
Pilot		1,156	8	1		10.00	7,610	9.9	3,800	8.7

This summary of the plant's approved display facilities is self-explanatory.

He knows that if improvements are made they will be reflected immediately in audited values which have the confidence of the buyer. Thus, the Traffic Bureau has afforded the plant operator protection for his investment

When all forms are audited and approved a certificate is given the plant owner. This certificate covers a space of 12 months' time. Then it is all done over again and a new certificate awarded.

and a means of estimating the market for future improvements to the limits of his territory.

The history, organization and operation of the Traffic Bureau make an outstanding example of what can be accomplished in the advertising field through a harmonious, coöperative effort to obtain scientific information of mutual concern to all parties interested.

CHAPTER 9

Some Laws of Psychology Applied to Buying and Selling

We Are All Creatures of Impulse

Little can be said about the science of psychology in the limited space available here. Yet, so important is an understanding of a few of the basic laws of the subject that they should not be omitted from a consideration of mass advertising. Furthermore, like most of the important things, these basic laws are so simple that they are easily grasped and even more easily applied.

One of the most fundamental laws of psychology is that at any given time and place a man will do the thing that he most wants to do. He may wish that he did not "have to" pay his taxes. He would like to use the money in so many other ways. But when he thinks of the penalties that would follow his failure to pay the taxes, he actually prefers to give his money to the tax collector, rather than to use it otherwise and suffer the penalties which would so surely follow.

Again, many people have an aversion to spending money. But most of them prefer to keep a respectable appearance before their neighbors. And when it comes to the final point of making a decision, parting with the money is actually less painful than appearing in shabby clothes, when friends and fellow workers begin to jeer at the unkempt appearance.

Very few things we do are the results of carefully thought-out and painstakingly worked-up plans. We all act impulsively, imitatively, according to habit, or instinctively many times for each occasion when we think through all the pros and cons and come to a logical decision about a course of action. This is true in selecting and buying most goods quite as much as in selecting food for lunch, following an accustomed route downtown, or in selecting the topics to read in a newspaper. Your food is chosen because you usually eat about the same things. Items vary from day to day, but a review at the end of each month would show about the same items consumed. Habit is the great force.

This is illustrated in following a habitual route to the railroad station or to the office. You deviate when you notice something that looks interesting on a new street and impulsively go that way. So with the columns you read in your newspaper. Some, probably most, of the headlines do not offer absorbing possibilities and are passed by. Then another item catches the eye, arouses curiosity, and you read it. Other columns and features you read out of force of habit. Each of these decisions is made without logical consideration. They seem the desirable thing to do at the time and under the circumstances. So the decision is made. As we shall see, most purchases are made with scarcely greater consideration. At least the method of making a choice will be about the same.

Similarity of Human Nature

One of the first things observed in psychology is the very great similarity of people, regardless of race, color, or economic levels of living. We all sleep about the same number of hours; we prefer the same range of temperature; we value the approbation of our friends and associates; we enjoy companions; we like sweet better than sour; we prefer light to darkness; we enjoy games. This list of our similarities can be greatly prolonged. Even with such a simple thing as strength of coffee, popular taste has been shown to vary only 5 to 10 per cent for more than 90 per cent of the American people. Our dislikes or aversions are almost as universal as our likes. We fear the unknown, avoid pain, however slight; we dislike loneliness; we hate to be crossed.

Even our mistakes are comparable. In each million letters dropped into the mail boxes of New York, New Orleans, London, Petrograd, Paris, Tokio or Calcutta, there will be about the same number without stamps, or without addresses, and about the same number that have not been

It is one of the laws of psychology that the great majority of people like the same thing.

sealed. These similarities make advertising possible. It is our differences that make salesmanship necessary.

To the big things of life, or those that we regard as of far-reaching importance, we give much thought and attention. In other words, we reason our way to a logical conclusion. In buying or selling real estate, there are many things to consider. Some are favorable; some unfavorable. In balancing the advantages against the disadvantages, a conclusion is reached. The reasoning may be good or poor, logical or illogical, but it is the basis of action. Usually much time and thought are involved in reaching such a decision. Data are investigated and compared, future contingencies are anticipated, records are gone over. But for most of us, real estate purchases are made only on rare occasions. And it is seldom that other purchases are as carefully considered. We buy because some one has recommended the product, because we have used it before, or because we feel that we know all about it, and have confidence that it will be satisfactory. Often this familiarity comes from seeing the advertising. Even when a customer gives some other reason for making a purchase, it may be the advertising that is fundamentally responsible. Walter Dill Scott[1] relates a story of this nature which happened to himself. He told the proprietor of a store that he came on the recommendation of a friend, but afterwards was unable to recollect that friend, but he did remember that he had been favorably impressed by the store's advertising.

A Few Basic Laws of Psychology

There are a few psychological laws that bear so directly upon our daily lives and in forming our likes and dislikes that they should be stated here. One of the most important of these is that we try to remember and repeat pleasant experiences. That seems so simple and such a common sense statement that we do not need to go to a psychologist to learn it, but, as we shall see presently, this is one of the fundamental laws that is frequently disregarded. It is the law that accounts for persons taking the same trip more than once, going to the same show twice, listening to the same songs, reading the same poems and playing the same games over and over again. The law also explains that the longer the interval of time after the experience, the less the inclination to repeat it. In shooting at a target, men frequently remain for a half hour, or more, yet once away from the gallery and the thing having passed out of mind, they will make no effort to visit the place again.

Dr. E. L. Thorndike states a law that is somewhat similar, which he calls the "Law of Effect." The essence of this law is that pleasant ideas and experiences tend to

[1] Walter Dill Scott, "Psychology of Advertising," Robert M. McBride & Company.

remain longer in the memory than unpleasant ones. There is an obvious attempt on the part of most people to forget unpleasant incidents and experiences. On the other hand, they like to remember the things that they enjoyed.,

Dr. H. L. Hollingworth has pointed out that all experiences involve a feeling response which psychologists call "Feeling Tone." According to the Law of Fusion, we remember experiences as being definitely colored by the feeling tone or dominant emotion of the occasion. We do not subdivide our sensations in memory, In attending a banquet, we may at the time say that one of the speeches was too long, or that another speech was entirely dry, but if the food was pleasing, one met old friends, enjoyed the toastmaster's quips and most of the responses, in a short time the event will linger in the memory as one decidedly pleasant. The same is true if the affair turns out unfortunately. If a waiter spills hot soup over the shirt front of a guest, the guest is very sure to remember it as being a very disagreeable evening. The unpleasant is so impressive that anything that may have been pleasant will fade rapidly from his memory in comparison with the intense feeling of irritation because of the accident.

These laws are extremely fortunate for advertisers. First of all, they provide a foundation and justification for making every advertisement as attractive as possible. If it pleases the reader, it will tend to remain longer in his memory. If he is pleasantly impressed by the advertising, he will be favorably disposed toward the advertiser. That is according to the Law of Fusion. Furthermore, if he is led by the advertisement to make a satisfactory purchase, he will be more inclined to respond to similar advertising the second time and will look forward to the purchase with more anticipation.

The owners of poster panels secure their income from advertising. In order for that advertising to be profitable to the advertiser and to the owner of the poster panel, it must serve some useful purpose for the reader. Too often the owner of the poster stand is interested only in pleasing the advertiser, but if the location of the panel is objectionable, or the advertisement that is placed upon it is irritating to readers, it is sure to be unprofitable to the advertiser and in the long run unprofitable to the owner of the stand.

The newspaper publisher sometimes finds it necessary to be indifferent and even antagonistic to the wishes of the advertiser in the selection of editorials and news matter. While he may receive his chief income from advertisers, in order to make his newspaper a profitable medium for them, he must please his readers who are their customers. The same thing is true with poster advertising. It must please the reader, or, at the very least, it must not antagonize him. A poster that irritates turns the reader against the advertiser as well as against the owner. The reader may be willing to forget his irritation and dismiss it from his mind, but that means the advertisement has failed, for instead of creating good will, it has only stirred up ill will and antagonism.

The Response to Suggestion

Most people are accustomed to believe the most of what they are told and what they read. They get their information almost wholly through these two sources. So unless there is some definite experience of the individual to the contrary, or unless the statement is otherwise at variance with his former experiences and beliefs, the reader will believe what he is told; and in the smaller things of life, he will do what he is told. Our police regulations, such as "One Way Street," "Do Not Throw Rubbish Here," and "No Parking On This Side," are suggestions that may be 'disregarded only at the danger of suffering a penalty. The child first obeys his parents, then his teachers, and then the policeman and the laws of his country, State and city. Having grown up with this attitude of obedience, it is natural for him to obey other instructions.

Inasmuch as we select most of our purchases on the recommendation of someone else, or in imitating someone else, a suggestion becomes one of the most important factors in all our buying. There are several laws in regard to suggestion that may be profitably considered:

1. Suggestion is stronger if positive than if negative. In general, it is better to tell people what to do than what to avoid. This is one of the oldest rules for advertising copy. It is true that most of our enacted laws and ordinances are stated negatively with much emphasis on "Thou shalt not." At the same time, every parent and every teacher knows it is easier to get compliance with the things that are desired by suggestion rather than by merely imposing prohibition. Instead of their peremptory, "Stop making so much noise in the house," the wise mother gets better compliance with a suggestion to "play outdoors for a time." The same thing applies to advertising. Advising the purchase of a car because it uses very little oil and gasoline is much more convincing than a warning: "Don't buy a car that wastes gas." The latter leaves the reader open to doubt. He doesn't know all the other cars, or their records for economy of operation. The assurance that car *A* is economical may make prospects want to investigate. Automobile advertising can scarcely do more.

2. A suggestion to be potent must not run counter to fixed experiences and beliefs. This is another excellent guide for the copywriter, for even if the advertisement states a fact, if that fact is so strange or unusual that it sounds exaggerated, then it will not be readily believed, if it appears in an advertisement. In other words, does it pay to invest good money in telling people what they do not believe after they have been told? How many times have we been advised to make our advertisements readable and believable, and yet we do not always do it.

3. Suggestion is oftentimes more effective if indirect than if direct. This is especially true when an idea can be given without an expressed command, for, although we are accustomed to obeying directions that are given us, we are sometimes irked by them. In other words, we feel that people are ordering us about unnecessarily or peremptorily. Sometime back, one of the leading paint companies published a series of advertisements showing an intelligent and attractive looking woman using paint for different purposes.

They's mostly out since they got that new

FORD V·8

This is indirect suggestion; a very forceful way to indicate how much the new automobile is enjoyed.

The copy explained how satisfactorily and easily the paint was applied in each case. The picture and the message gave the impression that it was the intelligent woman who was using the paint and recommending it. The reader easily put herself in the same class. If the woman in the picture could do it so easily and with so much satisfaction, she, the reader, could also do it. This was an example of indirect suggestion.

4. Suggestions gain force by repetition. There is an old adage to the effect that a lie repeated often enough will come to be believed, and there seems to be some grounds for believing that that is true. Probably this law gives the best explanation for the persistence with which old superstitions cling to life. Did any

one ever offer convincing evidence that 13 is an unlucky number; that potatoes will not grow to full size if "planted in a waning moon"? Can the reader point to any ill effects following when a black cat has crossed his path? Or when he spilled salt and did not throw some over his left shoulder? Or after walking under a ladder? Or by beginning a journey on Friday? Do storms really follow a ring around the moon, or a red sunrise, or come at the

This is a clever variation of form in presenting the message. The poster treatment adds to the effectiveness.

time of the equinoxes? There are thousands of people who believe these things, probably because they have been told them so often.

5. Suggestion gains in potency with the number who make the suggestion. That is a part of the mob psychology that should be understood. If one finds himself in a crowd of angry people bent on punishing some one and if all are of the same attitude and all repeat the same dire directions, such as "hang him," "tar and feather him," or "ride him on a rail," it is only a strong character who will contend against a suggestion coming from so many. In advertising, the application is slightly different, for instead of having an advertisement crowded with people, it is better to have a whole series of advertisements, each telling

the same story, but each telling it in a slightly different way. Ten or more years after the Camel cigarettes had been advertised by a series of posters in which different types of businessmen had been made to say, "I'd walk a mile for a Camel," the expression was in current use. Even the jokers and columnists had not forgotten it. Exact repetition may become wearisome and induce indifference. We have all passed street signs many, many times, yet because of the sameness, we fail to notice them. This is illustrated by the statement of a wise manufacturer who said that every 3 months he changes the form in which the rules for caution at his dangerous machines are given. For, if they are not changed, they soon become ineffective and are passed unnoticed. If the street signs were changed as often as twice a year, we would not ignore them.

6. Suggestion increases in potency with the prestige of the source. We may be skeptical of gossip or the accuracy of statements made in sensational newspapers and of rumors that are everywhere about, but statements which appear in a textbook, encyclopedia or other reference book are accepted at face value, if there is no evidence of inaccuracy at hand. This is because of the prestige of the source. Hence, in advertising, letters of recommendation, if sincere and genuine, may have great prestige and be strikingly convincing. Particularly will this be true if the one offering a testimonial is supposed to be an authority in the field. It does not follow that if some great musician recommends some cigarette or cigar that conviction will follow the statement. There is no reason why Percy Grainger should be an authority on cigarettes or cigars, but his recommendation for a certain make of piano would be highly convincing.

Size is another element that affects suggestion. Large fortunes, books, buildings, displays, rivers and

animals are impressive. Also, we think in terms of
bulk rather than of midgets. Ask almost anyone
which he prefers of two football players, two bridges,
or two buildings, and the answer will nearly always
be for the larger. Rare, indeed, is the individual who
will respond naming the smaller. A statement made in
an agate type in a classified column may not be convincing, but the same statement occupying a double
page is respected. This is one of the reasons why
outdoor advertising is so effective. It commands such
unusual space.

Age is another attribute that adds prestige and
impressiveness. A recent advertisement for an advertising agent stated that two clients had been with the
company over sixty years, others over fifty years,
still others over forty and thirty and twenty years. It
was the length of time, not the number, that was
impressive.

7. The intensity of the suggestion also adds to its
potency. A sudden call of "Fire" arouses emotions
so intense that immediate action is sure to follow
by all who hear the message. It is not always easy
or even possible to make an advertising message
intense. Sometimes such efforts become ridiculous.
The Diamond brand of tea may be the very finest
brand of tea on the market, but the frantic effort
of the advertiser to make the message so intense as
to be heeded by every reader is practically an impossibility. Gum chewing, the selection of an ice cream
at a soda fountain or the brewing of a cup of tea
are not matters of such importance to most people
that they would not smile at the advertiser who
becomes overserious in exaggerating the importance
of one of these products by intensive methods. The
artist frequently comes to the aid of such an advertiser by the skillful use of color and layout, and the
placing of the message with a degree of intensity

can be achieved. The reader will find more of this in the chapter on Art in Outdoor Advertising.

What Should an Advertisement Do?

To enumerate specifically what may be accomplished by advertising would make a very long list and would be of small service, but a few generalizations which attempt to establish standards may prove helpful in preparing or creating illustrations and copy. The purpose of most advertisements is to make immediate sales or to help make sales at a future time. We have often been told that sales are made in the mind, and it is the purpose of advertising to make readers see the desirability of buying the product presented. Seldom does an advertisement attempt to go the whole way and bring in the order. Of course, in mail-order selling, the advertising alone must make the sale, but mail-order selling is on the decline, and while there will probably always be some business of this nature, every year it seems to get less.

The classic requirements of advertisements are to attract attention, to arouse interest, to create desire, and to stimulate action. It is evident that where the advertisement is the only selling effort all these things must be accomplished, but with most advertising of the present day less is attempted than the classic demands required.

A businessman was more practical when he said he wanted his advertisement to be seen, to be read, to be believed and to be remembered. Another advertiser required his advertising "to repay the reader" even if he gave it but a cursory glance. In other words, he wanted his message to be attractive in form, so filled with information or helpful suggestions that the reader would be glad to give it attention.

A further consideration of the businessman's standard, given in the previous paragraph, may be enlightening. The matter of attention is no problem for outdoor advertising (see Spectaculars, Chapter 7, pages 123 and 124, or general observation). Perhaps a word should be said concerning the inclination of some advertisers to get attention to the message itself rather than to the object the message is supposed to sell. It is comparatively easy to get a picture which will attract attention, but the attention of the picture may direct the reader away from the product that is to be sold rather than to it. When an advertising man speaks of attention, he means centering the mind on the sale of the item about which he is writing. If there were no other reasons for preventing an author of advertising from signing it, I think this would be sufficient in itself. As an author, one is constantly, but perhaps unconsciously, making an effort to produce a composition that will reflect credit on himself. With so brief a message as most advertising offers, the temptation would be still greater to make the advertisement seem good rather than to make the product about which the message is written seem highly desirable.

Again, with outdoor advertising, there is little danger that the message will not be read. It is so brief. The picture, if well chosen, is such an integral part of the message that the reading is assured. For all this, the artist should make it easy to read. That means a style of lettering that is highly legible and so arranged that the eye follows easily from point to point to the end. In publication advertising, the size of the type helps to determine the length of line, but in each case six to eight words in a line offers the maximum legibility. Furthermore, the lines should be approximately the same length and size of type so uniform that no adjustment of the eye would be required in passing from one line to the next. The eye should run rhythmically across the column without any effort. In no case should valuable space be wasted with pictures or other decorative materials that do not help to tell the story of the product. The reader should be helped to grasp the idea quickly and clearly rather than confused with distracting features in the display.

Sincerity and Humor

A sincere, accurate statement about a product, or about an incident of news, is almost sure to be accepted at face value by most readers. The logic of the American people may be faulty, but their ability to recognize sincerity seldom errs. Many of our political campaigns demonstrate this ability. One of the hardest things in the world to fake is sincerity. Consequently, a writer should never be asked to make statements he does not implicitly believe. Common honesty demands this, but furthermore, good business demands it. Few indeed are the writers who can make up a story about merchandise and make it sound sincere. Very often to understate an advertising message makes it effective. John E. Powers, one of the creators of American advertising, was noted for this. An example comes to mind which Mr. Powers used in writing copy for Rogers Peet. It was a highly successful display card announcing: "Ties—25¢. Not as good as they look." Indeed, the history of advertising supplies many examples of this kind of copy. One advertiser maintained that exaggeration was so common in advertising copy that, if one did not enlarge upon his offering but tried to stick to the literal truth, his copy would seem tame and unimpressive in comparison with others. He felt that exaggeration was so much the order of the day that it could not be avoided with success. The author does not agree with that any more than did Mr. Powers in writing some of his most successful copy. Accuracy does not necessarily lead to dullness.

The businessman who wanted his advertisement to be remembered probably would have stated his thought more accurately if he had said that he wanted the offering to be remembered. Also, he wanted himself remembered as the one making the offer, and he wanted the product remembered. Many tricks have been tried to make the memory retentive, but few of them have been successful. Continued advertising seems to be the one sure way of preventing people from forgetting. This is true to such an extent that an advertiser who drops out is soon missed by the reading public which assumes that something has happened to his business. Readers can see no reason why a successful advertiser should discontinue advertising unless his product is no longer acceptable or unless something else has gone radically wrong. Both the laws of fusion and feeling tone, given above, present valuable hints for making an adver-

An excellent example of adapting humor to a sales message. The product could not be separated from the humor.

tising offering remembered. The more pleasing it is, the surer it is to retain a place in the memory. Also, the more pleasingly it is presented, the more acceptably it will be received.

I believe that all advertising must be profitable to the reader or it will not be profitable to the advertiser or to the medium which carries the advertising. Consequently, it is of importance to the one who owns the advertising medium to see to it that every offering that is made through this medium is suitable to his readers and is made in a way to be acceptable.

How Advertising Works

It is human nature to prefer the known to the unknown. We are suspicious of strangers who approach us on little provocation. We pass over the unknown newspaper and magazine on stands to select the favorites with which we are familiar. In all of our buying, we are much prejudiced in favor of the things we know about. This is wholly rational when it pertains to products we have already tried ourselves. But fortunately for the advertiser, it does not stop there. Things we have seen advertised extensively and which are familiar in appearance or in the appearance of the package are accepted almost as readily as the one we have tried and found satisfactory. This is in accordance with the old adage, "It must be good; it is so extensively advertised." Obviously, the basis of this statement is the understanding that an unworthy or unsatisfactory product cannot remain on the market for a great length of time. The advertising would of necessity cease after the inadequacy was discovered and the sales fell to the vanishing point. That the reverse has happened and that many products are advertised year after year to a great majority of people is evidence that these are meritorious. "They must be good; they are so extensively advertised."

As we have already seen, many products are bought on the recommendation of friends and acquaintances. This also includes the recommendation of those from whom we buy. We look to the grocer as one of authority on brands of foods. He knows all that his customers tell him, all that his manufacturers tell him, and all that he has an opportunity to learn in other ways. Consequently, he is in a position to recommend different items with a degree of authority. But this grocer is subject to the same influence by advertising as his customers. When he sees an extensive campaign for an item that he carries in stock, his confidence in that product is greatly strengthened and he feels able to recommend it without reserve. Another side of this is that he likes to have his recommendations accepted. He knows from experience that products that are widely advertised are much more readily accepted by customers than products little known. So, with the belief that the recommendation of an advertised article will be accepted, he is led to recommend such articles rather than the ones that are not advertised. The exceptions to this are the unknown items upon which the grocer may have a larger margin and from which he hopes to make a larger profit.

Almost every advertiser fifty years ago tried to make his advertising more pleasing by making it humorous. He thought that this assured both attention and reading. Perhaps that was true, but if the humor was in no way connected with the product or with the way it was offered, it merely occupied expensive space and helped to divert the reader's mind from his product rather than to it. Edward Balmer and Dr. Walter Dill Scott called attention to this fallacy in their early writings. The reaction resulted in sombre seriousness. Spending money was not a laughing matter to most people. So, for several years, the ultra seriousness of advertising was noticeable. Then some more human and more discerning advertiser discovered that, while spending money might not be a laughing matter to most people, for the most part it was nothing to weep over. Money was spent to provide a good time, or to buy a much cherished product. It was really a pleasure to buy articles that one or one's family wanted. Also, humor judiciously used might be an overture to the purchaser to get him in a good frame of mind before presenting a business proposition. This use of humor, especially when skillfully employed so as to lead into the subject, is still regarded as good advertising and especially as a good approach. When a pleasing advertising message leaves the reader in a receptive frame of mind, it has probably done all that is required of it in most campaigns, and because everyone enjoys humor of one kind or another, its judicious use in the advertising message is surely to be approved rather than condemned.

CHAPTER 10

Art and Outdoor Advertising[1]

Development of an Advertising Art

It is a far cry from the carved or painted symbols—sometimes, carved *and* painted symbols—which designated shops and taverns of Europe to the highly developed poster art of the present. The goat designating a dairy; a pair of shears, a tailor; and a bunch of grapes, a winery, resemble the modern commercial sign only in purpose. They both help to locate a business so that its customers can more easily find it.

For the painted bulletin and poster panel, there is no very close historical prototype. Probably the chief reason for this is that our modes of life, and particularly our commercial activities, have made necessary a much more extensive selling effort. At least, in consumer buying the sale is often initiated by the seller, which is the reverse of conditions when advertising was restricted to commercial signs. Things that the buyer may never have thought of owning are now so alluringly presented through the combination of pictures and language that new wants are created with great frequency. The difference between the two kinds of advertising is immeasurable.

[1] The material and largely the ideas for this chapter were supplied by Leonard London, art director of Outdoor Advertising Incorporated. Mr. London is one of the younger poster artists who is doing so much in adapting art to selling.

213

The evolution of commercial art to meet the demands of modern selling methods has required two centuries or more, for as early as 1700, history shows that eminent painters were interested in producing business signs.

That a poster is more than an advertising picture should be definitely understood. But a satisfactory definition has

Poster by Jean Carlu (French).

not yet come to the writer's attention. Perhaps by telling what a poster should do, Hamilton King has come as near as any one to explaining what a poster is. He says it should, "seize a moment, exploit a situation with one daring sweep of the pencil or brush. The poster is not a portrait, nor a study. It is a flash of line, a sweep of color

. . . all that can be told of a tale in the passing of an instant. It is dramatic and imaginative, yet it is saliently sincere."

Too often the art buyer wants a poster of the nature of a colored photograph, which defeats the whole plan and purpose of the composition. Charles Matlack Price empha-

Poster by Joseph Binder (Austrian).

sizes that the poster is not for study, but for the purpose of flashing a message, something on the order of a signal light. European artists grasped this conception before those of America.

The signs, particularly of France and England, reached a degree of artistic perfection by the middle of the 18th century. Such eminent names as Richard Wilson, George Morland, David Cox and John Everett Millais are identified with business signs.

During the evolution of the hand-painted sign, the publicly posted notice through the instrument of crude printing was also evolving. This form of publicity was usually a type set description of merchandise for sale and was instrumental in attracting the public to the merchant's shop. As the scope of this type of outdoor advertising widened, it became a trade influence.

Poster by Tom Purvis (English).

With the invention of the lithograph process by Aloys Senefelder about 1796, artistic scope of the posted notice broadened to become the poster. With the aid of this process, pictorial reproductions in quantity became possible. Due to the original limitations of this process, the first poster technique of simple, flat masses was established. The lithograph process is based on the affinity of one greasy substance for another and on the absence of this affinity between grease and water. Originally, a drawing was made on stone with a greasy crayon which contained soap among its ingredients. The drawing was fixed with gum arabic, and the whole was then saturated with water. The water was repelled by the greasy drawing but readily taken up by the

Poster by Hanns Wagula (Czecho-Slovakian).

absorbent stone. Ink, which adhered to the drawing only, was next applied by a roller and passed, together with a sheet of paper, through a press. Today, specially treated metal plates replace the cumbersome stones.

Through later mechanical improvements in lithography, more elaborate designs were accomplished and the technique in different countries took on its own national idiosyncracies. By 1900, various national schools of the poster were being established.

In England, the Beggarstaff Brothers; in France, Jules Chéret; in Austria, Mucha; in Germany, Sutterlin; and Penfield in America were laying the foundation for national poster techniques.

Of these, Chéret wielded by far the greatest influence, for it was he who was able to embody salesmanship in his designs. Others, many others, used the poster art for commercial purposes, but it was Chéret who combined picture and printing to tell a business story. He made the picture part and parcel of the message; and he did it with conscious purpose. In 1867, his advertising posters began to attract attention. Among the earliest was a theatrical poster of Sarah Bernhardt, which used about the same technique and a far higher degree of skill than is commonly seen in the foyers of theaters now—seventy years later.

Chéret continued his work until near the end of the nineteenth century, and by it earned the title of the "father of posters." He can with equal justice be called the first poster advertiser.

The American Poster Emerges

The beginning of variance between European and American poster technique dates back to the origin of the schools. The difference is easily explained. The modern movement, as early as 1900, was making an impression upon the art gallery conscious public of Europe. By the time the movement began affecting poster art, it had already gained some measure of public acceptance in Europe. It was not until some years later that this movement in any way affected the design of American advertising art or the American poster.

In each case of its application to the poster art of the different countries, the modern influence applied itself differently according to the temperament of the particular country. The poster in each country is accepted very much as any craft is accepted in the light of a somewhat patriotic pride. The German embraces the German poster in the same way the French embrace their own poster school. They encourage the development of the poster as an art more

Poster by Frederick Stanley (American).

than as an advertising medium that must have a very definite sales result in relation to expenditure.

With the standardization of American outdoor advertising in 1923 and the realization of the tremendous marketing influence outdoor advertising exerts, technical study was made of its art.

Definite consideration has been given to the type of circulation to be reached. At the present time, there are several different schools of American poster design. These are adapted to the various types of outdoor advertising appeal. The realistic illustrative school is generally better adapted to appeal to a pedestrian audience that may absorb the details that are vital to its selling story.

Specialists working in this technique are Haddon Sundblom, Andrew Loomis, and Frederick Stanley.

The broader techniques that may be absorbed quickly and from a distance are effective for displays showing to automobile and fast-moving mass traffic on the important streets, highways and boulevards. The range of these

Poster by Andrew Loomis (American).

techniques extends from the all-letter poster, of which Lucien Bernhard is an exponent, to the broad, illustrative posters by Howard Scott, Ronald McCloud, and Ronald McKenzie.

Poster by Howard Scott (American).

There are two methods to be followed in the creation and design of an American twenty-four-sheet poster.

One method is to allow the artist to design or compose the entire poster as well as rendering the finished drawing or painting.

The Coöperative Method

In the second method, which, owing to American advertising procedure, is more often used, a design is created in

Steps in creation of a poster.

rough form through the coöperation of an idea or copy man and a visualizer. This method permits greater opportunity to bring, through group creation, the design to a maximum efficiency. From this rough, worked out in the following manner, any selected school of poster art may work.

With the basic idea and copy theme established, the art director or visualizer usually makes a series of small or thumbnail roughs in black and white for the purpose of basic design and value contrast. He will approach his problem from more than one design standpoint. After

Poster by Leonard London (American).

studying his design for contrast, readability, pattern and balance, he will select his best designs for rendering in color.

The technique of building these thumbnail beginnings to finished poster art differs. In some cases a rough visual is rendered in colored crayon on a tissue layout pad. Another method is to render the rough in poster or water color. In either case, consideration is given to the relation of lettering and pictorial equality that the poster may have solid unity.

Depending upon the client's acceptance and the comprehensive quality of the rough, it may be enlarged to either an intermediate comprehensive size or finished sketch.

The sizes most convenient to work with are: thumbnails, 2 by 4½ inches; roughs, 4 by 9 inches; comprehensive sketches, 8 by 18 inches; finished sketches, 12 by 27 inches, 16 by 36 inches, and 20 by 45 inches. These sizes relate to the twenty-four-sheet poster, the actual size of which is 8⅔ by 19½ feet printing surface.

In the employment of the more illustrative schools of poster art, it is seldom that the specialized illustrator renders the original idea, layout, lettering or the reproduction of packages. For this reason, it is almost a necessity to employ the services of more than one artist.

It is very often the case that the creation of a poster has been dependent upon the thought and work of four or five persons. The technical considerations in the visualizing of a poster are many. The power to arrest attention, brevity, readability, color, fitness to product should be kept in mind in the approach to the poster problem.

Poster Essentials

Power to arrest attention depends upon the basic idea, the shape of the design, the balance of the composition, the technique by which the poster is rendered, and its fitness to its audience. Designs that will arrest and hold the attention of one group will be uninteresting to another. A poster designed to hold the attention and interest of the woman shopper of mayonnaise will obviously not carry the same elements that attract and hold the interest of an automobile tire buyer.

The technique of poster art usually determines the type of circulation which it will interest. Once the interest has been captured, the selling message, whether it be word or pictorial, must implant itself quickly in the mind of the observer. For this reason, brevity is necessary.

"It must be well designed, well colored, well printed and well drawn," says Charles Matlack Price, "and these qualifications are stated in their order of importance."

The lettering of the word message and product name in a poster should be bold and clean-cut in order to have the maximum of readability. This readability is also affected by the color relation of the lettering and the field upon which it is placed. Clean cut silhouette contrast to background should be attained if readability is not to be impaired. The entire ensemble should generally reflect the type of product so that it may reach its proper type of circulation.

The effect of combined color, design, illustration and lettering that would smartly reflect the La Salle automobile would be weak and ineffective for a truck poster.

Color Applied to Posters

To understand fully the relation of color to outdoor advertising art, a knowledge of color attraction and visibility, psychology and chemistry is a distinct advantage. The poster requires more technical consideration of its color than any other medium. To a great extent, the general effectiveness of the outdoor advertisement is dependent upon its color effectiveness.

The first consideration of poster color is correlated with basic design, in so far as the silhouette pattern of the design is the basis of the value contrast of the poster. A light object is best contrasted upon a dark ground, and vice versa. With the elements of the poster properly allotted in black and white pattern contrast, it is a simple matter for the visualizer or artist to translate the design into color, the contrast of which will be both visible and arresting. Warm versus cold colors offer a further instrument of contrast to the poster designer. The warmer colors of red, orange and yellow advance to meet the eye while the cooler blue, green and violet recede.

Large areas of neutral color increase the intensity of vivid color, enabling the designer to center attention upon the most important element of the poster.

Color, too, may further the impression value of the poster's own graphic meaning. The tranquility of blue is well known, while red is violent and arresting. Yellow is a color of gayety and delicacy. Green is restful, while orange, the second complement, is vigorous. The third complement, violet, is negative and somewhat associated for many centuries with mourning. There are further color associations; however, these are the basics. They are founded not upon superstition but upon psychological effects determined by research in color.

In any medium of advertising utilizing color that is exposed to air, wind and sun, color chemistry plays a vital part. The effect of the sun on some inks, exposed to it over a protracted period of 30 days, is to bleach or, in some cases, to oxidize the colors. Large areas utilizing color of this type should be avoided. Where it is vitally necessary to the design to use color of this type, guarantees should be given by the printing agent attesting to the durability of the ink to be used. The durability of colors of the magenta family is doubtful in many cases, but ink that will stand up may be obtained at a small premium in price. To a lesser degree, there are greens of the emerald family, mineral oranges and Italian blues that are not dependable.

The study of color in all its phases requires far more space than can be devoted to it here, but it cannot be too strongly urged to understand fully the practical phases of outdoor advertising.

Reproducing Poster and Painted Display Designs

Reproduction of the twenty-four-sheet poster is accomplished by the lithographic process, which has reached a degree of efficiency that will permit the reproduction of any number of colors and any type of design including color photography. Owing to the large size of the finished twenty-four-sheet poster, it is printed in sections.

Before the adoption of zinc plates for lithographic printing, the cumbersome weight of lithographic stones determined the size of the printing sheet. At the present time, the lightness of the metal plate allows a larger sheet to be used, which increases the printing efficiency. There are now ten mammoth sheets in a standard twenty-four-sheet poster. The term, "twenty-four-sheet poster," while still specifically used to identify this type of poster, is technically obsolete. These sheets are printed by multiple color impressions of many plates. The sheets are then collated and folded in order for later assembly on the poster panel.

Painted bulletins are standardized structures upon which designs are manually reproduced; these bulletins fall into two classifications.

The bulletin of preferred position, usually displayed to concentrated circulation, is located in the central business districts and on the important streets and boulevards. In some instances, in highly congested areas of heavily populated cities, these bulletins are located on roofs. For that reason, designs for this type of display must be exceedingly visible and readable. It follows, naturally, that word copy be reduced to a minimum and that any illustration must be bold.

The second classification of painted bulletins is the highway bulletin. This, owing to the speed of its circulation, must also be readable and bold. It is not advisable to suggest that highly modeled or intricate illustration be applied to bulletin display. Owing to the fact that these designs are reproduced by a painter manually enlarging from the sketch, the absolute exactitude of the reproduction cannot always be expected. This condition may be overcome by the use of flat and simple technique. Since all colors cannot be guaranteed permanent, this type of work is somewhat controlled by a standard range of color. The reason for this slight color limitation is to be found in the chemistry of color. Colors of aniline bases that oxidize in the sunlight must be eliminated in bulletin display which is exposed to the sun over a period of 3 to 4 months.

The third classification of manual reproduction is a wall display, which, in some cases, necessitates the reproduction of a design directly upon brick. The color limitation for the brick wall is slightly greater, owing to the porosity of the brick absorbing the oil of the paint. In consequence of this absorption, there is a tendency for the pigment to fall or blow away. For this reason the use of certain types of blues and certain tints, unless specially mixed, is inadvisable. Designs for this type of display should obviously be utterly simple and flat.

Color Applied to Painted Display

Standard basic bulletin colors for use in painted display, together with a uniform identification by name and number, have recently been established by the Outdoor Advertising Association in coöperation with advertising agency representatives, Outdoor Advertising Incorporated, the National Outdoor Advertising Bureau, and the manufacturers of bulletin colors.

The colors, twenty-six in number, are those which have proved most dependable for painted display by actual experience.

This is not intended to imply that they are the only colors which can be used for painted display copy. However, tints or shades of any of the twenty-six colors are not as dependable from a life-of-color standpoint. The general rule that governs is that predominance of color as against predominance of white gives the best results under exposure to light.

In matching colors to be used in sketches with the basic bulletin colors, the match is made when completely dry in as much as colors in the wet state usually appear brighter.

In executing copy on the painted display bulletin, the bulletin face is first coated with white before applying the colors called for by the copy in order that the resulting color tone will be uniform.

All manufacturers of approved bulletin colors guarantee that any of the basic bulletin colors supplied by them will match the standard basic bulletin colors in accordance with their uniform identification name and number.

In order to maintain a positive color control, all parties at interest are furnished with a basic color chart on which are placed vitreous enamel paddles of the twenty-six standard basic bulletin colors. These vitreous enamel color standards are nonfading, and through their use the advertising agency, the plant owner, and the manufacturer of bulletin colors are enabled to coöperate in insuring the use of the desired colors and hence faithful reproduction of copy.

The colors by name and number are as follows:

Light Yellow 35	Medium Green 12
Lemon Yellow 37	Blue 25
Medium Chrome Yellow 38	Light Blue 22
Medium Orange 42	Medium Blue 20
Orange 13	Dark Blue 7
Light Red 2	Dark Blue 7½
Bright Red 40	Cream 29
Maroon Red 3	Light Brown 8
Tuscan Red 18	Medium Brown 6
Light Green 11	Dark Brown 92
Pale Green 93	Gray 46
Emerald Green 91	Light Gray 3
Light Green 17	Dark Gray 5

Design for Painted Display and Electric Spectaculars

The method of design for this type of outdoor advertising display is similar to poster design. However, the size and shape are not always constant. Size varies with different types of bulletins, and rough-sketch proportions must be in accordance.

The highway bulletin proportion is roughly one unit high by four units wide. Preferred-position bulletin proportions vary. A safe average is two units high by three units wide. Painted walls and wall bulletins are usually upright and average to a proportion of two units high by one unit wide.

In the preparation of art for painted display, visualizing follows the same routine as in the visualizing of the poster.

In considering artists to render the finished sketch, semiflat or poster flat technique should be of prime consideration. The word-copy should be bold, brief and simply designed. Finished-sketch size should be somewhat smaller than the poster finished sketch size, as this drawing must be conveniently handled by the painter upon a scaffold.

This type of display demands of the designer not only great visualization powers but also a technical knowledge of light effects and their mechanical control.

It is advisable in designing for the electric to seek the assistance of engineers familiar with the technicalities of the spectacular electric display. What may seem an obviously simple action upon the face of the structure is often ingeniously controlled by a very intricate mechanism. In designing for the electric sign, color becomes a highly technical problem of light visibility.

In order of their light visibility standard bulb colors are as follows: white, yellow, flame, orange, green, blue and red.

The neon tube, which is used alone or in conjunction with bulbs, while more economical to operate, has somewhat greater action limitations due to its shape. However, a clever designer can work effectively through the combination of neon and bulb.

The visibility of the neon tube, in order of its colors, is white, gold, red, blue and green.

The Appeal of Color

Perhaps a few words should be added about the appeal of color, which outdoor advertising provides so profusely. Indeed the posters and painted bulletins provide the highest grade of art that a large majority of the population sees with any degree of frequency. They are referred to by an educator as "the poor man's picture gallery."

Human nature is attracted by beauty and repelled by ugliness. As the eye is so constituted that it sees only color, the difference between those two extremes is largely the presence or absence of color; its pleasing or displeasing use. Instinctively one's mind turns to color when the word "beauty" is mentioned. The most beautiful things we know are the ones which are most profuse in color—flowers, paintings, scenery, faces. Gala occasions and festivities are marked by color.

On the other hand, things that are depressing are connected with the absence of color—a "gray day," a "drab

Without color such picture appeal as this loses much. What there is here is in the boy. In the beautifully colored original, the Coca-Cola also stimulated the appetite.

life," "dark hours" are significant in that they are colorless. It would be a somber crowd indeed if all color were absent from dress. A room decorated and furnished in black, white and gray at best would be a gloomy room. Even the building which does not reflect a ray of color is regarded as cold or severe.

Color stimulates the appetite as well as delights the eye. One assumes that what looks good to eat *is* good to eat. Red apples, inferior in flavor, will outsell the best apples of another hue, except to the connoisseur. In metropolitan districts especially, that is true to such an extent that nearly three-fourths of the choicest apples put up under the Hood River, Big Y and Skookum brands are of a red color. Red cherries also outsell white cherries in about the same proportion, although, of course, with cherries the so-called white cherries have a strong color element. A red and

HOW 24-SHEET POSTERS ARE PRODUCED BY LITHOGRAPHY

A FINISHED 24-sheet poster is approximately 104 inches high by 234 inches long and is usually lithographed on ten sheets of paper, each about 43 inches by 60 inches in size, two of which are cut in half lengthwise to size 21 x 60, thus making twelve sheets to a 24-sheet poster.

The original sketch from which the lithographer works is either an oil painting, water color, pastel, colored photograph or color photography.

The first step is making a magic lantern slide from the sketch and this slide is then put in a projecting or enlarging camera which projects the whole design up to the full size of the 24-sheet. This is projected in a dark room, onto blank paper, full size and arranged in exactly the same way the final sheets will be lithographed and posted.

Tracings in conte crayon are then made of all details of the design onto the blank sheets, from which offsets are made onto the large plates of grained zinc on which the various colors are lithographed. A different plate is used for each color needed. Each of the twelve sheets that produce the complete poster must be printed in the number of colors necessary to produce that particular portion of the poster, some sheets taking up to eight or nine colors while others may take only one or two. Thus some 24-sheets require as many as sixty or seventy printings, where others may only take ten or fifteen, according to the design.

Each of these plates is lithographed by hand by skilled poster artists, using greasy crayon work onto the grained

Progressive Color Steps Used in the

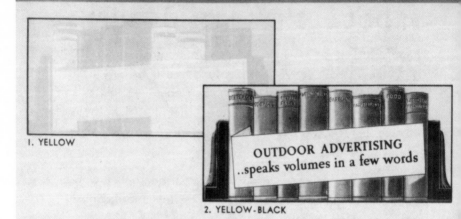

1. YELLOW

2. YELLOW - BLACK

OUTDOOR ADVERTISING
..speaks volumes in a few words

3. RED

YELLOW - BLACK - RED

OUTDOOR ADVERTISING
..speaks volumes in a few words

4. L. BLUE

YELLOW - BLACK - RED - L. BLUE

OUTDOOR ADVERTISING
..speaks volumes in a few words

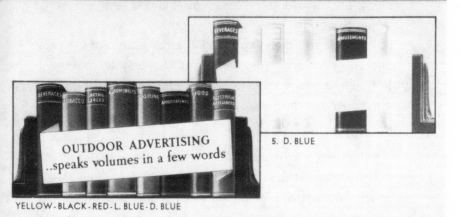

5. D. BLUE

YELLOW·BLACK·RED·L. BLUE·D. BLUE

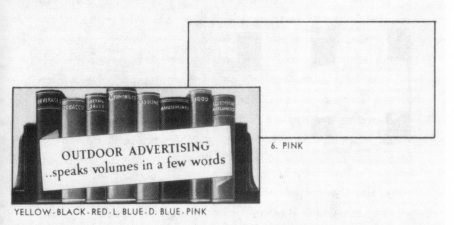

6. PINK

YELLOW·BLACK·RED·L. BLUE·D. BLUE·PINK

FINISHED POSTER

7. GREEN

YELLOW·BLACK·RED·L. BLUE·D. BLUE·PINK·GREEN

zinc plate, following the design as enlarged by the camera. When the various colors are run on top of each other on each sheet, the blending of all the colors used must produce an enlarged reproduction of the original painting. In the press room, the sheets of zinc plate are bent around a cylinder on the large rotary presses used to print the posters.

When the printing plate attached to the cylinder of the press revolves, it first comes in contact with a water roller, which deposits a film of water over the surface of the zinc not occupied by the greasy crayon on the part that is to print. Then the ink rollers deposit ink on the greasy portions but the ink is repelled by the water on the zinc portion. The paper then passes through between the cylinder and a blanket and gets the impression, after which the same process is repeated until the required number of sheets are run off in the required number of colors for each sheet. As an example — five thousand posters in thirty printings require 150,000 impressions to complete.

The sheets are then trimmed, allowing proper overlapping at sides and bottom of each sheet for pasting. Then they are collated in sets and folded in sections so the various pieces will unfold in the proper order for posting. The last step is to wrap them in bundles for shipping.

Much progress is being made in producing pictorial sections of posters by halftone with enlarging cameras. This is particularly adaptable and desirable in reproducing color photography subjects now gaining in popularity.

yellow peach will far outsell white peaches except again to the connoisseur. Yellow and green grapes have to be preceded by a considerable amount of consumer education before they can compete with the more beautiful purple grapes.

The appeal of color is so profoundly instinctive that all governments recognized it in choosing flags, pennants, paper money and even in postage stamps. Important papers, especially evidences of debt, such as stocks and bonds, which are to be sold to the public, are traditionally made artistic partly through the use of color.

CHAPTER 11

Public Policy of Organized Outdoor Advertising[1]

Tolerance Replaces Animosity

Distribution is the problem of the hour. A great public service is rendered by anybody who finds purchasers for worthy products. It is to facilitate distribution that outdoor advertising has been developed. It has become an industrial medium of vast importance. Both its prosperous existence and its proper regulation are matters of public concern.

The story of its evolution has been the story of other great industries. In its "frontier days" the attitude of many of its promoters was "the public be damned." This naturally resulted in widespread and even vicious resentment. Zealous but unthinking people raised the counter-cry "the industry be damned." Compromise or reasonable adjustment seemed impossible. For a time it looked like a fight to the finish.

More recently, however, both sides have discovered that their interests are identical. Intelligent coöperation has accordingly replaced unintelligent controversy. Nobody who appreciated the importance of a low cost and effective distribution of products would seriously advocate the destruction of the outdoor medium. No thoughtful operator

[1] Much of the material for this chapter was furnished by former Senator George Wharton Pepper. The discussion of police power is quoted directly from Mr. Pepper.

in the industry would willingly mar the charm of a land-scape or sacrifice beauty to commercial utility.

The practical problem is to preserve and effectuate a great and indispensable medium of distribution and, at the same time, confine its operations within the bounds of reason and good taste. Efforts at solution are being continuously made, and there has been much progress. While the legal rights of industry, property owners and public have not been overlooked, the amicable formulation of a public policy is obviously preferable from every point of view.

Difficult Legal Problems

Were legal controversy inevitable, the relative rights of the disputants would not be easy to determine. This is one of the reasons why coöperation is better than warfare. The industry would rely on the fundamental right of the citizen so to conduct a lawful business as not unduly to injure the rest of the community. Here the word "unduly" would be the point of controversy. The property owner desirous of leasing his land for advertising purposes would rely upon freedom of contract and his basic right to make a lawful use of his land. Hence the dispute would center upon "lawfulness." The public would resort to the State's power of taxation and to the exercise of the so-called "police power."

The *right* to raise money by taxation is, of course, undoubted, though the wisdom of using the taxing power as a means of regulating industry is far from clear. Regulation of advertising by taxation has little to commend it from the point of view of economics. If such a tax is laid upon all advertising, the tax will inevitably be passed on to the consuming public in the form of higher prices for the necessities and comforts of life. Advertising is merely an effective means of making sales and the cost of making sales is one of the elements which determines the price which the consumer must pay.

Control by Taxation Objectionable

A tax, then, upon all forms of advertising is objectionable because it burdens the consumer. A tax upon a particular form of advertising may not greatly burden the consumer but is unjustly discriminatory in favor of the forms of advertising that are not taxed and disadvantageous to the medium selected for taxation. The financial returns from a tax upon a single medium are not likely to be sufficiently large to justify the tax as a fiscal measure, while the inequality of its operation is sufficient to condemn it when judged by the standard of a square deal.

The "police power" is that relatively small portion of sovereign power which has not been subjected to much constitutional restraint. Experience has shown that in order to safeguard the health and morals of the community and, in emergencies, its safety, the sovereign must be left free to act without being limited by ordinary constitutional limitations.

Two illustrations will make this point clear. Normally, if it is to the public interest that private property be taken from its owner, he must first be adequately compensated. If, however, a destructive conflagration is spreading, a building in the path of the fire may, without compensation to the owner, be demolished in order to check its progress. Again, if the sovereign determines to prohibit the manufacture of alcoholic liquor, the distiller whose business is ruined has no right to compensation for the resulting loss. All rights are said to be held subject to the exercise of the police power. It is a power which belongs exclusively to the several States of the Union. Each State has all the power which has not been delegated to the Federal government, or limited by its own constitution. Of course, this extra-constitutional power has never been thus granted. It follows that the Federal government has no police power, in this technical sense, because it possesses only those powers which have been conferred upon it.

The Police Power

In a legal controversy between a State or municipality and the industry, the question involved would be the scope of this police power. Does it extend beyond the sphere of health, morals and safety? Does it extend to the protection of the aesthetic interests of the community? Can a man be prevented from building a house deemed ugly by everybody but himself? If so, is the restriction valid everywhere or does it apply only to parkways and other points of special scenic significance? If the latter, how is it to be determined whether the element of "special scenic significance" is or is not present? Obviously, these are difficult questions to answer. Different courts would be likely to give different answers to them. The parties to a particular dispute ought to be able to answer them more satisfactorily than by recourse to the courts. In Massachusetts an amendment to the State Constitution has been adopted and upheld under the terms of which the legislature may exercise wide powers of regulation. It is a matter of opinion whether the subject is one that can be satisfactorily dealt with in this way. Certainly it is to everybody's advantage to reach results by reconciling different interests whenever such reconciliation is possible.

The Actual Beginning of Coöperation

An early step toward reconciling the interests of the industry, of the property owner and of the public was taken in 1930 when the Outdoor Advertising Association of America, Inc., resolved as follows:

To work for the recognition, protection and conservation of the natural beauties of landscapes in rural areas and the protection of the health and safety of the transient and resident population while traveling on the public highways.

At that same meeting, with respect to its legislative policy, the Association resolved that it would support present laws and proposed legislation which

(1) is not discriminatory to the rights of any business or the legitimate use of private property;

(2) does not represent an especial tax upon the machinery of distribution of which Outdoor Advertising is a part.

Following the adoption of these policies, the officers of the Association were authorized to coöperate with other organizations interested in the subject of "Roadside Business and Rural Beauty" in working out policies and a plan of action which would accomplish the greatest good in the public interest.

In furtherance of this objective, the National Association of Real Estate Boards joined with the Outdoor Advertising Association of America, Inc., in inviting representatives of interested organizations to attend the Conference on Roadside Business and Rural Beauty Jan. 8, 1931, at Washington, D. C. The United States Chamber of Commerce furnished the facilities of their headquarters and acted as host. Former Senator George Wharton Pepper acted as chairman of the conference.

Sufficient progress was made at the conference to justify the appointment of a continuation committee for the purpose of formulating a plan, endeavoring to interest other organizations in the subject and work of the conference and then to call another conference when they were ready.[1]

[1] The long study and negotiation which led to final action in 1933 follow: A second conference was held Apr. 10, 1931, at Washington, D. C., in the headquarters of the United States Chamber of Commerce. There was presented to the conference by the National Association of Real Estate Boards a suggested "Bill for an act to create a state-wide scenic highway system for the purpose of conserving the amenities of the landscape and developing a scenic highway system for the use and enjoyment of the people of the State," which provided that "the owners of at least three-quarters of the frontage on each side of a highway in rural areas not less than one-half mile nor more than ten miles in length might petition the State to develop the scenic character of the highway and in return convey by appropriate instrument to the State such rights in the property as would be necessary to protect the view and control the occupancy of a marginal strip of land of adequate width, such instrument not to be effective until the State had

Crystallizing the Policy

After two years and more study and conference the following resolution and statement were formally adopted:

Whereas, it is the purpose of the Outdoor Advertising Association of America, Incorporated, and its members to conduct the business of Outdoor Advertising with due consideration of the public interest and welfare and to give the encouragement of the organization and the support of the medium to projects either community, state or national in scope which are of benefit to the public;

---

acquired by gift, purchase or condemnation the same rights to the remaining one-quarter of the frontage of such strip."

It was the sense of the majority of the conferees that the suggested measure was worthy of consideration by the organizations which they severally represented and that the Continuation Committee should be charged with the responsibility of receiving reports from the organizations as and when they acted upon the draft.

The national directors of the Outdoor Advertising Association of America, Inc., met in Chicago June 26, 1931, and unanimously agreed to coöperate with the organizations participating in the Washington Conference on Roadside Business and Rural Beauty in furtherance of the principles set forth in the suggested measure.

This does not mean that such a bill, if enacted, would represent a final solution of the problem, but, it at least recognizes a principle analogous to zoning as one of ways and means of coping with the problem of the roadside.

At Detroit, in November, 1931, on the occasion of the forty-first Annual Meeting of the Outdoor Advertising Association of America, Inc., a complete exposition of the entire matter was made before the members of the Association. The officers were authorized to prepare a tentative draft of a proposed policy for the Association and to place it before those organizations which were represented at the Washington Conference and all others having indicated their interest in the subject.

On Jan. 12, 1932, a tentative draft of such a policy, together with a letter of transmittal signed by the president of the Association, was distributed by mail and personally to national and State governmental authorities, civic and commercial leaders and organizations.

Those addressed and personally interviewed were requested to outline any criticism of the tentative plan or suggestions which they believed should be incorporated in the Public Policy to be adopted by the Association.

The opinions received indicated keen interest in the subject in general. They made a composite picture of the many ramifications of this complex problem. Such a picture was helpful in the formulation of a public policy and in the evolution of voluntary regulations for the industry. This policy and these regulations were duly incorporated in the resolutions given above.

Therefore, Be It Resolved, that in furtherance of this purpose, the Outdoor Advertising Association of America, Incorporated, in convention assembled at its forty-third Annual Meeting in Louisville, Kentucky, the 31st day of October, 1933, declares the following to be an official statement of the Public Policy of this Association:

It is the desire and intention to so conduct the business of Outdoor Advertising as it relates to the roadside in rural areas as will be for the conservation of the natural scenic beauties of landscapes and the rural amenities, such as monuments, shrines, relics, or objects of national, state or community public interest, for the establishment of recreational areas along such highways, for the safety, welfare and full enjoyment of the public using the highways and the orderly and appropriate development of business in relation to such highways in rural areas.

Realizing that the accomplishment of this objective is fraught with the age-old problem of reconciling utility and beauty, recognizing the complexities inherent in the situation because of the divergence of viewpoint and interest of the property owner, commercial supplier and highway traveler, and believing that it is only through co-operative and co-ordinated planning by all parties at interest along definite lines that any progress toward the desired end can be made, this Association views the problem as one requiring consideration and action on three distinct bases, as follows:

First: The education of the general public to the social value inherent in the roadside in rural areas.

The Association pledges the assistance of its organization and the force of the organized outdoor advertising medium in co-operation with any and all individuals, organizations, and channels of publicity working for this common end.

Second: The reasonable regulation of commercial occupancy of the roadside in rural areas by the state.

Third: The establishment and execution of a comprehensive and progressive program of state planning.

A Statement of Policy

It is the firm belief of the Association that the full realization of the objectives of the Conservation Movement will be attained only when brought under a progressive program of state planning.

In this direction, the acquisition of new rights-of-way for highways or the improvement of those existing should be so planned as to provide for securing land necessary for adequate parking and recreational areas, turn-off and resting facilities, and such other provisions as are necessary for the safety, comfort and enjoyment of those using the highways.

Many students of this subject have, through their experience and by trial and error, proved that no permanent progress can be made except through an authoritative over-all agency having discretionary powers within the limits established by the best zoning practice. These limits are such as to encourage the best in public initiative and to provide for the contingencies in specific areas, thus enabling improvement and development to take place progressively and with due regard for cost to the public and infringement upon private rights.

The application of the principle of zoning resulting from the study and analysis of land use and state planning by an over-all agency should result in the orderly and appropriate development of business and commerce with due regard for the convenience and general welfare of rural residents and the traveling public in rural areas, as well as the future growth and development of business and commerce throughout the state consistent with the conservation of the natural beauties of rural landscapes.

Regulations Are Definite

The "Voluntary Regulations" provide that

(1) No advertising structure will be located or maintained:

    (*a*) within the right-of-way of any highway or public road; or

    (*b*) upon private or public property without a lease or consent; or

    (*c*) upon the inside of curves or in the vicinity of railroad or railway crossings or highway intersections in such a manner as to create an obstruction of view constituting a hazard to traffic; or

    (*d*) on streets and on those portions of streets which are purely residential in their nature or in any other locations where the resentment of reasonable-minded persons would be justified; or

(e) on streets facing public parks where the streets surrounding the parks are residential; or

(f) continued in operation unless it is and continues to be in good physical condition, equivalent to the specifications of the Outdoor Advertising Association of America, Incorporated; or

(g) so as to obstruct a beautiful vista or the panoramic view of natural beauties of landscapes; (in this con-

Outdoor advertising encourages good citizenship through careful driving.

nection, the Outdoor Advertising Association of America, Incorporated, and the related State Associations will co-operate with the authorities of the State Departments of Conservation, Forestry, and Highways having jurisdiction of identification, development and preservation of such views); or

(h) so as to encroach directly upon the related amenities of an historical monument, shrine, relic, object, or place; (in this connection, the Outdoor Advertising Association of America, Incorporated, and the related State Associations will co-operate with recognized historical societies for the designation and protection of such places); or (*i*) which will directly encroach or intrude upon the beauty or dignity of the approaches and entrances to Federal, State, County Parks (in this connection, the Outdoor Advertising Association of America, Incorporated, and the related State Associations will co-operate with the National Park Service and the State or County Departments having jurisdiction for the establishment of the zone of influence of such approaches).

(2) No advertising copy of any character will be posted, painted, placed, or affixed in any way upon rocks, trees, fences, or barricades.

(3) No advertising structure owned or operated by a member of this Association will display copy which is critical of the laws of the United States or of any State, or which induces a violation of Federal or State Laws, or which is offensive to the moral standards of the community at the time the copy is offered for display, or which is false, misleading or deceptive.

The Future Should Be Amicable

As a result of such intelligent approaches as these, it is becoming increasingly clear that there is not nearly so much conflict of interest as was at first supposed. There are commercial and undeveloped areas from which the element of scenic beauty is wholly absent. There are scenic areas in which outdoor advertising is altogether out of place, not merely for aesthetic reasons but because it actually has no commercial value. Where the distance is considerable between an advertisement and a market, the impression made by the former may have entirely disappeared before the latter is reached. It is also coming to be realized that regulation by taxation is unsatisfactory because the effect of the tax is to drive the plant owner to the least costly locations, and these are the very ones which are apt to have scenic significance.

On the whole, the outlook for public, plant owner and industrialist is a hopeful one, provided always that the approach to all problems continues to be intelligent and good tempered. No observer of the situation can doubt the wisdom of such central organization of the outdoor industry as will establish and maintain effective standards of public service and increase, through intelligent educational work, a better appreciation of the outdoor medium both by industrialists and the general public.

CHAPTER 12

Relationship with Other National Organizations

Outdoor Advertising Industry's Standard of Ethics

Since the muckraking books dealing with advertising started rolling from the press ten years ago, there has been a veritable wave of criticism of advertising and its methods. In all candor, it must be admitted that some of this criticism has had a reasonable foundation. Much of it has been grossly exaggerated and inaccurate and a little downright vicious. The criticisms usually center on the inaccuracies and overstatements of advertising and some upon its vulgarities. The outdoor advertising industry has been least deserving of censure for any of these lapses. It was one of the first media carefully to censor copy and exclude everything that could, with any degree of reasonableness, be regarded as offensive. Furthermore, the outdoor advertising industry has adopted the policy of controlling the locations of advertising displays so that no fair-minded person finds serious grounds for criticism. The following quotation from the constitution of the Outdoor Advertising Association of America, Inc., sets forth not merely the ideals but the rules of practice which guard against offense both to public morals and public taste.

In the preamble of the Association's constitution, the aim of the Association is succinctly stated:

To provide for the American business community an efficient and economical instrument of distributing, merchandising and advertising; to insure, through standardization of practice, facilities and structures, a readily available and flexible, scientific advertising medium; to conduct the business with due consideration of the public interest and welfare; to advance the common interests of those engaged in the business of advertising.

One of the outdoor advertising industry's contributions to safety.

The standards of copy provide that no advertising structure owned or operated by a member of the Association will display copy which is critical of the laws of the United States or of any State, or which induces a violation of Federal or State Laws, or which is offensive to the moral standards of the community at the time the copy is offered for display, or which is false, misleading or deceptive.

"A man is known by the company he keeps" is an adage continuing to live because of its verity. In a somewhat similar way an industry can be judged by its responsiveness to social demands. Also, an industry may be further judged by the support it gives socially-minded institutions and organizations. The Outdoor Advertising Association of

America, Inc., may well be proud of the generous support
it has given many such groups, a few of which are listed
below, with at least a summary of the aims of each as
specifically set forth in their constitutions and bylaws or
by formal resolutions.

Some of these organizations have a deep interest in
advertising. With some, it is direct and specific. With
others, the interest in advertising may be less fundamental

A local poster with a strong appeal to charity.

without being less active. The advertising practitioner
as well as students of that subject should be acquainted
with these associations and clubs. That is another reason
for reviewing their activities here.

Association of National Advertisers, Inc.

This organization has over 300 members, who represent
the leaders in the manufacture of products having national
distribution in connection with the marketing of which
advertising is used as an aid to selling.

The A.N.A., as the association is called, stands for
greater effectiveness and economy in the field of distribution. It acts as a clearing house of information for the
benefit of its members regarding methods and research
developed in the fields of marketing, selling and
advertising.

The A.N.A. has accomplished much in the field of advertising during its more than twenty-five years of existence. A few examples follow:

1. Participation in the establishment and development of the Audit Bureau of Circulations, Inc., to audit and certify to circulations of member newspapers and periodicals.
2. Establishment and joint development of the Advertising Research Foundation with the American Association of Advertising Agencies, to conduct research on subjects of interest to advertisers.
3. Establishment of and joint sponsorship with the American Association of Advertising Agencies, and the Outdoor Advertising Association of America, Inc., in the Traffic and Trade Researches at Harvard University and the formation of the Traffic Audit Bureau, Inc., for the evaluation of outdoor displays.

The American Association of Advertising Agencies

Its membership consists of 124 of the leading advertising agencies operating over 200 offices throughout the United States. These agencies handle approximately 75 per cent of the total national advertising appropriations in all media.

The work of the Four A's, as this association is known, since its formation in 1917, has been primarily directed to raising the standards of the advertising profession and the improvement of advertising agency services, methods, technique and interrelationship.

The agency relationship with advertisers, media owners, and its effect upon the public is set forth in the following declaration:

To preserve friendly relations between all advertising agencies and insure such coöperation as will promote excellence of service; to secure the benefits of a free discussion on cost systems with a view to giving an ever-increasing quality and quantity of service

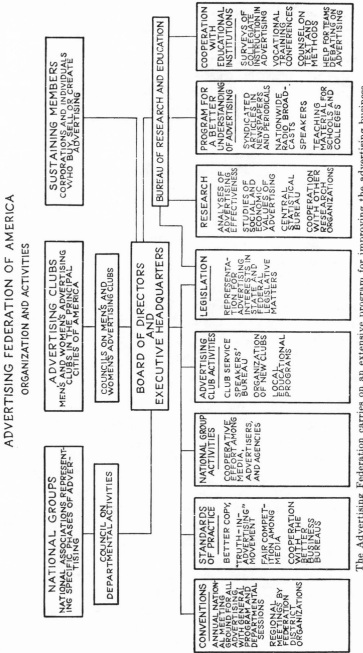

The Advertising Federation carries on an extensive program for improving the advertising business.

without unduly increasing our cost of operation; to bring out into the open, full and free discussion of trade conditions, volume and needs of the trade, and to develop, for the benefit of all concerned, sound commercial conditions throughout the country in the hope that the possession of accurate information with respect to the conduct of business, and actual trade conditions relating thereto, will benefit the advertising agency business as a whole, benefit business in general and the public at large.

The joint sponsorship of the Traffic and Trade Researches and the formation of and participation in the Traffic Audit Bureau with the organized advertiser and outdoor advertising, as stated above in the A.N.A. outline, is typical of the constructive work of the Agency Association.

An organization chart appears on page 19.

Advertising Federation of America

This organization, originally formed as the Associated Advertising Clubs of America in 1905, is made up of local advertising clubs and national associations representative of all organized advertising media. An organization and activities chart appears on page 247.

The objectives of the Federation are as follows:

1. To provide a common forum and a central medium for coöperative effort on behalf of all individuals and groups interested in advertising.
2. To elevate the standards of advertising practice and to combat any unfair competitive methods in its sale.
3. To help increase the effectiveness of advertising as an instrument of distribution, with its resulting benefits to business and the general public.
4. To determine and disseminate more accurate knowledge of the functions of advertising in business, and its social and economic values.
5. To aid in raising the standards of education and training for advertising practitioners.

The code of ethics contained in the Declaration of Ideals and Principles adopted in 1932 is as follows:

1. We agree to conduct our business with a due recognition that truth, honesty and integrity must be the basis of every sound transaction; consider the mutual interests of supplier and consumer and, therefore, avoid anything tending toward misrepresentation, indecent or misleading advertising, deceptive methods or the promise of performances that cannot be reasonably fulfilled.

2. We desire to maintain the constructive elements in competition, those elements of initiative, intelligent and efficient effort that benefit the consumer; and remove those practices in competition that are of no benefit to the consumer and that are destructive of the whole mutuality of interests. We, therefore, agree to develop in competition a friendly emulation in the improvement of the service to the consumer; and eliminate unfair practices, injurious and discriminatory methods, tending to destroy both the efficiency of business and the capacity of the consumer to purchase from business.

3. In the final analysis, business health depends upon the efficiency of the service to the consumer and, therefore, his interests are paramount, not only to himself but to our business. Therefore we will seek in all our endeavors to provide a more efficient service through increased capacity and knowledge, so that our responsibility in this direction will be fully discharged.

4. The big problem of modern industry is to bring the product from the point of production to the point of use with the greatest efficiency and with the least waste. Advertising has an important part to play in the solution of this problem and, therefore, we agree to bend our greatest efforts in this direction by the more practical use of these principles, a more effective comprehension of the problem itself and greater progress in the promotion of better practices in our own business and our contact with others.

What Organized Advertising Has Accomplished

A few of the outstanding accomplishments of the Federation are:

1. The starting and sponsorship of the Truth-in-Advertising movement.
2. The establishment and support of the Better Business Bureaus nationally and in the principal cities.[1]
3. The sponsoring and passage of state laws prohibiting fraudulent, deceptive and misleading advertising.

The thousands of Girl Scouts and their millions of friends greeted this poster with enthusiasm.

4. Coördination of all advertising interests in matters of mutual concern and the minimization of unfair competition between mediums of advertising.

Organized outdoor advertising actively participated in the accomplishments of the Federation outlined above and supports both morally and financially the annual programs for the improvement of advertising standards carried on by the Federation.

The three associations referred to above, namely, the A.N.A., Four A's, and the A.F.A., constitute over-all national organization in advertising, representative of advertiser, advertising agency and medium producer. They gave their helpful advice and counsel to the Outdoor Association in connection with the formulation of the public

[1] "The Fight for Truth in Advertising," by H. J. Kenner, 1936, is a reliable history of this movement.

policy and voluntary regulations of organized outdoor advertising. The public policy which has the endorsement of these three associations is outlined and explained in Chapter 11.

Chamber of Commerce of the United States

The membership of the national Chamber, formed in 1912, is composed of local and state chambers of commerce and commercial trade associations.

As an active member, the Outdoor Advertising Association has given its material and moral support to the con-

This poster, like that for the Girl Scouts, was displayed by the outdoor advertising industry for the purpose of promoting good citizenship.

structive work of the national Chamber in the interest of American business and the public.

The code of ethics of the Chamber of Commerce of the United States is as follows:

1. The foundation of business is confidence, which springs from integrity, fair dealing, efficient service, and mutual benefit.
2. The reward of business for service rendered is a fair profit plus a safe reserve commensurate with risks involved and foresight exercised.
3. Equitable consideration is due in business alike to capital, management, employes and the public.

4. Knowledge—thorough and specific—and unceasing study of the facts and forces affecting a business enterprise, are essential to a lasting individual success and to efficient service to the public.

5. Permanency and continuity of service are basic aims of business, that knowledge gained may be fully utilized, confidence established and efficiency increased.

6. Obligations to itself and society prompt business to strive unceasingly toward continuity of operation, bettering conditions of employment, and increasing the efficiency and opportunities of individual employes.

7. Contracts and undertakings, written or oral, are to be performed in letter and in spirit. Changed conditions do not justify their cancellation without mutual consent.

8. Representation of goods and services should be truthfully made and scrupulously fulfilled.

9. Waste in any form—of capital, labor, services, material or natural resources—is intolerable, and constant effort will be made toward its elimination.

10. Excess of every nature—inflation of credit, over-expansion, overbuying, overstimulation of sales—which create artificial conditions and produce crises and depressions, are condemned.

11. Unfair competition embracing all acts characterized by bad faith, deception, fraud or oppression, including commercial bribery, is wasteful, despicable and a public wrong. Business will rely for its success on the excellence of its own service.

12. Controversies will, where possible, be adjusted by voluntary agreement or impartial arbitration.

13. Corporate forms do not absolve from or alter the moral obligation of individuals. Responsibilities will be as courageously discharged by those acting in representative capacities as when acting for themselves.

14. Lawful coöperation among business men and in useful business organizations in support of these principles of business conduct is commended.
15. Business should render restrictive legislation unnecessary through so conducting itself as to deserve and inspire public confidence.

American Marketing Association[1]

This Association has in its membership, on the one hand, teachers of general and agricultural marketing, sales management, retailing, wholesaling, advertising and other marketing and allied subjects in schools of collegiate standing and those engaged in marketing research for the government and other public or nonprofit institutions. On the other hand, the membership includes those engaged in these activities in business.

This Association has the following objectives:

1. To foster scientific study and research in the field of marketing.
2. To develop sound thinking in marketing theory, both as regards the formulation of points of theory not already covered and as regards the formulation of new theory.
3. To improve marketing research methods and technique.
4. To mold public policy relative to marketing problems.
5. To study and discuss legislation and court decisions regarding marketing.
6. To improve marketing personnel and to study personnel problems.
7. To contribute to the improvement of the teaching of marketing.
8. To publish a journal in order to record permanently progress in the field of scientific marketing.
9. To encourage and to uphold sound, honest practices and to keep marketing work on a high ethical plane.

[1] Formerly the American Marketing Society and the National Association of Marketing Teachers.

The Outdoor Advertising Association has been a member of this organization for many years and received therefrom the inspiration and the sense of responsibility to place the attributes, processes, and organization of outdoor adver-

A Red Cross poster that was widely displayed and greatly admired.

tising before the teachers and students of marketing in its many phases in the interest of better understanding.

Public and Civic Welfare Organizations

The following organizations compositely represent national movements and carry on activities which are in the interest of the general public welfare:

American Association of State Highway Officials

American Association of State Motor Vehicle Administrators

American Red Cross

Christian Endeavor Society

Mobilization for Human Needs (Community Chests and Councils, Inc.)

National Tuberculosis Association

Girl Scouts, Inc.

Boy Scouts of America

American Legion

Veterans of Foreign Wars

Organized outdoor advertising has for many years been happy to give its moral and material support to the public welfare work of these organizations through the personnel of the membership of the Outdoor Association and the force of the outdoor medium. Examples of display contributed to these organizations are shown on pages 244, 245, 250, 251 and 254.

CHAPTER 13

Case Histories

A Few of Hundreds

The purpose of this chapter is to tell briefly some of the salient facts that have been important to the success of well-known outdoor advertising campaigns. There have been many thousands of advertisers who have used outdoor advertising extensively and have found it profitable. The author is not attempting to make out a general case for outdoor advertising. It is an established medium, and oldest of all media. Its effectiveness and power are acknowledged. Rather by selecting a few cases and giving their results and the means of accomplishment, the reader may better understand something of the method that has been followed in these different campaigns. Advertising without plan, regardless of the medium used, is seldom successful. There should be a definite aim and a definite plan to achieve that aim. Merely that outdoor advertising has been extremely profitable for one firm or one product does not give assurance that it would be equally profitable for another firm or product, even though there was a similarity in the two products and in the two sales organizations. Careful study and keen observation is necessary to make advertising successful. Extent of sales is no longer the final standard for measuring success. If one firm can sell its products with an advertising expense of 1 per cent, while its competitors are spending 2 or 3 per cent of sales to produce similar results, it is evident that the first of these, the skillful advertiser, has a great advantage over the others.

The cases selected here for discussion are not necessarily the ones that have provided the most striking successes. Sometimes the advertiser who has made a great success refuses to discuss his methods or results. He feels he might be supplying too much ammunition for competitors. Again, unusual results are achieved so quietly that no one outside of the organization knows the story. So it may be assumed that the following cited cases are by no means exceptional. In so far as possible, they have been chosen because they are typical.

No embarrassment will occur if in two or three or five years from the time this is written an advertiser, discussed here as an extensive user of outdoor advertising, does not use that medium. Some of the leading advertisers have the belief that they should rotate their primary medium. One year they use outdoor advertising extensively; another year, radio; and another year, newspapers or magazines; and then they come back to outdoor advertising and repeat the cycle. Outdoor advertising, like every other kind of advertising, is good when it helps to solve some very definite sales problem. Those in the business say it helps to flatten sales resistance. At one time, conditions may make it advantageous to use more outdoor advertising and another time to use less; meanwhile, it may supplement another campaign with other media chosen, because they help to solve a particular selling problem at the time.

Sunkist Advertising

The high lights of the advertising for Sunkist oranges was recently told in an interesting way by Mr. Sumner G. Hartshorn, Vice-President of Outdoor Advertising Incorporated. His discussion of the subject follows:

Picture yourself as a manufacturer with a plant which cannot stop. Day after day, six days a week, your product comes off the end of a finishing line.

Even worse: Your machinery is geared up to such efficiency that every year the number of units you produce materially increases —as much as 5, 10, 20%.

Now let us presume that your production is pretty well absorbed in good times. Although you must dump some of your product now and then the prices you receive for what you sell evens you up with a nice profit.

Then the depression hits. Prices drop. Demand withers up, almost dies. People haven't the money to buy your product nor the inclination if they had. It becomes the fashion to be broke.

November 1 to October 31	Packed box total output annually	Total advertising expenditures	Total outdoor expenditures
Boom years:			
1926–1927	22,266,540	$1,066,358.65	$40,482.26
1927–1928	19,493,236½	1,231,721.89	22,362.46
1928–1929	29,113,962	1,691,207.60	22,385.11
1929–1930	20,277,038½	1,306,064.27	48,071.17
Total..........	91,150,777	$5,295,352.41	$133,301.00
Depression years:			
1930–1931	27,784,676	$2,160,466.01	$486,774.75
1931–1932	25,433,742	1,469,369.36	320,627.05
1932–1933	23,829,800½	1,300,396.24	386,225.80
1933–1934	26,517,000½	1,526,969.06	327,643.02
Total..........	103,565,229	$6,457,200.67	$1,521,270.62
	* * *	* *	
1934–1935	31,290,548½	$2,082,819.59	$567,783.74
1935–1936	27,736,026½	1,483,397.01	377,022.60

People brag about their losses, their misfortune. But your product continues to come off the end of that finishing line in a never-stopping stream and you feel that there's nothing you can do about it.

But there is something you can do, and a manufacturer in just this fix has done it. The story is a true business romance, far more thrilling than fiction.

The "manufacturer" is the California Fruit Growers Exchange composed of 13,500 judicious citrus farmers who know what the word co-operation means. Let's take a look at the figures.

For the four years prior to the depression the Exchange sold 91,150,777 packed boxes of citrus fruits, an average of 22,787,694 yearly. Just because a depression came along, nature did not reduce the supply of citrus fruits. In fact she increased the supply. And on top of this she increased the supply of competitive citrus fruits from California, Florida, Texas, and elsewhere. Then to make matters worse, producers of pineapple and tomato juice saw a good chance to muscle in on the breakfast fruit market. They wasted no time—started in with aggressive campaigns in 1930 and have continued them ever since.

Now to a lot of people that would be a hopeless situation. To the California Fruit Growers Exchange it was merely a challenge and here is how they met it.

First, the Exchange held its advertising assessments solid, 10¢ per box on lemons, 5¢ on oranges and 3¢ on grapefruit.

Second, it overhauled its advertising appropriation with a view of stepping up its selling efficiency.

Since 1907 the Exchange had been doing a consistent advertising, job establishing the appetite and health value of oranges and lemons through reason-why copy. As a result of this advertising, men and women were thoroughly conscious that oranges tasted good and were healthful.

The depression created an emergency which called for more drastic measures—advertising which would sell oranges day after day—to secure the action which was needed.

It was no longer necessary to tell all the "reasons why" because people already knew them. A picture of a man drinking orange juice meant that orange juice tasted good and was healthful.

A picture of mother giving orange juice to her baby meant that doctors and mothers approved the feeding of orange juice to infants.

A picture and a line summed up the previous advertising into one capstone and that capstone might be called action.

Here is how the budget was changed.

The Exchange spent a total of $5,295,352.41 for advertising in the four years prior to the depression, $133,301.00 or $2\frac{1}{2}\%$ of which was outdoor. In the four years during the depression it spent $6,457,200.67 for advertising, $1,521,270.62 or $23\frac{1}{2}\%$ of which was in the outdoor medium.

Here are the results as shown in the Exchange's sales of citrus fruits:

1926–1930, the four years prior to the depression—
Number of boxes sold.............. 91,150,777
1930–1934, four years during the depression—
Number of boxes sold.............. 103,565,229
1935–1936, two years of recovery—
Number of boxes sold.............. 59,026,575

Thus for 13,500 citrus growers has outdoor advertising demonstrated its ability to change sales from long haul hopes to quick reality.

Chevrolet Motor Company

The Chevrolet, together with the Ford, year after year, supply automobile purchasers of America with fully one-

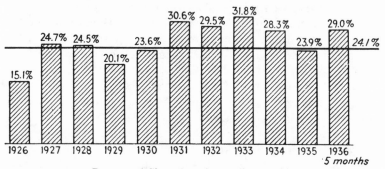

Per cent of Chevrolet sales to all cars sold.

half of the cars that are bought, and it is significant that these two leaders in the field, sometimes one ahead in sales and sometimes the other, should be the most extensive users of outdoor advertising. With new models, Chevrolet leads in adopting improvements that have been found on higher priced cars. The increase in size, greater power, ease of control, streamlining, improved ventilation, and whatever may be applied to enhance the beauty and add to the comfort of the rider has been added from year to year, all of which has been attractively presented in the poster advertising. Many of these improvements have come through the extensive investigations made by the General Motors Consumer Research Staff, headed by

Mr. H. G. Weaver. Mr. Weaver's questionnaires have become so well known that they are anticipated every season, and owners of cars of all makes are glad to contribute their own ideas of what is good and what is poor in the design and service of cars. Of course, this does not pertain to the real engineering problems but rather

A commercial sign which helps car owners to locate Chevrolet dealers and service stations.

to the refinements which add to the luxury of operating a fine car.

Mr. C. P. Fisken, advertising manager of the Chevrolet Motor Company, has the following to say of the Chevrolet's advertising:

Chevrolet is not an "in and outer" in advertising. We believe in advertising. And we use it extensively. But in using it, we do not expect it to do the impossible. We know that weak, spasmodic campaigns and half-hearted efforts do not pay. Advertising must be right. It must be productive of sales. Therefore, in our research work, our planning, creating, and developing of advertising, we exercise every care to insure its being a success.

In arranging our advertising plans, outdoor has a prominent place. In fact, during the last decade, it has been one of the two media ranking at the top in our program. It is probably the most consistent of all the various media we use, being wide open to view all of the time—every day—week in and week out.

This quality of consistency in outdoor advertising and the consistency with which it has been used is one of the factors behind the consistent demands for Chevrolet cars so graphically shown in Chevrolet's share of new car sales in the chart on page 260.

Chevrolet's new car sales during the last ten years have varied probably the least of any automobile's which shows how well production, advertising, and selling are geared to keep Chevrolet up at the front.

How much of a factor outdoor advertising has been in this success is difficult to determine. Whatever credit goes to advertising goes to the whole program which included all the major media. However, the fact that it has been used so consistently for so long a time is the most convincing evidence that outdoor ranks high.

Coca-Cola

Three outstanding American fortunes have been made in the sale of a 5-cent article: a soft drink, a chewing gum and a chocolate bar. Two of these have been outstanding advertisers and have used outdoor advertising extensively. The third has done very little consumer or other advertising.

Coca-Cola is a business of the first magnitude, even in the United States where big business is proverbial. Moody's rates Coca-Cola with assets at approximately $70,000,000 and annual profits running over $20,000,000, and these are the result of the sale of just one product.

In terms of cities, towns, villages and hamlets, Coca-Cola has what might be called a universal sale. Also, it is sold in a very large variety of stores: soda fountains, drugstores, wayside stands, grocery stores, restaurants, hotels, ice cream parlors, boats and dining cars, in recreation centers, parks and wherever people gather for rest or refreshment, Coca-Cola is to be found. A field force of service salesmen promote the sale of Coca-Cola at soda fountains. Their duties include the placement of advertising material at the place of sale; they aid in the fountain-operating problems; and in other merchandising activities that are differentiated from the usual salesman's job of securing orders. Salesmen and advertising representatives of the franchised bottlers offer similar merchandising aid to bottler outlets.

A few years ago, the Department of Commerce made a survey of the drugstores in St. Louis. In this survey it was shown that of the total business done in drugstores, the fountains account for 26.1 per cent of sales, 29.5 per cent of gross profit, and 31.8 per cent of net profit. Independent studies show that in drugstores from coast to coast one of every three fountain customers buys Coca-Cola, and one of every five customers for Coca-Cola makes other purchases in the store. So the contention that Coca-Cola has become a staple is well authenticated.

An article of such wide sale and with such a wide range of customers naturally leans heavily upon outdoor advertising to promote these sales. It is advertised through posters and other outdoor display which no one can help but see. The idea of the display is also carried into the stores where the purchases are actually made. The most interesting signs and the most ingenious devices for reminding people of their favorite drink are posted in all stores where the product is prominently displayed and sold.

No one advertising medium can claim the credit for the marvelous business that has been built up for Coca-Cola. All the major media have been used and used successfully, and while point of purchase advertising was the first sales promotion used, no other medium has been used so continuously and consistently over a long period of time as outdoor advertising. It has contributed its share to the marvelous growth of this unique business.

Two electric spectaculars which help to light Michigan Boulevard and keep people along that thoroughfare thinking of a popular fountain drink and of a new type of passenger train. The display is at the junction with Randolph Street. The Chicago and Northwestern and Union Pacific railways sponsor the top; the Coca-Cola Company, the other. For night display, see page 124.

Ethyl Gasoline

Paul E. McElroy, advertising manager of the Ethyl Gasoline Corporation, says:

Ethyl gasoline is made by adding "Ethyl Fluid" to regular gasoline that must exceed certain minimum specifications of both the oil companies that handle Ethyl and the Ethyl Gasoline Corporation. The result is "first grade" motor fuel that sells at, and justifies in all-'round quality, a premium over regular gasoline.

It is sold at the same service stations that sell the regular or "house" brands of some hundred and thirty oil companies including nearly all the leading refiners and distributors in the United States and Canada. The usual selling efforts of the refiner, distributor, and dealer, however, are not brought to bear directly on the sale of Ethyl. The purchase of Ethyl by car owners is essentially a matter of consumers' choice, which naturally puts a heavy burden on the advertising.

This burden is borne largely by outdoor advertising combined with general magazines and trade, farm, and aviation publications. The reasons for giving outdoor such an important place in the program are simple:

Ethyl's market is the motorist . . . every motorist. If he is already using Ethyl, he must be kept as a user. If he is a prospective user, he must be persuaded to try Ethyl.

And one of the best ways to present Ethyl to all these motorists is through poster advertising along the main routes of travel.

The best time to present Ethyl to the motorist is when he is most likely to be in a receptive frame of mind in regard to trying Ethyl. That time is when he is on the streets and highways and needs gas.

In fact the ideal time to present Ethyl would seem to be just before the motorist makes up his mind to pull into the next service station for gas—and posters come closest to serving this specific need.

Even if the motorist does not see a poster just when he decides to buy gas—the chances are that he has seen several shortly before and has been impressed by the Ethyl advertisement so that it is natural for him to pull up to a pump displaying the Ethyl trade mark and say: "I think I'll try Ethyl this time."

And when the motorist tries Ethyl, the primary purpose of advertising has been achieved.

Instead of supporting dealers handling only one brand of gasoline, our advertising is effective as applied to dealers of most of the refiners in the United States and Canada since they sell a premium grade of motor fuel bearing the "Ethyl" brand on the pump. Thus, what might be termed a multiplicity of dealer value is derived from our advertising.

During the depression when the demand for all products, but particularly higher-priced products, was being tested severely, Ethyl started using outdoor advertising in combination with its other media and has used it consistently for the past four years. The purpose was threefold; to hold present customers, to develop new ones, and to show gasoline dealers that Ethyl was very much "in the picture" in the selling of gasoline.

The wisdom of this policy is demonstrated in a steady increase in Ethyl sales since 1933. Last year's sales were 26% ahead of the 1935 sales and there is every indication that this gain will be extended in 1937.

Ford Motor Company

Older readers will remember that Henry Ford employed very little advertising in the recognized media when making and selling his Model T car. He made a substantial automobile, simple in design and construction, at a minimum price. It was the first car that literally millions of families ever owned. This car and its method of sales were not materially changed until 16,000,000 of them had been sold.

In 1927, Ford brought out the new model to conform more to the appearance and comfort of competing cars than had been possible with the Model T; some four years later the Ford V-8 followed. It is significant that, as the quality of automobiles has improved, the trend of prices has been down. Also, as the style element has become more fundamental, advertising has increased in amount and improved in quality. That is in accord with the law which Lee Mahin stated some twenty years ago. In effect he

said, "It pays to advertise only those articles which are
bought from choice, not of necessity"—like nondescript
fuel. The more particular one is in making a choice, the
greater opportunity the advertiser has. Certainly that
law is illustrated in the Ford advertising.

The Ford V-8 is advertised in all the major media. It is
one of the two best selling cars and holds its place because

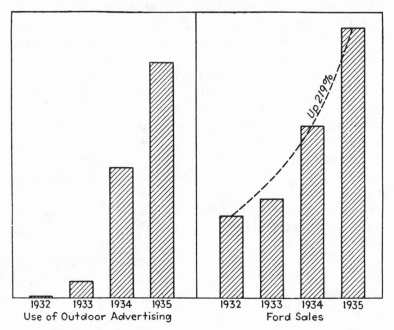

Use of Outdoor Advertising   Ford Sales

of appearance, service and comfort, as well as low price.
Appearance and style are qualities which appeal to the
imagination rather than to the reason, as do commensurable
factors.

The Ford radio programs are of two classes. One is a
very high type of musical entertainment with a brief
discussion of some social or economic topic, with reference
only to the Ford and Lincoln Companies as sponsors.
The other radio program is of the popular entertainment
class, but also contains a minimum of sales talk. The Ford
exhibits at the various expositions have helped to convey

the idea of mechanical precision with which the Fords are built, but conveying the ideas of style and ease of riding and beauty have largely been left to outdoor advertising, particularly to posters.

The poster advertising for the Ford V-8 started in 1933, but did not get fully under way until the following year. The car itself was shown in its most attractive colors in every poster. The campaign was extensive. So between the Fords on the roads and the Fords in the posters, it seemed that the Fords were everywhere, and the slogan, "Watch the Fords go by," became a veritable byword.

In using posters, Ford had added a powerful force to its selling efforts and one that provided coverage of every prospect in the market—executives of big organizations who might buy Fords as a second car for running about, office clerks or stenographers who wanted a stylish car within the bounds of strict economy, salesmen who had to cover a great deal of ground and at the same time keep their costs down, mechanics, service station attendants, people in the trade, families who wanted a good buy in car value—practically everyone was a prospect and posters reached them all.

It didn't matter whether people traveled by automobile, train, bus, streetcar or by foot—outdoor advertising presented the Ford V-8 to everyone, all over town. Day in and day out, at every turn it was Ford V-8 again and again.

Car owners and prospective car owners alike were never allowed to forget the advantages and joys of motoring; in particular, the advantages offered by the Ford V-8, such as style, beauty, speed, smartness, convenience, comfort, safety, economy, endurance and value—all of which were so well presented in the Ford series of posters.

A few weeks before this was written, the 25,000,000th Ford car rolled off the assembly line. An official company announcement at the time stated that this was the first time in the history of the industry that an automobile had ever reached such an extensive sale. There had been no change in ownership and no change in the name of the Ford car. The period of manufacture had extended over approximately one-third of a century.

Jantzen Swimming Suit Campaigns

The Portland Knitting Company, incorporated in 1910, a little later changed its name to the Jantzen Knitting Mills. It did not reach sales of national proportion until

Such advertising as this has helped to change bathing suits into swimming suits

1920. From that time on it grew rapidly and is now a leader in the field.

Mr. J. A. Zehntbauer, president of the company, gives the philosophy behind the advertising of the Jantzen Knitting Mills as follows:

Swimming suits appeal to the active young people on the go, and it is these same people who are out the most times and go the most places, and see the most outdoor advertising. They see our posters at a time when they are most interested, when they are on their way to the beach or the lake, to a weekend at some resort or on vacations. Then their thoughts are easily centered on the subject of swimming suits, which are essentially for outdoor wear. The greater the popularity of outdoor life, the greater will be the use of swimming suits. Then the more people who are out of doors, the greater will be the number who see Jantzen posters.

The evolution of the swimming suit is perhaps the most spectacular change in clothing that occurred from the late nineties to the early thirties. The style element has become predominant, and the striking pictures on the posters have largely promoted the vogue from year to year, until the cumbersome habiliments of the nineties gave place to the revealing one-piece suits currently worn. It is the boast of the Jantzen Company that they changed *bathing* suits to *swimming* suits. The poster has been an important part in popularizing the simpler and more comfortable one-piece suit, for men as well as for women.

The growth of Jantzen outdoor advertising is compared with the growth in sales in the following chart.

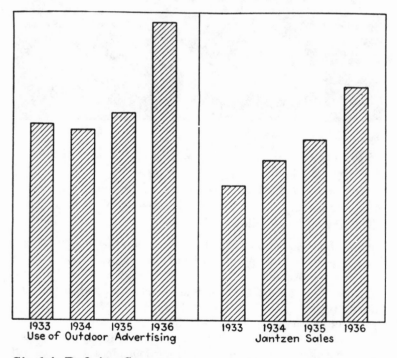

1933 1934 1935 1936   1933 1934 1935 1936
Use of Outdoor Advertising   Jantzen Sales

Sinclair Refining Company

Perhaps no one has seen the "market on wheels," as the automobile market is called, more clearly and appealed to it more directly and effectively than the sales organization of the Sinclair Refining Company. Sylvester Morey, advertising manager of that company, discussed his conception of this market and the best way to reach it, as follows:

For some products it may be difficult to put one's finger "here" and say, "This is the market for our products." But in the marketing of gasoline and oil, one can be pretty definite: The Market is the Motorist.

Every time he starts his car he uses gasoline and oil. The more he drives, the more he uses. The greater the number of motorists or the greater the volume of traffic on our streets and highways—the greater the market.

Traffic is what brings business to the service stations where gasoline and oil are sold. So that in planning advertising for such products, first consideration should be given to automobile traffic.

As a basis for determining just where service stations should be located in developing dealer-service organizations, most oil companies have made extensive studies of the various factors which were considered as having a bearing on the volume of business done by service stations in different parts of the country.

The results are conclusive in that it has been found that the volume of business at service stations invariably paralleled the volume of passing traffic. Therefore, the most important factor in the selection of service station locations is traffic.

The same general principle applies to advertising. It is obvious that the job advertising has to do for gasoline and oil companies is to reach this traffic from which their business is derived. The more directly it can be reached and the more often . . . the better.

Like service stations, outdoor advertising is placed with traffic as its objective. Along any of our commercial streets in the cities and towns throughout the United States, we see a service station —a poster—another service station—another poster—and so on and on.

Both are located where the motorist sees them. Both serve the travelling public. Service stations sell gasoline, oil, and lubrication service. Posters inform people regarding products that will serve their needs. They tie in very well in their relationship to the motorist.

While this situation in advertising applies to practically all the larger oil companies as far as their market is concerned, each company has its own particular ideas regarding advertising copy for the presentation of its products to this travelling market.

The Sinclair advertising campaign through 1934, 1935 and 1936 had two copy themes which were original and unusual. One was the extensive use of the dinosaur and the other was the lifting power of gasoline. This series

Posters tell motorists the merits of the advertised brand just at the time they need the product.

showed the S. S. Leviathan, the Statue of Liberty, Empire State Building, and other well-known buildings and structures with a discussion of the height to which a single gallon of Sinclair gasoline would raise them.

Mr. Morey concludes his discussion with the following paragraphs:

While the two principal factors—adapting advertising to traffic and developing the specific advertisements—have been discussed, there are other contributing factors that have a bearing on advertising to the motorist. Probably most important is the time people spend outdoors.

Among the influences that take people outdoors, it is likely that the automobile ranks first. It is used by many as a necessity and by everyone for the sheer joy and pleasure to be derived from being out—going places—seeing things. Of importance also are the labor-saving appliances in the home which allow people more time to be out. Even such activities as shopping, going to the movies, sports, and other forms of recreation, all play a part in the general trend to outdoor life and help to swell the volume of traffic on our main routes of travel.

There is every reason to believe that these factors will continue to play an important part in people's mode of living and that they will continue to take people out; and, so, shall continue to help swell the market of motorists as well as contribute to the value of outdoor advertising as an excellent medium for reaching the motorist.

The Southern Pacific

Seldom have either posters or painted bulletins been used in a major campaign to sell a service, but in the following paragraphs Mr. F. Q. Tredway, general advertising manager of the Southern Pacific Company, relates how his railway utilized outdoor advertising profitably. He writes:

New life, as it were, seems to have been injected into the railroads; and, as a result, the volume of passenger traffic, which had been steadily falling off, is now showing a substantial increase.

To give you an idea of the extent of the decline in railroad travel, here are some figures from the 1936 Edition of "A Yearbook of Railroad Information."

CLASS I RAILROADS

Year	Passengers carried	Passenger-miles	Passenger revenues
1920	1,234,862,048	46,848,667,987	$1,288,503,573
1929	780,468,302	31,074,134,542	873,564,246
1932	478,800,122	16,971,044,205	377,095,346
1935	445,872,300	18,475,571,667	357,904,808
1936	485,000,000[1]	22,000,000,000[1]	411,000,000[1]

[1] Approximate.

While the latest figures show a very gratifying increase, this improvement in business did not become apparent until the railroads had become thoroughly aroused to the seriousness of the situation and had taken definite action in improving their service and in presenting the advantages of their service to the public.

I know in our own case we experienced something of the difficulties common to most roads. One of the most important factors was the competition from private automobiles. This form of competition is particularly keen in our Pacific Coast territory where the climate is mild all the year round, and the highways paralleling our rails are noted for their excellence.

For many years we, like the other railroads, had no tangible advantages to offer the motorist. It was difficult to impress him with our advantages. Rail fares were higher than he felt like paying. Air-conditioning had not been perfected. Our service was safe, but until recently motorists didn't seem to be much interested in safety.

When the depression hit, Southern Pacific redoubled its efforts to increase passenger business. Fares were reduced to 2¢ a mile, and even less for round trips. Many trains were air-conditioned. Schedules were speeded up.

With more tangible advantages to offer motorists, we began to appeal directly to them in our publication advertising. Among other things, we coined the slogan, "Next time, try the train."

The more we and our agency thought about this slogan, the more we were convinced that its proper place was on the highways, where motorists would see it while actually driving their cars.

Our reasoning was something like this:

Thousands of people never even think of the train for travelling unless on a trip of considerable length. Thousands of people have never been on a train since air-conditioning and lower fares were inaugurated. Let us, therefore, tell these people about the advantages of travel when they are in a receptive mood. Let us say to them: NEXT TIME, TRY THE TRAIN, and give them a "reason why." In the hot country let us tell them that the train is cool. On dangerous mountain roads let us remind them of the safety of train travel. On crowded highways, let us tell them they can relax on the train. Let us remind them that train fares are 2¢ a mile.

How could we best present our story to the public?

We discussed the pros and cons of the different media that might be used, weighed their various advantages and disadvantages, went over the whole story with both our advertising agency and the different media representatives.

If we were to direct our efforts towards reaching people along our own lines and reaching them when they were using their automobiles instead of our trains, then our advertising would have to be flexible enough to permit our adapting it to the different territories served by our lines. The copy would also have to be adapted to each territory at a minimum expense.

Our decision was—to use painted highway bulletins.

They could be selected to cover the main highways paralleling our lines and copy could be adapted to present any particular message that we wished for any territory we served.

This flexibility in the outdoor medium made it ideal for our purpose, and sixty locations were selected for highway bulletins on main highway thoroughfares paralleling our main lines in California and Oregon. We were assisted in selecting our locations by a representative of Outdoor Advertising Incorporated whose experience in this work was very helpful.

The bulletins were first painted in April, 1936, and our campaign was under way.

In rounding out the complete display of bulletins, every care was taken to insure receiving a maximum value from each bulletin and to insure our having the proper coverage on all the important highways along our lines.

Our advertising copy is simple and strong, with terse messages that cannot fail to register in the minds of our prospects. So that as far as getting our story across to the public is concerned, we are sure of that.

Outdoor advertising copy can be dramatized to create just the right atmosphere for featuring the advantages of travelling by train. The richness and variety of the colors used help in presenting our story attractively and appealingly. The huge size of painted bulletins, $12\frac{1}{2}$ feet high by 42 feet long, attracts attention and helps to register the message. And the constant repetition with which they keep reminding people over and over again to try our railroad for comfort, safety, economy, and convenience is bound to have a tremendous influence in impressing the public with the advantages of using our lines.

The comment aroused with these bulletins was astonishing. Although our company was an old advertiser, we had never had such response to our advertising.

General Electric Coöperative Campaign

For more than ten years the General Electric Company has been carrying on a coöperative outdoor advertising campaign for its electrical refrigerators. This company did not enter the electric refrigerator field on a large scale until 1927, after many other manufacturers had already established names for themselves.

The basis of coöperation was an allowance to the dealer of $10 for each refrigerator. Painted bulletins and posters were both chosen as ideally suited to reach the many prospects for this new commodity. During this first year, General Electric sold 24,820 refrigerators, or 6.8 per cent of the total new electric refrigerator sales.

In 1928, outdoor advertising was increased. Painted displays were used extensively, particularly to reach the markets of higher purchasing power where electric refrigerators found their best market. As the market began to widen, posters came into even greater use. Five poster designs and three painted bulletin designs were offered the dealers. General Electric refrigerator sales for the year jumped to 28 per cent of all electric refrigerator sales.

Posters and painted bulletins continued to be used in 1929, with great increases in some parts of the country. Spectaculars and semispectaculars were purchased in key metropolitan centers, on the same coöperative basis as paint and posting. Outdoor billing reached a half million dollars. General Electric increased its sales to 39 per cent of all electric refrigerator sales, and became the leader in the field.

In 1930, the use of posting was again increased to reach a more general market as more and more people became prospects for electric refrigerators. The factory's order of 3,000 Christmas posters was jumped to 4,500, and all of these were used to fulfill the demand of dealers. In spite of the depression, practically all of the eighty General Electric distributors increased their sales 30 per cent over 1929, both in dollar value and number of units. General

Electric sales reached 40 per cent of all electric refrigerator sales.

Both posters and painted bulletins were continued in 1931, although posters made a still further gain as General Electric began developing an ever wider market among the great mass of middle class prospects, particularly in the smaller cities and towns. Additional electric spectaculars were purchased in various distributor territories.

One of the General Electric displays used in its coöperative campaign with dealers.

In illustration of the place that the outdoor medium had come to hold in the advertising plans of General Electric, Mr. Walter J. Daily, sales promotion and advertising manager of the Electric Refrigeration Department, in speaking before the 1931 Advertising Federation of America convention in New York City, said:

I think, in order to explain how we use outdoor advertising, I should explain our advertising and sales promotion function. First of all, we lay out the schedule for our distributors and dealers, not only in advertising but sales promotion work, in November, for the following year. We schedule newspaper advertisements, direct mail, outdoor advertising, window displays, literature, and everything that goes into the making of a well-rounded program.

We place outdoor advertising where we think it belongs as a part of the picture. We use all kinds of it, mostly posting panels, painted bulletins, semi-spectaculars and spectaculars. Our panels, painted bulletins and semi-spectacular signs multiplied nearly three times in the first five months of 1931 over 1930.

We tried outdoor in three cities of 50,000 population without anything else—without newspaper, direct mail. Those three fundamentals, of course, usually go together with us. We tried newspaper advertising alone, also, and in both cases it worked pretty well, but where we put them together we got over three times the efficiency as when we used one or the other by itself. While each one can stand on its own feet, I think we get the most benefit when we work as a unit.

In 1932, the coöperative arrangement between the factory, distributors and dealers was continued on practically the same basis as in 1931, with all three contributing to the space cost, according to the number of refrigerators purchased by the dealers, with the factory supplying posters and imprints free.

An indication of the fact that the market for electric refrigerators was still an extensive one, and consequently one that was ideally suited to the outdoor medium, only 18 per cent of the wired homes in the United States were as yet equipped with electrical refrigeration—82 per cent or 16,942,250 homes were prospects.

In 1933, coöperation was offered during the months of March, April, May and November. The feature of the 1934 coöperative campaign was the introduction of the new Liftop model and the introduction of the 5-Year Protection theme in the standard model.

In 1935, poster advertising was extended to cover all twelve months of the year, with special emphasis being laid on March, June, September, and November.

With sales of all household refrigerators, for the first 7 months of 1936, 30.7 per cent in excess of those of the corresponding 7 months of 1935, General Electric dealers had accumulated sufficient advertising credits to purchase poster advertising on an ever-increasing scale.

The 1937 campaign was in full swing at the time this was written. This year, in addition to the coöperative arrangement, the General Electric Company has placed directly from the factory a 2-months' campaign in the smaller cities and towns of the country.

That the market for electric refrigerators is still a great, far-flung one, is evident from the latest statistics available

The "staff of life" also responds to good poster advertising.

at the beginning of 1937. Only 41.1 per cent of electrified homes are equipped with electric refrigeration, leaving a vast market not yet touched. This is a sufficient reason for the General Electric to continue its outdoor advertising.

Local Campaigns

It will be noted that the foregoing all pertain to national campaigns, but outdoor advertising also lends itself to sales promotion in limited territories. Perhaps the baking industry offers the best example of individual campaigns, extending only to one city and its trading area, although the dairy industry, hotel and bank advertising are almost as prevalent. A good example of a bakery campaign is the Fischer Baking Company of Newark, N. J., which was delivering its small output twenty years ago with one horse and a wagon. Their leading product was an excellent rye bread which was appreciated by the German people who lived in one district of Newark. An outdoor advertising salesman convinced Mr. Fischer that a little good advertising would help his business. The first campaign consisted of five painted walls in the German section of Newark. The effects of the advertising were felt immediately, and it was extended, other products being mentioned as the campaign increased in its coverage. In time, painted walls gave way to posters and the number of these was increased from year to year.

The Fischer Baking Company has grown to be one of the largest independent bakeries in the country and requires over 250 trucks to distribute its product throughout New Jersey and metropolitan New York. During this time, many advertising media have been used, but outdoor advertising has remained the backbone of the campaign of this baking company.

An equally interesting story comes from Mobile, Ala., where, at the turn of the century, Gordon Smith, Jr., employed five people and had a capacity of 600 loaves of bread a day. In 1909, Mr. Smith did some experimenting with advertising. He bought a painted bulletin and carefully watched developments, which began to show immediately. Today Gordon Smith's company owns four modern bakeries with a daily capacity of 102,000 loaves. Increased sales have been accompanied with increased advertising, which has resulted in greater sales. So the happy spiral has continued. Now, the advertising includes a representative poster showing, a number of painted walls, two unilluminated and two illuminated bulletins, and two neonized bulletins. In all, 65 per cent of the appropriation goes for outdoor and point of sale advertising.

Near the close of 1935, the *Bakers' Weekly* made a little survey of the extent to which baking companies were using outdoor advertising. The result of this study was published in the issue for Nov. 30, 1935. First the article discussed the "Big Four" of the baking industry—Continental, General, Purity and Ward. It was shown that, in 1932, 29.6 per cent of the combined advertising of these huge concerns was given to outdoor advertising. Two years later, that proportion had been increased to 41.4 per cent. Most of the other media had either decreased or made a very small increase. The range of advertising for bakeries was exceedingly varied, ranging all the way from small

Readers are not allowed to overlook the fact that it is Bond bread which the young lady is enjoying.

commercial signs to three-sheet posters, twenty-four-sheet posters, painted bulletins and electrical spectaculars, which the *Bakers' Weekly* referred to as the "Big Bertha" of all outdoor advertising.

The Dayton Bread Company of Dayton, Ohio, was employing a striking spectacular at that time to advertise the excellent toast that could be made from its Miami Maid bread. From Portland, Ore., came a story of Davidson's Bakery, which was using twenty-four-sheet posters with fine success.

The Awrey Bakeries of Detroit, Mich., were running an outdoor advertising campaign made up of several different designs of posters, which was also true of the Hansen Baking Company of Seattle, Wash. The latter was featuring Olympic bread: "makes jellies taste better," "makes a

Dutch lunch taste better," and "makes every sandwich taste better."

The small amount of money that is necessary to put on an outdoor campaign was illustrated by the Zinsmaster Bread Company of Duluth, Minnesota, which started its first advertising campaign with a monthly appropriation of $40. Twenty years later, Mr. Zinsmaster was still using outdoor advertising extensively and had been a consistent buyer of poster space all that time.

Another campaign which started in a modest way was that of the New England Company of Hartford, Conn.

Two slices of browned toast can be made to look appetizing. The original package was also shown without seeming to intrude.

It began with a wall sign and increased the use of space as the business grew. This company also had wagon cards and dealer display made from the designs of their most interesting wall displays.

The Betsy Ross bread made by the McGough Bakeries Corporation of Birmingham, Ala., Kilpatrick's bakery in San Francisco, the Colonial Baking Company of Memphis, Tenn., and the Van deKamp's Bakeries of Los Angeles were among the other bakeries of the country that were using some form of outdoor advertising to stimulate business. It makes a good showing for bakeries and baked-goods stores.

Another interesting local campaign of a very different nature was that of Laird and Company of Scobeyville, New Jersey. This company was one of the oldest manufacturers of applejack in the United States. A keen outdoor advertising man saw the possibilities of developing the cider market for this company—cider being the source from which applejack is made. At the time advertising was first employed, the company was operating on a very small scale, crushing only about 160,000 pounds of apples and producing some 20,000 gallons of cider. That was in 1930.

A merchandising idea and an aggressive poster campaign did wonders for this old-fashioned product.

The advertising man suggested the use of a new container, a jug in the shape of an apple, which would identify the product easily and otherwise lend itself to advertising. In 1931, the first year of their advertising, the campaign was limited, but their business increased almost threefold. More extensive advertising from year to year has built up this business until now Laird and Company are the most extensive manufacturers of cider in the metropolitan districts, of New York and Newark. The story of their growth is told in the table on page 284.

With the new processes for making attractive posters in limited quantities, the possibilities of local outdoor advertising has been very greatly increased. Most of these new posters are well designed and attractive. They are made to fit the business better than the syndicated poster which was so popular a few years ago. Of course, with the painted walls and bulletins, there has never been the same difficulty

Year	Gallons of cider	Pounds of apples
1930	20,420	163,360
1931	58,140	465,120
1932	65,080	520,640
1933	69,176	553,408
1934	95,435	763,480
1935	84,639	677,112
1936	89,058	712,464

in getting the design well executed as with the three-sheet and twenty-four-sheet posters in short runs.

Local banks also find outdoor advertising especially attractive. There is a dignity about it which makes it popular with bankers. The Bank of America of California is a striking example of bank advertising. This bank has nine branches in the Golden State, and employs outdoor advertising so extensively that each branch is given liberal support.

The copy used by this bank on its posters, painted displays and spectaculars is varied and interesting. It has far less of the institutional flavor than most bank advertising. During the first depression years, emphasis was placed on "banking today for use tomorrow." Children and young people appeared prominently in the displays with such reminders as "Bank today for their tomorrow," and "Bank today on tomorrow for these [a group of young people] are America."

Other copy harmonized effectively with the state of mind at the time. One display showed the Bank of America pulling with Uncle Sam to relieve unemployment. Several others offered loans to "buy, build, modernize your home."

Then as prosperity began to return, automobile financing was offered and traveler's checks mentioned.

The institutional advertising was far more than an attempt to keep the name before the public—which in itself is seldom a sufficient reason for advertising. One poster advised readers that "California's ten largest corporations are depositors in the Bank of America." The time-plan loan service which this bank has encouraged was given special emphasis by a spectacular on Wiltshire Boulevard, Los Angeles. A large revolving hourglass tied in attractively with the theme and provided high attention value.

The Bank of America advertises to be "the largest bank west of New York," and financial writers have credited it with being the largest advertiser of any bank in the world with an appropriation of more than one-half million dollars a year. But it is not the immensity of the advertising or the great size of the bank which arouses our interest. It is the intelligence with which the bank is made to serve the public and the common sense way in which the bank calls that service to the attention of present and future patrons. Not all banks can be great, nor can they all be extensive advertisers, but every one can perform a useful service and every one can sell its service to patrons. The Bank of America has shown the way.

To Sum Up

Outside of the national field, it is conservatively estimated that 15,000 local merchants, covering a very wide range of industry and merchandise employ outdoor advertising to promote sales. The very widespread use of the medium is indicated by the fact that in two months of one year 4,800 advertising contracts were placed with the General Outdoor Advertising Company, Inc. A store or other local business would be unusual, indeed, if it could not profit by some judicious outdoor advertising.

Glossary

Agencies. As referred to in advertising, companies that specialize in handling advertising as a business. Agencies of recognized standing handle outdoor advertising just as they do other media—newspapers, magazines, or radio. They may place outdoor advertising orders direct with the plants or place it through National Outdoor Advertising Bureau, Inc. Their compensation comes principally from a discount or commission from the medium owner.

Angled. The position of a display. It is said to be angled when the face of the panel makes a 90-degree angle, or less, to the line of traffic.

Association. The Outdoor Advertising Association of America, Inc., a membership trade association, chartered under the laws of the State of New York.

Association standards. Standards of structural design, specifications and operating practice established by outdoor advertising plant owners through majority action in the Association.

Billboard. Formerly referred to an outdoor advertising display. Now it is an obsolete term.

Blanking. The matting of white paper between the lithographed design and the molding of a poster panel. It adds to the attractiveness of the poster as a mat adds to the attractiveness of a picture.

Bulletin spectacular. A bulletin upon which in addition to painted copy there has been superimposed electrical, mechanical or third-dimensional illuminated or animated copy.

Checking. This refers to the inspection of the showing. The plant owner drives the advertiser or agency representative about the city so that he may see each panel, bulletin or wall in his showing or display and know that his advertising is in good condition.

Circulation. The number of people to whom an advertising display presents a message, counted by the day, week, or month. The Traffic Audit Bureau computes the effective circulation of outdoor advertising as one-half the pedestrians plus one-half of the automobile traffic, plus one-fourth streetcar and bus passengers that pass a given display in a specified time.

Circulation value. The volume of traffic passing a given outdoor advertising location having a reasonable opportunity to observe the advertising message.

City painted bulletin. A painted display bulletin of any classification, located in urban areas.

City and Suburban Bulletin. A painted display bulletin located in urban areas, having a standard over-all face size of 12½ by 47 feet.

Commercial signs. Displays which are usually erected on buildings to serve as identification of the business, such as theaters, retail stores, restaurants and manufacturing plants. The principal difference between a commercial sign and other outdoor display is that the commercial sign is displayed at the place of sale only, while other outdoor displays are placed on leased or owned property at strategic points to reach the greatest circulation.

Coöperative outdoor advertising. That in which the manufacturer and distributor or dealer each share in the cost.

Copy. As referred to in outdoor advertising, it is the complete advertisement, that is, pictorial design, background, word copy, etc.

Coverage. In poster advertising, the use of locations so distributed throughout the market as to cover effectively the entire daily movement of traffic. In painted display or spectaculars, the use of one or more selected locations for the purpose of covering the traffic movement at strategic points of heavy circulation.

Custom-made posters. Handpainted, manugraphed, or screen-processed posters made in small quantities for use principally by local merchants in markets under 100,000 population.

Dealer imprint. A section of a twenty-four-sheet poster, usually 20 inches high by 19 feet 6 inches long, carrying the identification of the local retailer handling the product advertised. The dealer imprint represents about 20 per cent of the area of the poster.

Design. The finished drawing or painting used in the copy.

Effective circulation. The number of people by T.A.B. formula who have a reasonable opportunity to view the display daily in a definite location.

Half showing. An obsolete term which has been replaced by the term "representative showing."

Hand-painted posters. So called because of their process of manufacture. Their chief use is for local advertising where only a small number is needed or in connection with announcements when speed is essential.

Head-on. Position of a structure which is directly in frontal line of vision of traffic moving toward it.

High spot. A term which once designated preferred position. It is no longer in use (see Preferred position).

Highway bulletin. A painted bulletin located along heavily traveled highways. It is 12½ feet high by 42 feet long.

Highway wall. An advertisement painted directly on the side of a building along a main highway so that it shows to passing traffic.

Imprints. The strips of paper carrying the dealer's name which form a part of the poster usually at the bottom or top. They are generally used when the manufacturer and dealer share in the cost of advertising (see Dealer imprint and Coöperative outdoor advertising).

Intensive showing. Consists of either once and a half or twice as many poster panels as a representative showing and is used to provide intensified repetition and market coverage.

Lithography. The method most commonly used in the printing of posters. The range and variation in colors is practically unlimited. Lithography differs from ordinary printing and engraving in that the printing surface in lithography is flat, while with other methods the printing surface is either raised or depressed.

Location. The place where an outdoor advertisement is situated. Usually designated by naming street and number or naming two streets when the location is at a corner.

Metropolitan highway and railroad bulletin. An extra large painted display bulletin located along highways and transportation lines approaching metropolitan centers, having a standard size overall of 18 by 72 feet.

Minimum showing. Consists of half as many panels as a representative showing and is used in some few cases where it is considered necessary only to keep a limited campaign active.

NAC. "Net advertising circulation" is the Traffic Audit Bureau's standard unit of measurement of circulation value in outdoor advertising.

N.O.A.B. National Outdoor Advertising Bureau, Inc., acts as a central outdoor department for some 225 agency members. It functions as an extension of its member agencies' own departments in helping them to buy, place and service outdoor advertising.

National solicitor. An individual, partnership or corporation functioning as an agency and specializing in the sale of outdoor advertising (see Selling companies).

Neighborhood showing. A coverage of one or more neighborhood shopping districts by outdoor advertising.

Neon. Luminous tubing which has both night and day value for advertising.

Nonwrinkle posting. A method which consists of dampening the poster either before posting or during the posting operation and stretching it to its greatest extent in posting it so that when dried it presents a smooth surface showing no wrinkles.

O.A.A.A. Outdoor Advertising Association of America, Inc., is a national association of outdoor plant owners (see Association).

O.A.I. Outdoor Advertising Incorporated is a nonprofit organization, the national sales representative of the plant owners in the United States. Its functions are to present the medium to advertisers, agencies and selling companies, to collect market information, conduct surveys, plan campaigns, arrange schedules, and to develop copy and art work and do such other work as will be helpful in making outdoor advertising most valuable.

O.A.I. representative. An individual employed by Outdoor Advertising Incorporated to act as a national sales representative of the outdoor medium.

Opaque printing. A process for printing, usually by a series of screens, a color over other colors without losing any of the value of the top color. It does not permit blending of colors.

Overlay. A paper strip carrying dealer identification to be pasted upon a poster (see Dealer imprint).

Painted bulletin. Any outdoor advertising structure upon which the advertisement is reproduced in paint.

Painted wall. An advertisement painted directly on the wall of a building so that it shows to passing traffic.

Parallel. Position of a structure parallel to the flow of traffic.

Plant. The physical structures for outdoor advertising which may consist of any, or all, posters, painted displays and electric spectaculars.

Plant owner. A person or company that operates an outdoor advertising plant.

Position. The particular setting of the outdoor structure on a certain location, that is, the angle of unit, height from ground, direction showing, etc.

Poster panel. An outdoor advertising structure upon which an advertisement reproduced on paper is posted. This term ordinarily refers to a structural unit 12 by 25 feet used for displaying twenty-four-sheet posters.

Poster showing. The group of posters used to provide coverage of a market.

Poster, three-sheet. A small poster measuring 6 feet 10 inches high by 3 feet 5 inches wide (see Three-sheet panel).

Poster, twenty-four-sheet. An advertisement measuring 8 feet 10 inches high by 19 feet 8 inches long which is lithographed on large sheets of paper and posted upon the sheet-steel face of a panel 12 feet high by 25 feet long.

Preferred position. Painted displays of outstanding value located at downtown points of great circulation.

Public policy. A statement of the viewpoint and policy of organized outdoor advertising with respect to the regulation of commercial occupancy of the roadside in rural areas.

Public relations. Generally, the acceptance accorded the medium by the general public and the public policy, voluntary regulations and standards of practice in the organized industry which have a direct bearing on these relations.

Railroad bulletin. A painted bulletin located along a railroad right of way and showing to passing traffic.

Renewals. The posters usually sent to plant operators over the number actually required for posting. They are used to replace any posters that may become damaged.

Repaints. The repainting of copy of painted displays, either new copy or the same copy may be used.

Representative showing. The intensity of poster display generally used to provide complete market coverage.

Selling companies. These are similar to advertising agencies except that they confine their activities to the outdoor medium. They usually sell direct to the advertiser, place the business they secure direct with plant owners and handle the complete servicing of outdoor campaigns.

Semi-head-on. Position of a structure which is slightly to the right or left of the direct line of vision of traffic moving toward it.

Semispectacular. A painted bulletin with the addition of special treatment (see Bulletin spectacular).

Sketch. Usually, the preliminary rough of the copy with colors to be used indicated.

Sniping. Advertising copy or signs of any character or size, posted, painted, placed or affixed in any way on buildings, fences, rocks, trees, barricades without consent. Such advertising is not approved by the Outdoor Advertising Association of America and is not carried on by members of the Association.

Solar print. An enlargement made from a negative through the use of an enlarging camera and highly sensitized paper by means of daylight.

Space position. The angle of an outdoor display in relation to the movement of passing traffic. It is quoted in value by the T.A.B. formula.

Spectacular electric display. Advertising copy, usually animated, constructed from sheet metal, wired for sockets and Mazda lamps or luminous tubing, or both, with copy action controlled by flashers, circuit breakers or motographs, and attached on an open-faced steel structure built specially for the purpose.

Standard showing. Any one of the recognized poster coverage intensities, namely, minimum, representative or intensive.

Standard structures. The various types of outdoor advertising which have been adopted and built according to the standards approved by the Outdoor Advertising Association of America, Inc.

Standards of practice. The methods of operation for both poster and painted display plants approved by the Outdoor Advertising Association of America, Inc.

Store bulletin. A painted display bulletin located on the side walls of retail stores in urban shopping areas, having a standard height of 9 feet 10½ inches over all and varying in length from 11 feet 6 inches to 26 feet 3 inches.

Streamliner. A new type of painted bulletin developed with a view of presenting a modern atmosphere to the whole advertisement.

Suburban bulletin. A painted display bulletin of any classification, located in suburban areas.

T.A.B. Traffic Audit Bureau, Inc., is a nonprofit organization representing the Association of National Advertisers, Inc., the American Association of Advertising Agencies, and the Outdoor Advertising Association of America, Inc. Its directors consist of representatives from these three associations. Its functions are to collect and record authentic data on the coverage, space position and the circulation of outdoor advertising, and to apply this circulation data to markets and market areas in a scientific manner.

Three-sheet panel. A poster panel of small size, usually located on the side walls of retail stores in urban shopping areas, having a standard over-all size of 8 feet 7 inches by 4 feet 10 inches.

Voluntary regulations. A set of standards of practice which govern the placement and operation of outdoor plants in a manner consistent with the public policy of the business.

Wall bulletin. A painted display bulletin attached to a wall, located in urban areas.

Appendix

[1] The information was assembled from material supplied by Judge E. Allen Frost.

NAME: Associated Bill Posters and Distributors of the United States and Canada

Date	Place	President
1902, July	Milwaukee, Wis.	Charles F. Bryan
1903, July	Atlantic City, N.J.	Barney Link
1904, July	St. Louis, Mo.	Barney Link
1905, July	Montreal, Que.	Barney Link
1906, July	Chicago, Ill.	Thomas H.B. Varney
1907, July	Niagara Falls, N.Y.	Thomas H.B. Varney
1908, July	Detroit, Mich.	George L. Chennell
1909, July	Atlanta, Ga.	George L. Chennell
1910, July	Chicago, Ill.	P.J. McAliney
1911, July	Asbury Park, N.J.	P.J. McAliney
1912, July	Minneapolis, Minn.	Charles T. Kindt

NAME: Poster Advertising Association, Incorporated

Date	Place	President
1913, July	Atlantic City, N.J.	Charles T. Kindt
1914, July	Atlantic City, N.J.	E.L. Ruddy
1915, July	Atlantic City, N.J.	E.L. Ruddy
1916, July	Atlantic City, N.J.	John E. Shoemaker
1917, July	Atlantic City, N.J.	John E. Shoemaker
1918, July	Chicago, Ill.	Edward C. Cheshire
1919, July	Atlantic City, N.J.	Edward C. Cheshire
1920, July	St. Louis, Mo.	Milburn Hobson
1921, Oct.	Detroit, Mich.	J.H. Brinkmeyer
1922, Oct.	Richmond, Va.	J.H. Brinkmeyer
1923, Oct.	Cincinnati, Ohio	W.W. Workman
1924, Oct.	Detroit, Mich.	W.W. Workman
1925, Oct.	Kansas City, Mo.	Harry F. O'Mealia

NAME: Outdoor Advertising Association of America, Incorporated

Date	Place	President
1926, October	Atlanta, Ga.	Harry F. O'Mealia
1927, October	Atlantic City, N.J.	Clarence U. Philley
1928, October	West Baden, Ind.	Clarence U. Philley
1929, October	Atlantic City, N.J.	Clarence U. Philley
1930, October	Milwaukee, Wis.	George W. Kleiser
1931, November	Detroit, Mich.	George W. Kleiser
1932, October	French Lick, Ind.	George W. Kleiser
1933, October	Louisville, Ky.	George W. Kleiser
1934, October	Chicago, Ill.	George W. Kleiser
1935, November	New Orleans, La.	W. Rex Bell
1936, October	Atlantic City, N.J. and New York City	W. Rex Bell
1937, October	St. Louis, Mo.	W. Rex Bell

Form 2—Page

No._____

(Office use—do not fill in)

AGREEMENT
of the
Outdoor Advertising Association of America, Inc.
To Recommend a Source of Business to Its Members

WHEREAS_____
has filed with the Outdoor Advertising Association of America, Inc., a statement of information regarding its organization set-up, operating policies, the extent of experience of its personnel, its credit responsibility, and a list of the accounts handled, all of which have been found satisfactory as of the date of this Agreement; and has further pledged its adherence to the policy of the Association governing the relationship between Sources of Business and Association Members hereinafter set forth in detail, now, therefore, in consideration of the mutual covenants and agreements herein contained, this Agreement witnesseth that:

(1) The Association hereby recommends to its members the said

_____
as a source of outdoor advertising business;

(2) The period of time covered by this Agreement is from
_____ to _____
It is understood that this Agreement does not include the statistical service of the Association, but that this agreement of recommendation entitles the above named source of business to subscribe thereto;

(3) This Agreement shall be binding upon the Association only after it has been executed by the president, vice president in charge of the Business Development Division, and the general manager or the secretary of the Association;

(4) It is further understood and agreed that the Association shall have the right to cancel and terminate this Agreement at any time upon written notice served by the Association upon the above-named source of business if it is believed that any or all of the terms contained in this Agreement are being violated by the above-named source of business. Such cancellation or termination shall take effect upon service of such notice. It is, however, further understood and agreed that the Association will reinstate this Agreement if an explanation satisfactory to the Association is made promptly by the above-named source of business;

(5) It is also agreed:

    (a) That all dealings with members of this Association will be based upon the principle of equality of treatment set forth in the following resolution and the source of business unqualifiedly subscribes to the provisions of this equality of treatment resolution, both in principle and in practice:

"RESOLVED, that it is a fundamental principle of the Outdoor Advertising Association of America, Inc., to promote among its members the policy of equality of treatment and service to all advertisers and an equality of opportunity among all solicitors and agencies.

To effectuate this principle, every member of this Association who gives to one or more advertisers either rates or showings more favorable than those enjoyed by others shall be bound to refund to all advertisers whose contracts are current such part of this consideration paid by them as is necessary to equalize them with the most favored advertiser. And no member of this Association shall, by concession of free space, by discrimination in rates or otherwise, enable one or more solicitors or agencies to offer to advertisers terms more favorable than are available for all";

(b) That members of the Association will not be requested to post or execute painted display copy in conflict with the following excerpt from the standards of practice of the Association:

"No advertising structure owned or operated by a member of this Association will display copy which is critical of the laws of the United States or any state or which induces a violation of federal and/or state laws, or which is offensive to the moral standards of the community at the time the copy is offered for display, or which is false, misleading or deceptive."

In this connection, the Association stands ready to give consideration to any copy submitted to its headquarters office for determination as to whether or not it may be in violation of the foregoing copy standards;

(6) It is further understood and agreed that the Association's recommendation is predicated upon the following:
   (a) Declaration of Purpose.
   (b) Definition of the Classifications of Outdoor Advertising.
   (c) Requirements of Sources of National Business.
   (d) Requirements of Association Members.

(a) It is the purpose of the Association:
   (1) to adopt and administer policies designed to insure equality of treatment and equal opportunity to all advertisers, advertising agencies and exclusive solicitors in their use of the Outdoor Advertising Medium and in all relations the Association or its Members may have with them in connection with such use;
   (2) to likewise insure to the Members of the Association the benefits of the policy of equality of treatment and equal opportunity.

(b) Outdoor Advertising consists of three classifications, viz.: National, Local and Co-operative.

NATIONAL

On national business, an agency differential computed upon members' published prices and terms may be allowed to sources of national business recommended by the Association.

The term "national business" shall refer to outdoor advertising of any product or service which is the subject of national or sectional distribution.

LOCAL

On local business, members may grant recognition upon such terms as may conform to local requirements; provided, however, that any agency differential paid on local business shall not exceed nor shall terms be more favorable than those granted to recommended sources of national business.

The term "local business" shall refer to outdoor advertising of any retail merchandising or manufacturing business, product or service, the distribution of which is confined within the metropolitan zone or recognized retail trading area in which the related contract is to be performed.

CO-OPERATIVE

Co-operative business shall be classified as national business; provided, however, that if on the portion of such co-operative advertising to be paid for by the distributor and/or the retail outlet the member assumes the credit risk, renders service and makes collection in keeping with the terms of the related contract, then such portion shall be deemed to be local business.

The term "co-operative business" shall refer to outdoor advertising of any product or service which is the subject of national or sectional distribution for which outdoor advertising payment is made in part by the manufacturer, his distributor and/or his retail outlets.

(c) Sources of National Business to secure and retain the recommendation of the Outdoor Advertising Association of America, Inc., to its Members must conform to the following standards:

The Source of National Business shall

(1) possess and maintain a credit rating commensurate with the scope of its operations and shall furnish credit statements when and as required by the Association;

(2) establish an outdoor advertising department with adequate personnel possessing a sufficient technical knowledge to represent its clients effectively in presenting and servicing the medium of outdoor advertising;

(3) maintain or employ an art department informed in the special technique of outdoor advertising design as applied to poster advertising, painted display advertising and electric and spectacular display advertising;

(4) prepare or cause to be prepared at its expense the necessary specifications, blue prints, solar prints and pencil layouts when distributing painted display or electric and spectacular display copy to members;

(5) procure the special forms necessary to the efficient placement of outdoor advertising business.

It is understood that the terms and conditions set forth in sublet contracts and in written or verbal instructions in relation thereto shall not be in conflict with the terms of the Agreement Recommendation, especially as they relate to equality of treatment and the Association standard of service as outlined in paragraph numbered 5 of the "Requirement of Association Members";

(6) possess and maintain adequate knowledge of poster advertising, painted display, electric and spectacular advertising, including the circulation, advertising and price values in all such forms of outdoor advertising;

(7) install and maintain currently adequate statistical records of poster advertising facilities and rates;

(8) not represent to any advertiser that it can purchase outdoor advertising in any form at prices and terms more favorable than those available to any other recommended source of national business.

(9) make prompt payment for services rendered by members of the Association within 30 days of the expiration of each month's service covered by contract.

It is understood that if payment is not made within 60 days of expiration of a given month's service, the subject source of business shall be considered delinquent and no agency differential shall be allowed on any business executed for the subject source of business until the delinquency has been liquidated. And, further, that if the period of delinquency extends for more than 90 days beyond the expiration of any month's service, the recommendation of the Association of the subject source of business shall be withdrawn;

(10) not request members of the Association to accept commitments for space subject to less than 60 days notice of cancellation or deferment of posting date, unless the space allotted to such commitment can be sold to another advertiser by the member;

(11) not request members to post posters or execute painted display copy which is critical of the laws of the United States or any state or which induces a violation of federal and/or state laws or which is offensive to the moral standards of the community at the time the copy is offered for display, or which is false, misleading or deceptive.

The Association will give consideration to any copy submitted to its headquarters office to determine whether or not copy may be in violation of the foregoing standard;

(12) make arrangements with members for verification and evaluation of outdoor advertising under contract in their respective territories as far in advance as possible to conserve the time of all concerned.

Complaints with respect to the service delivered in relation to the provisions of the governing contract shall be called to the attention of the member at the time the verification and evaluation is made.

It is understood that if service shortcomings are not corrected promptly by the member, the source of business shall file formal complaint with this Association.

The recommendation of the Association may be withdrawn at any time for nonconformity with the foregoing requirements.

(d) Members of the Association in their relationship with sources of national business must conform to the following standards of practice:

The Members of the Association shall

(1) adopt no standards of recognition at variance with those herein contained, nor sublet business which in the usual course would be placed through a recommended source of national business;

(2) allow the customary agency differential to all recommended sources of national business; provided, however, that if a source of national business becomes delinquent, the provisions with respect to delinquency set forth in paragraph numbered 9 of the "Requirements of Sources of National Business" shall apply;

(3) not allow an agency differential to unrecommended sources of national business;

(4) not render any service such as dealer contact work, merchandising assistance, preparation of designs and layouts, estimates, checking, or any similar or other service which is not likewise available upon the same terms and conditions to every recommended source of national business;

(5) fulfill the service requirements of all accepted contracts. It is understood to be the obligation of members to accept only such contracts as require the Association standard of service as set forth in the service rules and regulations of the Association and in keeping with the equality of treatment resolution which requires that members shall not by any concession, discrimination, or otherwise, give to one advertiser or his agent terms or service more favorable than are available to all.

If complaint is filed that the service provisions of the contract as accepted have not been complied with after verification and evaluation, the member shall immediately make the necessary corrections and advise the related source of national business;

(6) furnish to the Association statistical information such as coverage allotments, rates, prices and terms relating to the outdoor advertising facilities which they operate.

Changes in the statistical information are subject to the following:
(a) Notices of change of rate, allotment, and/or terms of discount shall be effective only on January 1st of any year;
(b) All such notices shall be filed with the Association at least 6 months and 15 days prior to January 1st, and members are urged to give as much additional previous notice as possible to expedite notification to recommended sources of national business.

The Association furnishes the statistical information to recommended sources of national business at a cost commensurate with its value as may be determined from time to time by the Association.

Dated at Chicago, Illinois, this _____ day of _____, 193__.

OUTDOOR ADVERTISING ASSOCIATION OF AMERICA, Inc.

By _____
President

By _____
Vice-President in Charge of Business Development Division

By _____
General Manager

By _____
Secretary

The foregoing expresses the understanding with the Outdoor Advertising Association of America, Inc., under which the undersigned acts and which the undersigned approves and accepts.

Signed _____
Company Name

By _____
Name   Title

Date _____

Index

303

Titles in This Series

1.
Henry Foster Adams. Advertising and Its Mental Laws. 1916

2.
Advertising Research Foundation. Copy Testing. 1939

3.
Hugh E. Agnew. Outdoor Advertising. 1938

4.
Earnest Elmo Calkins. And Hearing Not: Annals of an Ad Man. 1946

5.
Earnest Elmo Calkins and Ralph Holden. Modern Advertising. 1905

6.
John Caples. Advertising Ideas: A Practical Guide to Methods That Make Advertisements Work. 1938

7.
Jean-Louis Chandon. A Comparative Study of Media Exposure Models. 1985

8.
Paul Terry Cherington. The Consumer Looks at Advertising. 1928

9.
C. Samuel Craig and Avijit Ghosh, editors. The Development of Media Models in Advertising: An Anthology of Classic Articles. 1985

10.
C. Samuel Craig and Brian Sternthal, editors. Repetition Effects Over the Years: An Anthology of Classic Articles. 1985

11.
John K. Crippen. Successful Direct-Mail Methods. 1936

12.
Ernest Dichter. The Strategy of Desire. 1960

13.
Ben Duffy. Advertising Media and Markets. 1939

14.
Warren Benson Dygert. Radio as an Advertising Medium. 1939

15.
Francis Reed Eldridge. Advertising and Selling Abroad. 1930

16.
J. George Frederick, editor. Masters of Advertising Copy: Principles and Practice of Copy Writing According to its Leading Practitioners. 1925

17.
George French. Advertising: The Social and Economic Problem. 1915

18.
Max A. Geller. Advertising at the Crossroads: Federal Regulation vs. Voluntary Controls. 1952

19.
Avijit Ghosh and C. Samuel Craig. The Relationship of Advertising Expenditures to Sales: An Anthology of Classic Articles. 1985

20.
Albert E. Haase. The Advertising Appropriation, How to Determine It and How to Administer It. 1931

21.
S. Roland Hall. The Advertising Handbook, 1921

22.
S. Roland Hall. Retail Advertising and Selling. 1924

23.
Harry Levi Hollingworth. Advertising and Selling: Principles of Appeal and Response. 1913

24.
Floyd Y. Keeler and Albert E. Haase. The Advertising Agency, Procedure and Practice. 1927

25.
H. J. Kenner. The Fight for Truth in Advertising. 1936

26.
Otto Kleppner. Advertising Procedure. 1925

27.
Harden Bryant Leachman. The Early Advertising Scene. 1949

28.
E. St. Elmo Lewis. Financial Advertising, for Commercial and Savings Banks, Trust, Title Insurance, and Safe Deposit Companies, Investment Houses. 1908

29.
R. Bigelow Lockwood. Industrial Advertising Copy. 1929

30.
D. B. Lucas and C. E. Benson. Psychology for Advertisers. 1930

31.
Darrell B. Lucas and Steuart H. Britt. Measuring Advertising Effectiveness. 1963

32.
Papers of the American Association of Advertising Agencies. 1927

33.
Printer's Ink. Fifty Years 1888–1938. 1938

34.
Jason Rogers. Building Newspaper Advertising. 1919

35.
George Presbury Rowell. Forty Years an Advertising Agent, 1865–1905. 1906

36.
Walter Dill Scott. The Theory of Advertising: A Simple Exposition of the Principles of Psychology in Their Relation to Successful Advertising. 1903

37.
Daniel Starch. Principles of Advertising. 1923

38.
Harry Tipper, George Burton Hotchkiss, Harry L. Hollingworth, and Frank Alvah Parsons. Advertising, Its Principles and Practices. 1915

39.
Roland S. Vaile. Economics of Advertising. 1927

40.
Helen Woodward. Through Many Windows. 1926